Sheila

To my own Sheila, Paola,
and in loving memory of my late father, Arthur

Sheila

The Australian ingenue
who bewitched British society

ROBERT WAINWRIGHT

ALLEN&UNWIN

First published in Australia in 2014 by Allen & Unwin
First published in Great Britain in 2014 by Allen & Unwin

Allen & Unwin
c/o Atlantic Books
Ormond House
26–27 Boswell Street
London WC1N 3JZ
Phone: 020 7269 1610
Email: UK@allenandunwin.com
Web: www.allenandunwin.co.uk

Hardback ISBN 978 1 74331 682 5
E-book ISBN 978 1 74343 156 6

Index by Puddingburn Publishing Services
Set in 12.5/18 pt Minion by Post Pre-press Group, Australia
Printed and bound by CPI Group (UK) Ltd, Croydon, CR0 4YY

10 9 8 7 6 5 4 3 2 1

CONTENTS

PROLOGUE

A PRINCESS RETURNS

The lady graced, rather than sat on, the hotel couch; at ease, as one might have expected, in the luxury of her temporary surroundings. Her face, famed in her youth for its ethereal beauty, was still bright and eager, her make-up spare. Wide clear eyes creased faintly when she smiled, framed by thick, carefully styled silver hair that sat shoulder-length—longer than in her heyday, when she had helped make short, sharp hair fashionable. *Pixyish*, an admirer and frustrated suitor had once described her. That compliment still held true four decades after it had been given.

But she had some other, special quality. Her interrogator, the women's magazine journalist perched on a chair opposite, scrambled mentally for the phrase that might definitively encapsulate the woman before her. It was on the tip of her tongue, and yet somehow elusive. *Prim* or *matronly* did the lady a disservice, despite the cascading strings of pearls around her throat and the modest length of her skirt in this summer of 1967. Even *graceful* was too simplistic an assessment of a woman with an air that evoked much, much more. Then it came to her—*regal*. She had a bearing that could only have come from a life of stature.

The lady's name was Princess Dimitri Romanoff, but she was Russian only by name. As Sheila Chisholm she had been born and raised on a sheep and horse station on the Goulburn Plains in southern New South Wales, where she defied her parents and smoked at the age of twelve and rebelled against well-meaning but demanding governesses: "Mother told me she would never keep on a governess who was unkind to me so, whenever they actually tried to teach me something, I said they were being unkind. Governesses came and went like butterflies. I was a monster," she confided to the journalist, with a half smile and only a hint of contrition.

But this same wilful child would become as intimate with royalty as any Australian woman of her time. Born into a family that had helped settle and explore Australia and then craft the European settlement from the days of the early fleets, Sheila, as she would always call herself, left Australia as a teenager in 1914 just as political rumblings stirred fear of a war in Europe. She would return home just three times in the next fifty years—her first visit as the wife of a Scottish lord, her second as the wife of an English baronet, and now as the wife of a Russian prince. Through it all, she remained quintessentially an Australian country girl.

"I married all my husbands for love," she'd told a throng of media waiting at Sydney Airport when she had arrived a few days earlier. "I certainly didn't care about titles, and none of them had any money."

In the forty-eight hours since arriving in Sydney the prince and princess had lain low, taking their time acclimatising to the twin demands of time and seasonal change. They had come from the twilight and damp cold of an English winter to the glazing, steamy heat of an Australian summer; the temperature had bubbled at over 102 degrees Fahrenheit (39 degrees Celsius) when they'd arrived at Sydney Airport and sat in a room with a broken air conditioner while three television stations took their turns interviewing the couple. One reporter, sensing their distress, had offered Prince Dimitri a glass of water. His reply—"No thank you; I never drink water"—delighted them; they interpreted it as the motto of a vodka man without knowing he had once made his living selling whiskey.

Sheila knew the impact of change more than most. Her life had been shattered twice by world wars—her first marriage devastated, at least partly, by the impacts of the Great War on her psychologically-fragile husband and the life of one of her sons taken in battle during World War II.

———

Traumatic upheaval had haunted her generation, as the man who now sat beside her could testify. As a young man Prince Dimitri had escaped the violence of the Bolshevik Revolution, which had claimed the life of his uncle, the last Tsar of Russia,

Nicholas II. His family had been under house arrest for eight months before they were rescued and taken to London; he was one of only thirty-five of the famed Romanoffs who survived. In reply to a question from the magazine writer, he recalled: "We slept in our clothes, always hoping for escape. We were starved." He had survived, rescued by the English King, George V, but, notwithstanding his grand title, he had spent most of his adult life working, including some years in the United States as a factory worker making refrigerator parts.

His wife's life had been the opposite: born in the obscurity of the Australian bush but, by a combination of fate and opportunity, finding her way to the centre of the world, in London. In her heyday the public had been fascinated by Sheila's life, which had been reported on regularly over the years, not only by Fleet Street but by newspapers across the United States and the sub-continent. Back home, even the smallest regional papers had carried regular reports gleaned from the wire services, for readers eager to explore her success and wonder how a young woman from the plains outside Canberra had managed to spend half a century inside the palaces, mansions and clubs of the rich and powerful.

Sheila's story was deliciously evocative, as the reporter would observe in her feature article for *The Australian Women's Weekly*: "When you talk to [her] the air seems to fill with the ghosts of a long-ago glittering world, with the sound of far-off trumpets, the swirl of beautiful Court dresses, the flash of light of ceremonial swords."

The newly federated Australian nation was still finding

its feet when Sheila Chisholm left its shores with her mother Margaret—wife of the pastoralist, grazier and prominent racehorse breeder, Harry Chisholm—and headed for the social glamour of Europe: "Canberra didn't exist when I left," she reminisced; the national capital was still a political wilderness in the middle of nowhere, with barely a shovel hole. Its development would be further delayed when the Great War was declared a few months later, which meant she had not seen it until now.

This trip home—for that's the way she would always feel despite the infrequency of visits—was a sentimental pilgrimage of sorts. Her last, thirty years ago, had been to see her mother, who was then seriously ill; there had been little time for sightseeing. The onset of World War II a few years later would prevent her returning for her mother's funeral. After that, there was little reason to make the arduous trip, which in those days meant hopping from continent to continent and cost the equivalent of two years of a working man's wages.

Now she wanted to reconnect with the place and the people she had left behind: "I want to see the Blue Mountains again—and a koala farm. I want to surf again, to see if I can surf without being knocked over." It was no idle wish.

There would also be time to visit friends in high places: "First, we go to Canberra to stay with the British High Commissioner, Sir Charles Johnston, and his wife Princess Nathalie, who is Dimitri's cousin," she explained matter-of-factly, unselfconsciously name-dropping, although strangely neglecting to mention that another cousin was Prince Philip,

Duke of Edinburgh and husband of Queen Elizabeth. "Then back to Sydney to do all those things I dream of. And I want to meet all my old friends again, and have Dimitri meet them."

What about change? They had seen so much in their lifetimes, the reporter suggested. Princess Dimitri nodded: "I was reared in a world of servants and chaperones. Today the young have no chaperones and almost no help, and they manage their lives magnificently. I'm not bothered by Beatles haircuts. Half the boys at Eton have long hair, and it horrifies their fathers. But what does it matter? Basically, they're very much alive, and they just want to be different. They're very tough."

She might have been speaking about her own resolute determination, after arriving in London half a century before as one of a handful of Australian-born women making their way in a society that demanded blood and position as an entry card. Somehow, her personality and beauty—in that order—would open doors and not only invite her into the most inner of sanctums but allow her to stay and become a leading figure in a society that might otherwise have ignored her.

There would be great highs —the patronage of kings, movie stars, celebrated writers and even heroes. She would become a fashion icon, among the first to go hatless and adopt the daring hairstyles of the raging 1920s and 1930s; she would grace magazine advertisements for beauty products, pose for famous photographers and be pursued by the world's richest and most eligible men.

As the limelight of her youth faded, she would reinvent herself as a businesswoman and a celebrity travel agent: "I started it as just a counter in Fortnum & Mason's with a staff of two," she explained about her business. "I couldn't even read a balance sheet, but somehow the thing snowballed. Now we employ two hundred in our London office and we have branches everywhere, even in Australia.

"I was chairman of the company for a long time, though still unable to read those balance sheets! Now I mainly help with publicity. I can be very useful persuading our friends to use the agency, and, oh, yes, in persuading them to pay up. The rich don't pay, you know. No, they don't, Dimitri."

Dimitri smiled quietly. He understood his wife's subtle point. There was a perception in society that the powerful classes were, by definition, also the wealthy. But, as their own lives would show, the richness was in the experience.

TO PROVE THAT A GIRL COULD DO IT

It was a farewell tea, or at least that's the way the occasion would be described in the social pages of *The Sydney Morning Herald*. In hindsight though, this casual social event was probably more a beginning than an end. The young woman at the centre of attention was on her way to adult life—with all its possibilities and pitfalls.

On the afternoon of March 31, 1914, eighteen-year-old Miss Sheila Chisholm and a few dozen friends and family chatted over tea and sandwiches beneath the arches on the first-floor balcony of the grandest establishment in Sydney, the Hotel Australia. Out on the balcony, they chose to ignore the hotel's interior splendour, with its soaring red marble Doric columns and mahogany staircase, so as to relish the autumn sunshine and the noise of the city and Castlereagh Street below.

Not far away, in the midst of the harbour jostle lay the

steamship SS *Mongolia*, due to leave the following morning for a six-week voyage to London with a cargo of the best of Australia's produce—wool, leather, fur, tin, copper and lead, as well as cases of refrigerated meat and meat extract, crates of apples and boxes of pearl shell. The ship would also carry a human cargo—up to 400 first- and second-class passengers plucked from the Australian capitals—as she made her way around the southern coast and then across the Indian Ocean toward Africa, the Suez Canal and on to Europe. Among those who paid £45 for passage, the equivalent of seven months' wages for a working woman, were Sheila Chisholm and her mother, Margaret, who were travelling to Europe for at least six months—France, England, Germany and Italy—hence the farewell gathering.

Australia may have grasped a degree of political independence after its declaration of federation in 1901, but its upper echelons remained firmly attached to the matronly bosom of England; the wife and only daughter of prominent grazier and bloodstock agent, Mr Harry Chisholm, were joining the great annual migration of well-to-do families paying homage to the rituals of British society.

It was daunting and exciting, particularly for a young woman who had spent the best part of her life on a grazing property named "Wollogorang", a local Aboriginal word meaning "Big Water" because the property bordered a large lagoon, which was a two-day ride south of Sydney and 60 kilometres from where Canberra would eventually rise.

Like her father and older brothers, John and Roy, Sheila

had been born in the main bedroom of the two-storey stone homestead and reared in the practical, if privileged, colonial environment of working men. Her birth notice in *The Sydney Morning Herald*—sans the names of either the mother or daughter—had reflected a world that was spare, both in its comforts and attitude to women: "CHISHOLM—September 9, the wife of Harry Chisholm, Wollogorang, Breadalbane, a daughter."

When the baby was finally named, she was christened Margaret Sheila MacKellar Chisholm, but from an early age she would go by her second name, taken from the heroine of a book that had inspired her mother, who eschewed her husband's suggestions of naming her after one of two godmothers or Queen Victoria, as "the idea of the former is mercenary and the latter snobbish".

Despite the challenges of a rural life, Sheila was brought up in what she later described as "an atmosphere of love and sympathy. I adored my mother and father." Harry Chisholm was tall and prematurely silver-haired, with the firm-eyed gaze of a man who spent his days in the sun. In the months before his daughter was born in 1895, he had pursued his love of racehorses by establishing what would become Australia's largest bloodstock agency. He was a hardened businessman but at home Sheila would recall a doting father who filled her head and heart with stories about heroic bushrangers like Captain Thunderbolt and quoted poems from Adam Lindsay Gordon. He couldn't resist his young daughter, even her habit of referring to him by his nickname, "Chissie", something his sons would never dream of doing.

Sheila

Harry had known Margaret MacKellar since they were children and married the slim, fair beauty when she turned sixteen. "She was an extremely intelligent woman, twenty years ahead of her generation and a suffragette at heart," Sheila would recall in her unpublished memoir, which she would begin penning in the late 1940s. "Had we lived in England, I can easily imagine her doing violent things and being under the influence of Mrs Pankhurst."

The family homestead was an English retreat inside a spare colonial landscape of "brown rolling country, purple hills beyond and gentian-blue skies". The main building was pale yellow washed stone with French doors opening onto trim lawns with English oaks and elms, and a wooden bridge leading to a pond surrounded by willow trees, all created seventy years earlier by her paternal grandfather, James Chisholm, son of a Scottish soldier who arrived in Australia with the Third Fleet in 1790. Her father had inherited Wollogorang after his older brother, Jack, had died when thrown from his horse. Jack Chisholm's ghost is said to still haunt the homestead.

This was a wealthy household, with a main house containing dining room, drawing room and her mother's sitting room downstairs and her parents' private rooms upstairs. There were also two wings: one for Sheila, her brothers and guests, and the other for the household staff of five, including Sheila's nanny, whom she called "Ninget". Sheila would always remember the wallpaper in her bedroom, patterned with clusters of tiny roses "all seeming to have little faces. I constantly counted them as I lay in bed—an eccentricity I have to this day."

Her childhood home was "beautifully run but old-fashioned and rather shabby", always with masses of flowers arranged by her mother, who wore elaborate, clinging dresses known as tea-gowns in the evenings while her father and brothers wore dinner jackets, a formality that was rare among station owners.

———

John, or "Jack" as he was known, and Roy were seven and four when their sister was born: "They had both prayed ardently for a baby sister and I became a toy to them. They alternately spoiled and teased and tormented me. I was rather a timid child, but I tried to be brave and to do all the things my brothers did because they were proud of me and said I was almost as good as any boy.

"I was sensitive and imaginative with large, hazel eyes and a pale, heart-shaped face and short hair. I was allowed to go about in riding breeches except on Sundays when we all went to church. Then I had to wear a stiff muslin frock with a wide sash bow at the back. The parson and his tiresome wife usually had luncheon with us afterwards. I disliked her because she constantly remarked: 'Little girls should be seen and not heard'. She never said anything disagreeable about the boys. I hated being a girl and used to pray that God would turn me into a boy overnight."

The conflict of being a female in a male world and being expected to behave in a certain manner would be a constant struggle and a mark on her life, Sheila once making herself sick by drinking a bottle of Worcestershire sauce when challenged by her brothers "to prove them wrong and in defence of my sex". She adored the wildness of her fourteenth-birthday present, a black mare named Mariana, which she rode with deliberate abandon and laughed when the grooms told her she would "break her bloody neck".

These were important statements of independence, perhaps not so much intended for those around her but to satisfy herself, like the day she harnessed Mariana to a cart called a longshafter and, without telling anyone, drove to the nearby village of Breadalbane to collect the mail, only to be thrown and almost killed when her horse bolted after being confronted with a rare sight on country roads—a motor car: "It did not teach me a lesson," she wrote. "Nothing ever does."

Sheila loved the farm, separated from the main house by a dusty ribbon of road, but was caught between its mystery and its horror; delighted at the overnight arrival of baby pigs, goats and cows, and disgusted yet intrigued by the bloody slaughterhouse: "I occasionally sat on the fence and watched the pen man cut a sheep's throat and then skin the poor animal."

The shearing shed was the real attraction, with its rough workers like Jock, who had amputated his own foot with an axe rather than let the poison from a tiger snake kill him. The shed was no place for a girl, he told her, before allowing her a turn at being a tar boy, to dab and brush tar to seal nicks on sheep when the shears drew blood. "This made me feel most important, but I was always sorry for the sheep, their lives seemed to me to be hideous: they were eternally herded together in their thousands, driven for miles amidst clouds of dust in the burning sun, dogs snapping at their heels, kicked and cursed, then shorn and often badly cut. No wonder they looked so bewildered!"

The young girl sat enthralled on top of the 6-metre fence of the "round yard" to watch her brothers break horses. By the age of nine they had taught her to ride any horse, swim and crack a stock whip. She had killed her first snake and watched it be devoured on an anthill and once galloped for hours at dawn in a wild kangaroo hunt with her brothers and a pack of dogs. "It had taken months to persuade an apprehensive mother and indulgent father . . . that I was old enough and could ride well enough to go out with the boys. I had a strong will and I knew it. I was excited and secretly terrified . . . my heart beating so fast I could hardly breathe . . . but of course, I never admitted it."

She kept a variety of pets, including a piglet and a lamb born on the same day, which she fed with a bottle and which followed her everywhere. When a pet died, she would arrange an elaborate funeral service. The body of the animal would be placed on a goat cart, which the gardener then led to a pet cemetery near the orchard. Sheila followed dressed in the robes of a nun: "The ceremony would always include Mummy and Ninget . . . and occasionally Jack and Roy if they felt in the mood. I would read a few words of the burial service and a cross with the animal's name on it would mark the grave."

Of all her animals it was the rabbits she collected that especially caught her heart; forbidden creatures she'd hide in the wine cellar when the government inspectors arrived every few months, trying to eradicate the introduced menace that was so out of control across Australia that if Sheila gazed off into the distance at dusk their sheer numbers made it look as if the hard brown land was moving.

As always though, there was a practical side to rural life: "Although my heart always ached for the rabbits, once they were dead it seemed different. Jack and Roy taught me to skin them expertly in 30 seconds. I was proud of the achievement."

Occasionally Sheila would remove herself from the male world of the station and lie in the long grass of the orchard beneath the pear trees, where she would construct plays in her head, once convincing her brothers to dress up and put on a play she had written about a woman who ended up as a convent nun because of unrequited love.

Margaret Chisholm, encouraging her daughter's creative spirit, gave her a bound copy of Elizabeth Barrett Browning poetry for her fourteenth birthday, as well as a copy of *The Rubáiyát of Omar Khayyám* and Thomas Hardy's *Tess of the D'Urbervilles*. Her imagination soared: "I sometimes dreamed of flying to England and America in an airship, not unlike *Arabian Nights* and magic carpets.

"I suppose I was a queer mixture of romanticism and boyishness. I wrote these sentimental poems and stories, and yet was really happy with my horse and dogs and particular family pets. I liked to go out all day and help to round up the sheep and cattle, and I once swam my horse over a swollen river for a bet. I was quite unconscious of my looks."

Jack and Roy would certainly not tolerate any notion that their sister was anything but a tomboy, washing her face under an old pump near the kitchen the day they detected she had a dash of powder on her nose and teasing her about having a 43-centimetre waistline. Sheila accepted it with good grace but was embarrassed when they found her secret book in which she wrote her poems and began tittering over a verse titled "Is It Love?":

> Is it love, this nameless longing?
> This aching, lonely feeling,
> that round my heart seems stealing,
> and makes my pulse race.
> Is it love that makes me want you?
> Feel I cannot live without you,
> is it love that makes me doubt you?
> With your strange, elusive face.

Despite the isolation Sheila had several girl friends, relationships mostly made when the family rented a house in Sydney each year during the late summer. Mollee Little was her best chum, one of five children of the prominent pastoralist and businessman Charles Little, who had settled his family in a grand old mansion called Brooksby House, at the bottom of Ocean Avenue as the slope of Darling Point flattened out and slid into Sydney Harbour.

Mollee would come and stay at Wollogorang for holidays where they memorised *Alice in Wonderland* and read the poems of Baudelaire, talked about life and love and confided in each other: "We wondered what was just around the corner, beyond the lagoon—unknown, intangible, mysterious, exciting things—the places where you will never be, the lover you will never know. We didn't really understand half the time what we were talking about. We decided that when we married, we must feel like the poem by Elizabeth Barrett Browning, 'A Woman's Shortcomings'":

> *Unless you can think, when the song is done,*
> *No other is soft in the rhythm;*
> *Unless you can feel, when left by One,*
> *That all men else go with him;*
> *Unless you can know, when unpraised by his breath,*
> *That your beauty itself wants proving;*
> *Unless you can swear "For life, for death!"—*
> *Oh, fear to call it loving!*

Sheila's brother Roy was in love with Mollee, and Roy's best friend, a boy called Lionel who would also come to stay at the property, was infatuated with Sheila. Although Mollee felt the same about Roy, Sheila couldn't bring herself to declare romantic feelings for Lionel who pestered her about the future, promising to one day marry her and take her around the world in a "flying machine". Despite her rebuttal of Lionel's advances, they hung around with Roy and Mollee during holidays at Wollogorang as an "inseparable" foursome.

Sheila once tried to explain her feelings for a boy with whom she was quite happy to lie in the fields and wish on the evening star but knew she would never marry: "I suppose I loved Lionel in a childish way. I loved him as I loved my brothers only slightly differently which I couldn't even explain to myself."

⚬⚬⚬

As Harry Chisholm's business grew, so did the demands on his time in the city of Sydney, 200 kilometres to the north; here he made his way up the business and social ladders of colonial society, marking out his business territory in the heart of the CBD and creating his political base as a committeeman at the Australian Jockey Club.

Sheila had been educated at home for most of her formative years, making life as difficult as possible for the series of governesses who travelled out from Sydney only to be sent packing. This was the norm for girls, in a society moving only cautiously toward the notion that women were "robust" enough to tackle a formal education.

She and her mother would make the occasional trip to Sydney, usually catching a steamer at Kiama as it made its way up the coast from Melbourne. Sheila was gradually introduced into Sydney society circles, at first as a twelve-year-old dressed as "Cherry Ripe" at a children's fancy dress party at Government House and then graduating to being seen at race meetings as a seventeen year old—"Miss Sheila Chisholm, beech brown silk poplin skirt and coat, black hat with a crown of Bulgarian silk, finished with a long black quill."

The trips also meant she could catch up with Mollee, where the poetry readings and talk of love were replaced with high jinks, getting in trouble for wild pranks and dares, as Sheila would recall: "I'm afraid we were rather naughty, disobedient, wild girls and we did some pretty foolish things. We had a favourite expression 'I will put you on your mettle' which, on thinking it over, I suppose meant 'I double-dare you.'"

Their antics were at times dangerous, particularly at Bondi Beach where they loved body surfing and swimming out further than other swimmers, often out beyond the breakers despite warnings about sharks—"our boast was we liked to go out further than the furthest man"—until the day they watched the water boil crimson as a nearby swimmer lost his leg to a shark. "This episode dampened our enthusiasm for showing off."

The formal shift from country to city life came in 1912 when Wollogorang was sold after seventy years as the family home. Despite her deep passion for the property, Sheila would make just a bare mention of the sale in her private memoir, blaming it on an inability of her brothers to "get on together": "Chissie said he didn't want them to wait for him to die and so he gave them the money," she wrote. "Jack bought an enormous property in Queensland called Wantalayna. Roy bought a place called Khan Younis in NSW. Chissie and Ag [Margaret] decided to live in Sydney."

The Chisholms settled among the grand houses of Woollahra and Sheila finished her education at Kambala Anglican School for Girls in Sydney's eastern suburbs, where she was among the original enrolment of fifty girls who moved into the school's rambling premises overlooking Rose Bay.

It was a peaceful, uncluttered environment at Kambala, a name apparently derived from an Indian word meaning "Hill of Flowers", which was among the first private schools for girls established in Sydney as debate raged about the ability of young women to handle a male education curriculum. Until the latter part of the 19th century, girls had largely been educated at home but more and more schools were now opening, particularly to the upper classes, and Sydney University had recently even opened its gates to female matriculants. The girls at Kambala did not wear uniforms and were taught mainstream subjects such as English, French and Latin, as well as Mathematics and Science. Other classes offered included Elocution, Dress-making, Dancing, Singing, Music, Drawing and Painting. "The moral training of the girls, both in character and manners, is most carefully watched over," a prospectus of the day reassured parents.

But this breakthrough in education was a mere stepping stone on the long and difficult path to equality; for the moment, the expectation for most young women remained one of marriage and children: "Chased and chaste," her mother warned. Sheila's destiny seemed no different and, as she took leave of her friends at the Hotel Australia gathering, it was time for her to make the transition into the adult world—her finishing school would not be in the classroom but in the social whirl of Paris and Munich and possibly even in being presented as a debutante at Buckingham Palace.

Her parents had talked about it for years, particularly her mother: "She was ambitious for me and wanted me to finish my somewhat sketchy education in Europe—an idea that many parents acquired years later. Anyway, she argued, I was far too young to be married, even though Chissie reminded her she was sixteen when they were wed."

Margaret may also have been encouraged by a reading she once received about her daughter from a famous Chinese astrologer who told her that he couldn't tell her anything about Sheila's future because her stars belonged to the northern hemisphere and he was only able to read stars from the southern hemisphere. Chissie declared it hokum and dubbed her the "child of fate".

Harry Chisholm, easygoing and good-natured, particularly with his daughter, was not among the guests at his daughter's farewell that afternoon, or at least not mentioned in the list of mostly young friends who sipped tea and exchanged pleasantries for a few hours. He was probably in his elegant sandstone office one block away, at the corner of King and Castlereagh streets, his attention fixed on the annual Easter sales at his yards in Randwick where dozens of established thoroughbreds and 237 yearlings would go under the hammer.

Perhaps Chissie would have acted differently, and been more attentive to the plans of his wife and daughter and insisted they stay home, if he had had a more realistic sense of what lay ahead for his family and the nation. Even though there were storm clouds of war on the horizon the future must have seemed so bright and the possibilities endless. The threat of war in Europe simply seemed so far away, physically and politically. The First Lord of the Admiralty, Winston Churchill, had reassured them just a few days before that the British Navy was superior to the German fleet and that Australia was safe because of Britain's alliance with Japan.

But these assurances were naive, and the threat was real. Most of the dozen or so young men attending Sheila's farewell that afternoon would enlist within a year to fight for King and Country on the other side of the world. Many among them would return physically shattered or psychologically damaged, but other guests would not. William Laidley, a friend of her brother Roy, would be awarded a Military Cross for gallantry in August 1918, only to die a few days later amid the human carnage of the Somme.

The party moved inside as the afternoon breeze threatened to remove the ladies' hats and send them fluttering off the balcony and into the street below; it finally broke up so that Sheila and her mother could go home to finish packing for what they thought would be a six-month sojourn. Next morning, as Sheila boarded the *Mongolia* and waved goodbye to her father on the dock, there was no sense that it would be more than six years before she would see him again.

"I felt excited by the prospect of this trip but sad also," she would reminisce. "It would probably be enjoyable to see new places and meet new people and would only be for a few months. I hated the thought of leaving Chissie, my brothers, Mollee and my pets but to my surprise I hated to leave Lionel most of all. I suddenly realised I would miss him, and remembered how often we had both been entranced by the beauty of the black swans on the lagoon at sunset and by the brilliance of the multi-coloured parakeets that perched in the trees or wheeled screeching overhead as we rode through the paddocks in the early morning and the haunting scent of the wattle and the gum trees. He appreciated sunsets and dawns and black swans and white blossoms and the scent of wattle, and understood how it made one feel. But did he really understand?

"I felt these emotions so deeply myself that I wanted to share them with somebody else, even if I had to pretend. When I was very young I had always dressed up my dolls, and to me they became real people who thought and spoke and lived, exactly as I wanted them to think and speak and live. They also lived in imaginary dream houses, which I could see so vividly at night, just before going to sleep. Mummy warned me against this trait in my character. She said: 'You must be careful, this make-believe may bring you unhappiness some day. Do not try to turn people into what you want them to be; do not fancifully decorate them as one decorates a Christmas tree for, if you do, the awful moment will surely come when you will find the branches bare, stripped of all the ornaments of your lively imagination pinned upon them. It is better not to live in a world of dreams.'"

The Sunday Times newspaper also reported their departure, the short but prescient mention appearing in the social pages:

Mrs Harry Chisholm and her daughter, Miss Sheila, were among the travellers who left for Europe on Wednesday by the Mongolia. They have gone for a tour of Europe and expect to be away for some time. Mrs Chisholm was a Miss MacKellar and was one of the belles of Sydney. Miss Sheila Chisholm is very popular.

2

I THOUGHT THIS MUST BE LOVE

June 18, 1914: The London Season was approaching its peak and the attendant *Sydney Morning Herald* journalist, writing the column "A Woman's Day", was glowing in her delight:

At the moment the world amuses itself; the sun shines brightly, trees are at the zenith of their beauty, roses abound and, above all, it is Ascot week. To those who know England much is summed up in this sentence. Though Tuesday, the first day of Ascot races, was cold enough to demand wraps, we have had glorious weather ever since. On Tuesday Ascot was "cloaked". There has never been such a sudden dash into popularity as this incursion of the cloak. It swept everything else before it. Cloaks of fine cloth, of satin, taffetas, velvet and lace; no costume seemed complete without one. In the fine gossamer-like material the cloak simply hung from the shoulders of its wearer, looking, as the wind caught its voluminous folds, like a huge butterfly.

The Season was an event to embrace rather than to attend, created to give society women a reason to accompany their husbands to the city during the sitting of parliament; an endurance test of presentation and deportment. It lasted not for a few days or even weeks, but for months—from the middle of April, when the spring slowly thawed, through May with the court ball at Buckingham Palace and June when the crowds flocked to Epsom for the Derby and the Royal Ascot week. Then followed the Henley Regatta and the Eton v Harrow cricket match at Lords after which the crowds travelled to the Isle of Wight for the Cowes yachting regatta before the rich and privileged at last began packing up their city houses and shifting back to their sprawling, if crumbling, country estates.

And before the Season proper came the debutantes—a 200-year-old ritual, in which society mothers presented their teenage daughters to the royal court to signify they were now of marriageable age. This tradition had been begun in 1780 by George III, who held a ball each January to celebrate the birthday of his wife, Queen Charlotte; it had then become entrenched through the 19th century as a rite of passage—the sovereign's blessing.

By the 20th century the presentations were held through March, when the cold winds still blew up The Mall, forcing the young ladies in their virginal white gowns and plumed feathers to scurry across the gravel forecourt of Buckingham Palace, holding their trains in gloved hands as they disappeared through its austere facade. Once inside they would wait nervously in lines to be presented to the King and Queen; a deep curtsey to the Queen—graceful descent, left knee locked behind the right, arms by the sides to balance—then three sidesteps and another curtsey to the King.

There were three debutante presentations in 1914. Margaret and Sheila had missed them all by the time they arrived in London in the July after several weeks in Paris, but the rounds of garden parties and balls had only just begun as they rented a flat at St James's Court, in the heart of the city abuzz with society and those who wanted to be a part of it.

Sheila had been dazzled by the trip even before reaching Europe, the journey by ship accentuating the distance and cultural divide between her homeland and the rest of the world, as if drawn from the pages of the books she loved—"flying fish and sunsets across the Indian Ocean, rickshaws in Galle drawn by sweating, coloured men wearing only a loin cloth, the barren rocks of Aden, the stifling heat of the Red Sea. Then the wonder of the Suez Canal and the riotous colours of Port Said."

They had landed at Marseilles and joined a boat train to Paris where Sheila was immediately enchanted by the rich splendours of the city. They stayed at the Hotel Lotti, the city's newest and most fashionable hotel, and she pestered her mother into allowing her to go one night to the restaurant Maxim's, which had featured in the opera *The Merry Widow* that had toured Australia in 1913. Not one to let an opportunity pass, Sheila then revelled in the "shock and disapproval" of other restaurant guests when she accepted a dance invitation from a professional dancer: "He was a typical gigolo, I had never seen anything like him before."

Talk of war had forced them to abandon planned trips to Germany and Italy so Sheila and Margaret headed for London where there was another opportunity to be presented at the palace, this time as part of a select group of Australian women. The event was reported back in Sydney, Margaret and Sheila "among Australian ladies either attending or being presented at the drawing rooms at Buckingham Palace. Lady Samuel is presenting Mrs Chisholm and her daughter". Viscountess Beatrice Samuel was the wife of the British Postmaster General, Herbert Samuel, and an active member of the Women's Liberal Federation whose aim was to give women the vote.

At other times during the endless round of society events it was hard to get noticed in the crowd, particularly when the venue was one of London's most exclusive, the hostess among the most famous society women of her day and the room full of aristocrats:

July 20 Queensland Figaro and Punch: The unusually warm weeks which have preceded the end of the London season have driven some people out of town but there were still a number of parties every afternoon and evening . . . Lady Grey-Egerton gave a very large "At Home" at Claridge's last week. She wore a white lace silk gown and her daughter, Miss Aimee Clarke, wore powder blue cloth. Among the guests were many notable English people including the Countesses of Selkirke, Dudley, Limerick,

Lindsay, Annesley, Ranfurly and Brassey, Katherine Duchess of Westminster, Lady Blanche Conyngham, Lady Constance Combe, Lady Templemore, Lady Helen Grosvenor; and of Australian interest Lady Denman, Lady Reid, Lady Mills, Lady Fuller, Lady Coughlan, Lady Samuel, Mrs Collins, Mrs Smart, Mrs Primrose, Mrs Chisholm and numbers of others.

But the excitement would end quickly. No one had quite believed that war would be declared. The Germans didn't have the money to fight a war and, besides, they would be beaten within weeks or, at worst, months. But on July 28, a week after Lady Grey-Egerton's select gathering, the first shots were fired.

On August 4, Londoners crowded into the city centre to sing and cheer when the announcement was finally made that Britain had no choice but to enter the conflict that had been ignited by the assassination of Archduke Franz Ferdinand in Sarajevo. Any thoughts Margaret and Sheila might have had of booking their passage home to Sydney were now placed on hold. Sheila could hear the crowd from the apartment: "I have remembered all my life the dull roaring sound of the crowd that surged around Buckingham Palace. 'God Save the King' was sung over and over again," she would recall years later. "The cheering went on for days and nights. It was mob hysteria. It seemed a crusade. London was electric."

Margaret didn't know what to do. Neither did Chissie, who was keeping in touch by cablegram. Should mother and daughter remain in the relative safety of London or risk a three-month boat trip back to the sanctuary of Sydney? In the end the decision was made to stay. They were still in London in late October, when Roy Chisholm was married, not to Mollee Little as Sheila had expected but Miss Constance Coldham, daughter of a wealthy Queensland businessman and racehorse owner her brother had met. The wedding was celebrated at the Australia Hotel—the same place Sheila's farewell had been held seven months before. The Townsville Daily Bulletin noted: "A cablegram was received from Mrs Harry Chisholm, who is still away with her daughter Sheila on the wedding day."

And there was further important news for the family. Older brother John had joined the Australian Expeditionary Forces and was headed for Egypt in preparation for the push into France. "Jack", a lean, 6-foot-tall man with the ingrained deep tan of a grazier, cut a commanding figure and was assigned to the 6th Australian Light Horse Regiment and given the rank of sub-lieutenant. The regiment was part of the 2nd Australian Light Horse Brigade, which would be based at Maadi on the outskirts of Cairo where they would wait for orders.

Margaret Chisholm made up her mind—mother and daughter would go to Cairo to be near their son and brother.

<hr />

Margaret and Sheila left England in November through the fog that clung to Tilbury Docks, amid little of the fanfare that normally accompanied departing ships. These were serious times.

They arrived in Cairo in December, a month before Jack and Roy's childhood friend Lionel who had also signed up.

Meanwhile, Sheila and Margaret settled into the strange, almost twilight existence of a city that was being commandeered for war. The opulence of the colonial outpost remained, with hotels like the grand Shepheard's where they stayed, but this was a city in transition.

Sheila was one of few women among thousands of men, many of them young and single who accepted that the next day might be their last: "I was usually dressed in riding breeches or as a Red Cross worker, always surrounded by dozens of men in various uniforms," she would recall. "I had many would-be-admirers but they didn't interest me in the least."

Among them was a coterie of English aristocrats including the Duke of Westminster, "considered one of the most attractive men in England. I liked him but thought him rather old. I suppose he was thirty-seven at the time." Others included Lord Parmoor, and his brother Colonel Fred Cripps who would lead the last-ever cavalry charge against the Turkish guns at El Mughar and later become Chancellor of the Exchequer.

Her daily confrontation with death only drove Sheila and her companions to explore what they could of life, with sailing trips up the Nile in dahabiyas and crazy night drives in cars to see the Sphinx by moonlight, stars hanging like lanterns against the night sky. At other times Sheila rode Arab stallions out into the desert in the evening to watch the sunset, or at dawn to watch the sunrise.

Although there was an illusion of normality with lively bars and restaurants filled each night, Cairo had been converted into a sprawling hospital campus, where every available public building was emptied and refilled with iron-framed beds hauled from hotels, and others made locally from palm wood. Even before the medical staff faced the overwhelming influx of wounded Allied soldiers, they were challenged by infectious diseases; they were simply unprepared for the mammoth outbreaks they encountered of measles, bronchitis, pneumonia, tonsillitis, meningitis and venereal disease.

Alongside the arrival of the Australian divisions in January, the Heliopolis Hotel was commandeered to provide another 200-bed hospital; its lavish furniture and fine carpets were rolled up and carried away to be stored while its four floors were turned into kitchens and wings for officers, soldiers and nursing staff. Beds were placed in great hallways beneath marble columns and soaring curved windows. But this still wasn't enough. By late February an infectious diseases hospital, to treat an outbreak of measles, was housed at a local skating rink, and there were another 400 patients in a separate venereal disease hospital under canvas at the aerodrome.

Sexually transmitted disease, not war-related violence, was the greatest health risk in the months between December 1914 and April 1915. To try and limit its occurrence, the Australian and British commanding officers decided to create a series of clubs to try and corral their soldiers into an environment that might be safer than letting them loose into the local community.

The biggest soldiers' club was a converted ice rink at Ezbekiya Gardens in Cairo, which could hold up to 1500 people. It was a honey pot for young soldiers, who knew death was potentially just around the corner and approached life accordingly, and for "beauties from any nations tickled to be escorted by bronzed giants from Down Under", as one lieutenant would later observe. On Sunday evenings lanterns would sway and twinkle in trees against a sky heavy with the aromatic scents of the East, while the band competed with endless Arabic chants. The streets bustled day and night with a mix of horse-drawn carts and limousines.

On April 17 the officers of the Australian Light Horse hosted a dinner-dance—as a thankyou to the local people for their hospitality but also as a farewell from officers who knew many of their company would die in the coming months as they faced battle for the first time. The dinner was held at the grand Tewfik Palace, its grounds and terraces lit with rows of coloured lights and the ballroom decked with a combination of palm trees and roses. Among the guests were Margaret and Sheila Chisholm, happy to have been reunited with Jack after his arrival and unwilling to consider the worst-case scenario. The next morning Jack and Lionel were among the tens of thousands who left Cairo for the Dardanelles off Turkey, and a week later the fighting began with the ill-fated landing at Gallipoli.

No one was prepared for the reality of war, as an Australian government report prepared in the aftermath recorded:

The weather was beautiful, and anyone might have been easily lulled into a sense of false security. In April however, a trainload of sick arrived. Its contents were not known until it arrived at the Heliopolis siding. The patients had come from Lemnos and numbered over 200 sick. On the following day, however, without notice or warning of any description, wounded began to arrive in appalling numbers. In the first 10 days of the conflict, 16,000 wounded men were brought in to Egypt.

Sheila was a witness to the horror: "The news was appalling, like a nightmare. About 500 wounded were expected but 10,000 arrived."

A casino was taken over, then a sporting club, a factory, three more luxury hotels, even Prince Ibrahim Khalim's palace. By the second week of May 1915, the initial plans for one hospital of 520 beds had grown into eleven hospitals housing 10,600 beds, most of which were now being made of palm wood. By the end of August, the wounded and sick would number more than 200,000, handled by a daily staff of fewer than 400.

The crisis was not merely because of a lack of space and facilities but also a lack of staff; many nurses began to break under the strain. Reinforcements were on their way, but there was a desperate need for civilian help. Margaret and Sheila Chisholm were among a number of Australian women who volunteered to stay on and help.

Margaret, or "Ag" as Sheila began calling her mother in gentle mockery of Margaret one day declaring: "Goodness, I am becoming an old hag," had been working for the Blue Cross taking care of injured horses. She and Sheila also helped establish the Australian Comforts Fund, which provided basic items, such as blankets and socks, for the soldiers at the front; they spent hours each day going from one hospital to another, visiting men they didn't know, listening to their stories and providing reassurance.

Against protests from officialdom, they even provided free cigarettes to convalescing soldiers, rather than force the men to spend
their wage of 5 shillings a day on the tobacco they needed to take
their minds off the pain and horror.

Sheila worked alongside her mother tending the wounded
and dying, much to Ag's annoyance who thought her daughter,
aged nineteen, too young and delicate ("how it bored me to
be thought too young", Sheila would later recall). The young
woman, who a few months before had been dressed expensively
while attending parties almost nightly and mingling with the
upper echelons of London society, was now clad in the practical
garb of a hospital volunteer.

But she did not remain unnoticed, particularly when she
accidentally destroyed several thermometers by leaving them
for too long in boiling water and was relegated to cleaning
duties for a period. She would always cringe at any reminder of
that particular mistake.

Two decades later, at a reunion of nurses in Adelaide, her
contributions would be remembered. Miss Sinclair Wood,
principal matron of the Army Nurses Reserve, who was in Egypt
when the first wounded came back from Gallipoli would recall:

There were five of us at Mena Hospital, and one night we got
word that 248 men were coming. We set to and made up beds,
prepared wards, and waited. The men had been in the ship for a
week and no one knows what they had gone through. When we
got the opportunity to snatch two hours' sleep some of the Red
Cross women, among them Sheila Chisholm, who was one of the

loveliest girls I ever saw, came over, rolled up their sleeves and it was wonderful what they did.

A *Sunday Times* gossip column in early May 1915 described her as one of "four beautiful Australian girls to be seen in Cairo quite recently". It seemed she could not be mentioned without a comment about her beauty.

Margaret and Sheila had other roles outside the hospital, including organising the delivery of Australian and English newspapers so the men could feel as though they were still a part of the world outside the war. There were even moments of levity in the bleakness of the dusty city. The cable sent to Australia by Margaret to begin an appeal for newspapers mangled her surname, which appeared as "Mrs Chicolo". Not only did papers arrive in their thousands but more than a hundred letters came addressed to Mrs Chicolo, thanking a "foreigner" for her kindness. "Some of the epistles are written in French and Italian, and others from people I know," she told *The Sydney Morning Herald*.

———

In the bloody tide of death that accompanied the Allied invasion of the Gallipoli peninsula during the last weeks of April and the first weeks of May 1915, it is understandable that the details of a bullet wound to an individual soldier would escape the attention of military chroniclers, even though the injured man was a British peer. When a cable about this incident lobbed in London a week later, headed "Sub-Lieutenant FES Lord Loughborough", it gave scant information about the incident beyond the staccato: "Wounded in action nr. Dardanelles . . . reported from hospital Cairo . . . progressing satisfactorily . . . wounded right shoulder".

"FES" referred to the young lord's "regular" name—Francis Edward Scudamore St Clair-Erskine. He was the elder son of the Earl of Rosslyn and heir to a lifetime seat in the House of Lords at Westminster as well as Scottish lands a few kilometres outside Edinburgh, which included the world-famous Rosslyn Chapel.

His injury was inconsequential compared to the thousands of men lying in muddy fields with their innards ripped open or lungs filled with mustard gas; yet such was the British deference to its class system that the young peer's misadventure made a few lines in a *Daily Mirror* story which described the military folly as "The magnificent story of the landing of the Allied troops at the Dardanelles and their successful advance against the Turks".

It was a convoluted task deciding how to refer to such men of title in the field of war. "Francis St Claire-Erskine" would have been too plain, but "Lord Loughborough" gave no Christian name, hence the unwieldy combination. Peers were also entitled to ranks that set them above the ordinary soldier and were often slotted into roles that did not fit their capabilities. Because of this, there would be numerous examples of poor aristocratic decision-making, often with tragic consequences for ordinary soldiers.

Lord Loughborough—"Loughie", pronounced Luffy, to his friends—was twenty-three years old. Tall, rakishly handsome and affable, so far he had found it difficult finding a place in society beyond his birthright, let alone meeting the demands of the military. He had been in Rhodesia when the war broke out, but joined up within a month of returning to London in the autumn of 1914. On application, he had been assigned to the obscure new armoured car division of the Royal Navy Volunteer Reserve.

Loughie was dressed in his uniform when he appeared in a court in January 1915 accused of writing a bad cheque. According to the charge, he had, in April 1913, signed a cheque for £200 to cover a gambling debt. Not only had the cheque not been honoured, but it had been post-dated to November to cover the fact that Lord Loughborough had not yet come of age. The newspapers covered that case too and even published a small but embarrassing photo of the young man, head down, scurrying from the Courts of Justice in the Strand.

The reason that this matter had taken so long to get to court was that, two months after writing the cheque, he had fled to Rhodesia. At the time his father, Lord Rosslyn, explained publicly that celebrations for his twenty-first birthday would be delayed for a year while his son was "off farming". When he finally returned he would "probably hold a dinner", Lord Rosslyn said, without any mention of the pending court case.

It was the timeline of events that allowed the sitting judge of the King's Bench, Justice Rowlatt, to decide that, because Lord Loughborough had been still a minor when he wrote the cheque, his actions should be excused and the charge dismissed. It was a fortuitous escape and one from which an important lesson should have been learned but, alas, the incident would be the beginning of an ultimately tragic narrative.

For the moment though, Francis St Clair-Erskine would enjoy some good fortune, if going to war could be seen as such. Two months after his court appearance he joined the Armoured Motor Machinegun Squadron, which was stationed on the Greek island of Lemnos; he arrived in March 1915 as preparations gathered pace for the disastrous Gallipoli campaign which lay ahead.

Torn and faded war records do not reveal any details of when his squadron joined the landing, but it was likely to have been several days after the initial assault on April 25. On May 2 he was wounded, most likely by a Turkish sniper firing from trenches high above the beaches. The same day, at least a dozen men in his unit were killed. A wounded shoulder must have seemed a blessing in the circumstances—he was evacuated immediately, and lay in a Cairo hospital bed two days later.

It was here, convalescing, that Francis Erskine's life changed for the better when an Australian soldier was given the bed next to him. Jack Chisholm and Francis Edward Scudamore St Clair-Erskine—two elder sons of landed gentry from opposite sides of the world—found themselves in the same wartime hospital, and they would soon share another common bond.

Sheila met Loughie one day when she came to visit her brother in hospital. It was love at first sight, according to a later report in the Singleton Argus, which described Loughie as a "youthful warrior". He was instantly smitten by Sheila's dark beauty and frontier-like attitude and quickly made a play for her attention. She was at first distracted—just another admirer—but fell for his cultured English charm when he sat up with her all night nursing a sick stray dog she had adopted and called Treacle.

She recorded the romance in her memoir: "Loughie came to tea the next day. He was tall and slim, with thick brown hair and hazel eyes. He was witty and most attractive. I soon began enjoying his company. We read the Brownings. He pursued me relentlessly and I was flattered by his attention. He told me that he had fallen in love with me at first sight. He constantly said: 'I love you and you are going to marry me, you will like England and all my friends will adore you.'

"He was persistent. He said: 'I know I am wild, but with your love I will be different. I could do great things.' I believed him and I was fascinated by him. We seemed so happy together. I thought this must be love."

Margaret counselled her daughter against marriage—she was too young and her beau, as witty and charming as he was, had a reputation for being too wild. Her father, Chissie, would not approve.

But amid the Armageddon the warnings fell on deaf ears, as she later remembered thinking: "Too young, too young, wait six months, wait a year, wait while he goes back and probably gets killed. He loves me so much and I love him. He is sweet to me and fond of animals; can't we be engaged? I suppose Loughie was spoiled and perhaps not very reliable but he had a great attraction and such a wonderful sense of humour, and he always made me laugh."

Loughie returned to the Gallipoli peninsula, his shoulder mended, but remained only a few weeks before being injured again, this time "slight and entirely his own fault", according to his colonel who described him as "brave, crazy and foolhardy". He returned to Cairo where he soon proposed.

Their engagement was announced on July 20 in the *Daily Mirror,* which praised the young peer. The rush to the altar received the blessing of Loughborough's father, the Earl of Rosslyn, of whom the paper commented: "The Earl himself is, of course, one of our most versatile peers. He has been a good soldier, a fair actor, a talented editor and a very brisk war correspondent. He has made at least one speech in the House of Lords. Verily, a peer of many interests!"

On December 27, 1915, at St Mary's Church in Cairo, Lord Loughborough married Sheila Chisholm, a union described by the *News of the World* as one of the most interesting weddings of the war because of the match between an Australian commoner and a British peer, adding: "Like most Australian women she is a superb horsewoman and excels as a vocalist."

Another newspaper columnist noted: "It is refreshing to hear that an Australian girl, after a pretty little war romance, has married into the peerage. With some of Britain's lordlings it has been a not too infrequent habit either to marry a charmer off the music halls or else wed an American heiress. Now it appears they are marrying on the keep-it-in-the-Empire principle—at least Lord Loughborough has set a new and patriotic fashion in that direction."

3

"HELLO, CALL ME HARRY"

Sheila watched the man from the deck of the ship *Arabia* as it docked at Southampton. Loughie had pointed out his father's car, a large black Rolls Royce with gold handles embossed with the letter R above coronets—the Household of Rosslyn. Then the earl had stepped out, instinctively ducking his head as tall men do before straightening and taking the umbrella from the man who had opened his door.

It was April 1916, dull grey skies and raining and a year since the disastrous landing at Gallipoli which had brought her and Loughie together. The couple had returned to England because his armoured car regiment was being disbanded and Loughie had been granted leave to transfer his commission from the navy to the army where he would join the King's Royal Rifle Corps.

There was one unexpected shock as the couple was preparing to leave Egypt. News came that Lionel, who had still hoped that

Sheila would one day marry him, had been killed in action: "I was absolutely miserable, my first deep sorrow. I loved him but was not in love with him. I tried to make him understand, but he didn't want to understand. Later I received a snapshot of myself which was found in his pocket. I have thought of him all through these years."

Lord Rosslyn was on the dock to greet them as they stepped from the gangplank. He was not only tall but handsome, and a man well aware of his own charms: "Hello, call me Harry," he smiled, a suggestion that seemed quite natural to Sheila, given that she called her own parents Chissie and Ag.

Harry Rosslyn went on: "Well, m'dear, quite a beauty. Loughie, I admire your choice. Now let me see the famous engagement ring, of course I had to pay for it. My son has no idea of money, as you will no doubt realise only too soon, if you have not already done so. Has he told you how often I have paid for his debts?"

The last bit took her by surprise, not because of what he said but because a father would deliberately embarrass his own son in front of his new wife. Sheila smiled and said nothing as she walked to the car: "I was rather shy, unsophisticated. I thought to myself: 'Head high, walk very tall'."

Sheila was already aware that her new husband had a gambling problem. The morning after their wedding, spent in a splendid villa overlooking the Nile, he had insisted on attending a race meeting in Cairo where he promptly lost a month's pay as well as the cheques given by guests as wedding presents.

Loughie apologised, trying to placate her with promises of

a baby son "with your looks and my charm", but the disturbing pattern would continue over the next few months, his periods of leave dominated by nights of drink and gambling. She played down the significance of his problem, dismissing his faults as the "crazy exuberance of youth".

What was important was that he made her laugh, like the night he dressed her in the borrowed uniform of a young officer and took her to visit the "low night haunts" he frequented around Cairo. Her concerns were probably also allayed by his station in life. Money didn't seem to be an issue, particularly when she met his cousin Geordie Sutherland, a man so rich that he had lent the admiralty his 200-foot private yacht, *Sans Peur*, to be used as a patrol vessel.

Even so, Loughie's gambling bothered her and she made him promise that he would stop. It lasted until they were aboard the ship taking them back to England where he spent the nights playing poker in darkened cabins to avoid being spotted by German submarines. Their boat would be torpedoed a week later. Sheila found the trip exciting rather than frightening, but worried about her new husband: "He seemed to have quite forgotten his promises. I didn't remind him of them as I was determined not to be a nagging wife." It was a long drive to Calcot Park, the Rosslyn home near Reading where the earl's third wife waited with their two young children. She was a former actress named Vera Bayley but was known as Tommy, and was more than eighteen years younger than her husband and just five years older than her stepson.

Sheila's first weekend in England was strange; she was driven in a convoy of cars and servants to a country estate of Lord and Lady Tichborne where the men played golf and the women sat home knitting for the troops.

At dinner she was seated next to Lord Birkenhead, who turned to her and asked how many children she had.

"None," Sheila replied, to which Lord Birkenhead raised his voice:

"You should be ashamed of yourself; a young, strong, healthy, beautiful woman like you. How long have you been married?"

"Four months."

"Oh ... er ... I'm sorry. Well, when you do have a child take my tip and have a twilight sleep."

Sheila sat dumbfounded, unable to conjure a response to the inappropriate lord and glad when he "turned to the more interesting woman on his left".

The men played poker after dinner and, since no one offered to teach her how to play, Sheila went to bed with Loughie's promise of not gambling "too high" ringing in her ears. She sat by the dying fire in her bedroom, alone and frightened in a strange, cold house with strange people who knew each other and told jokes she couldn't understand. Her husband appeared at 5 a.m., drunk and having lost a large sum of money to his father, which the earl and the rest of the house found amusing the next day.

<hr />

There are two ways of viewing the life and times of Loughie's father, James Francis Harry St Clair-Erskine. The first would be to marvel at his adventures and nerveless deeds at the racecourses of England and the card and roulette tables of Monte Carlo where he won, and lost, money in sums few could imagine, let alone risk. The same attitude could be taken to his war stories, first as a soldier and then as a war correspondent during the Boer War, and his subsequent careers as a professional stage actor in London and New York (the first English peer to claim this honour), a newspaper owner and finally an author of some controversy. It seemed there were no bounds to his talents and derring-do.

But a more realistic assessment of the activities of the 5th Earl of the Scottish House of Rosslyn would provide a less charitable perspective. By his own admission Rosslyn, as he referred to himself, was a flawed man who laid waste to his family's fortune and estate, cheated on two of his three wives and mostly rebuked or ignored his five children. The earl was well aware of his failings when he wrote his 1928 memoir, titled *My Gamble with Life*. It began: "I was heir to an earldom, so respected in the Kingdom of Fife and throughout Great Britain, that to live up to my father's reputation—not to speak of my grandfather's, who died before I was born—was a matter of no great ease. I can remember my father boxing my ears and telling me that if I was not a bigger man than himself I should disgrace the name." And yet that's exactly what he did.

Just three months after his own father's death, the 21-year-old 5th Earl attended the Newmarket thoroughbred sales "in my dead father's fur coat and with a long cigarette holder" and spent £6000 on one horse and several thousand more on others. The rot had set in early and within six years he had gambled away the bulk of his £50,000 inheritance, the equivalent of A$10 million today, coming to a head in 1893 when he placed £15,000 on Buccaneer, which had triumphed the year before in the Gold Cup at Ascot and was his favourite among the racehorses he owned. The horse finished fourth and the earl faced financial ruin.

In a move of desperation he sold the stable of racehorses, including Buccaneer. In the light of day it must have seemed calamitous. The earl was also forced to sell the family's home, the cold and forbidding Dysart House at Fife in Scotland, to a linoleum manufacturer, along with his father's pride and joy, a steam-driven yacht "of great splendour". The family's silverware followed soon afterwards in a three-day sale at Edinburgh.

And there was more to come as Rosslyn continued to gamble. Ruin was inevitable and four years later, having lost an estimated £250,000 on horses and cards, the earl faced the ignominy of being declared bankrupt. He was banned from taking his seat in the House of Lords; having inherited an estate of more than 3500 acres, plus coalmines, he placed what little was left in the hands of a trust while he turned his hand to acting and journalism to earn a living.

There might be room for some level of sympathy for Rosslyn's plight, if only because his story was all too common among his titled peers, at a time when money was easy to obtain and borrowed off the back of family estates with no thought for the longer-term consequences. Most of the members of the gentlemen's clubs of London—places like White's and the Jockey Club—lived off borrowed money.

<hr>

Among the earl's closest friends was Queen Victoria's oldest son and the future King of England, Edward VII, who, as Prince of Wales, proposed the toast at Rosslyn's first wedding in 1890 to Violet de Grey Vyner, daughter of an English aristocrat. Violet was financially "plentiful" and for a time helped prop up her husband's wastefulness. So close were Rosslyn and the prince that two years later Edward became godfather to Rosslyn's first son, Francis Edward Scudamore St Clair-Erskine—Sheila Chisholm's new husband, Lord Loughborough.

But the marriage of Loughie's parents would only last a few years, doomed by Rosslyn's erratic behaviour and long absences from home. The pair had been estranged even before he filed for bankruptcy, from the time when he was caught buying a £2000 turquoise necklace for an unnamed "beauty of her day". The earl was confronted by his father-in-law and admitted to the purchase, but he insisted there was nothing untoward about the gift. Violet and her father begged to differ and, after a short, failed reconciliation, she moved into a property in York owned by her father. Repeated pleas by Rosslyn for her to return to him were rebuffed. Their children, Rosabelle and Francis, then aged five and four respectively, went with their mother and rarely saw their father again during childhood.

Rosslyn resigned his commission in the Fife Light Horse and took to the stage, forming a company of players—Lord

Rosslyn's Theatrical Performances—which toured the country for two years. When the South African wars broke out in 1899, he tried to rejoin but was rebuffed. Instead, he took a job as a war correspondent for the *Daily Mail*, witnessing the Battle of Ladysmith against the Boers and being taken prisoner twice.

On his return from South Africa, Rosslyn started his own newspaper and followed his dream of becoming a stage actor. In 1902, he headed for the New York stage, where he appeared in a series of small roles.

He also returned to the gambling tables of Monte Carlo, somehow convincing others to contribute £1200 into a syndicate through which he would run a complicated roulette scheme. The inevitable happened and that scheme eventually folded, but Rosslyn would return year after year with predictable results.

In 1905 he met and married an American actress, Georgina "Anna" Robinson—a marriage that officially lasted two years, but had quickly soured. He later accused her of being "a drug fiend and addicted to drink" and she, in turn, accused the earl of being a liar and a philandering wastrel.

The couple lived in London for the first year of their marriage and then used Anna's money to lease a castle in Scotland, so Rosslyn could entertain his friends in more style. But it had clearly been a hasty decision on both parts and they soon split up. In 1906 they somehow got back together and hired a yacht for a reconciliation cruise. But when he brought another woman aboard named Muriel Saunders, Anna erupted in anger and left the boat, never to see him again.

Muriel believed Rosslyn would marry her after his divorce from Anna Robinson. But he fled to South America for a year before venturing back to London where, by chance, he met another actress, Vera Bayley, whom he swept off her feet and married. He was thirty-nine years old and Vera, daughter of a professional soldier, had just turned just twenty-one, being only four years older than his daughter. The following year they had a son, James Alexander, followed by a daughter, Mary, in 1912 and a third child, David, in 1917, six months after his older son, Loughie, had become a father and he a grandfather.

Some years later, as her daughter's marriage began to unravel, Margaret Chisholm revealed to Sheila a conversation she'd overheard back at the Shepheard's Hotel after the wedding ceremony: "I cannot understand how they could have allowed their child to marry into that effete, unreliable family," the unidentified person remarked.

But it would have made no difference to her strong-willed daughter: "Ag had tried to explain the facts of life to me but I didn't want to listen. I thought I knew everything."

4

A SON AMID THE AIR RAIDS

To marry into the British aristocracy was an exciting and daunting prospect for any young untitled woman, let alone for a stranger from the colonies. Yet, almost from the moment she arrived in London, the new Lady Sheila Loughborough was not only accepted, but feted, by society.

News of their marriage had taken time to penetrate the roar of wartime gunfire, and details of the union and how they had met changed ever so slightly from one version to another, but there was a clear sense of acceptance in the tone of the media coverage that found its way into the social pages of the major newspapers.

Some reports were matter-of-fact and recognised that wartime marriages were frequently precipitous—often desperate and tragically fleeting when, as in many cases, the husbands later failed to return from the Front. But other accounts were more enthusiastic and almost whimsical about wartime love, as in the following item from a "Ladies' Letter" column published in the *Camperdown Chronicle*:

Whenever you hear that two adventurous spirits have just murmured the usual "I wills", if you've any room left for feminine curiosity under those tight waists they make you wear nowadays, you wonder how they first came to meet, and where it was that he realised she must be his little too-tums for ever. Well, in the case of young Lord Loughborough, who was married at Cairo the other day, these details are frightfully romantic, with a background of Armageddon and a nasty noise of guns going on all the time. Lord Loughborough, who is the Earl of Rosslyn's heir, and an officer in the RNVR, has been at the Dardanelles, and so has a certain Tommy Kangaroo, a member of the Australian Contingent. Miss Sheila Chisholm is this soldier's sister, and she journeyed with her mother all the way from Sydney to be near her brother. In Cairo she met Lord Loughborough who was wounded, and—well, the orange-blossoming went off without a hitch.

To others she arrived as a woman of substance in her own right. *The Sunday Times* reported:

Lady Loughborough has been a most energetic worker for the Australian wounded in Egypt, and it was her mother, Mrs Harry Chisholm, who started the Empire Soldiers' Club at Heliopolis, a club that was greatly appreciated by thousands of Anzacs and others. It is a fine building, situated opposite Luna Park, near the

No. 1 Australian General Hospital, where numbers of Australian and New Zealand women in Egypt gave their services to comfort and cheer their men. The refreshments were provided at cost price. The average daily takings were £60, which is an evidence of how much the club was appreciated.

But despite this media acceptance, behind the scenes Sheila was desperately unhappy, other than her husband alone among much older strangers at Calcot Park where they continued to stay. It had been a mistake for the young couple, who should have been striking out together establishing a home of their own. Instead, the only time they seemed to spend in each other's company were the forays to London.

They usually stayed at the Ritz—opened a decade before by hotelier Cesar Ritz and already among the city's finest hotels, with bathrooms in every bedroom, walk-in wardrobes and brass rather than wooden beds—and attended dinners chaperoned by Loughie's cousins, the Sutherlands: Geordie's sister Rosemary and wife Eileen, whose influence would help Sheila ease her way into society.

But the weekends also gave Loughie, unfit for service due to his wounds, an opportunity to misbehave. His gambling had been barely tolerable in the surreal atmosphere of war, but now that they had returned to the genteel, safe environs of London it had become a worrying aspect to his character.

Sheila recalled one weekend, which she described as typical: "We dined and went to a play and I felt we were closer than we had been for some time. When we got back to the hotel he put me in a lift and said: 'Goodnight, be a good little girl while I go out with the boys. I won't be late.'"

"Please take me with you," she implored, fearing a repeat of the poker night when they'd first arrived.

"Most unsuitable, my child, it is what we call a 'tarts' party."

Sheila could not sleep and when Loughie finally returned near dawn they sat crying together in the luxurious suite. Just as he had done before, her husband promised that he would never do such a thing again, then went out and bought her a fox terrier she named Billy.

Sheila somehow found a way to blame herself, finding it difficult to tell her mother exactly what was happening and that her marriage, less than a year old, looked to have been a mistake and doomed for failure: "There was no doubt that Loughie was difficult but he had such charm and sweetness at times, although he was definitely a weak character," she would write on reflection. "I didn't know how to cope with him or my life and unfortunately there was no sign of a baby. I thought if I produced a son then things might get better."

In early September Margaret finally saw through her daughter's obfuscation, realised she was in crisis and took the next ship from Egypt to London where she arranged to talk to the Rosslyn family lawyers about the possibility of divorce. It was not an easy proposition because Britain's restrictive laws would not give women the same rights as men for another seven years. But to her surprise, the senior partner agreed wholeheartedly, commenting: "I advise you to take your daughter back to Australia before they break her heart."

But the divorce did not go ahead. Instead, Margaret persuaded the earl to finance the young couple into a London residence—a white, stuccoed, late-Georgian townhouse in Stanhope Place on the fringe of upmarket Hyde Park in the city's north-west where the homes were smaller than the grand mansions of Belgravia but generous enough to house a modest staff—generally a butler, a cook and two maids—who lived and worked in the basement floors and ascended, unseen, to the upper floors using internal staircases.

But as he gave with one hand, Harry Rosslyn took away with the other. Just as his son and daughter-in-law were moving into their first marital home, he placed a front-page advertisement in *The Times* to announce that he would not be responsible for his son's debts. It read:

WARNING to MONEYLENDERS—Messrs Terrell and Varley, as solicitors for the Earl of Rosslyn, are instructed to give notice that his Lordship is aware that his son, Lord Loughborough, is being tempted by moneylenders and touts to borrow money. The Earl of Rosslyn himself is his son's largest creditor and persons lending Lord Loughborough money are WARNED that Lord Rosslyn is not responsible for his son's debts and will not make himself responsible for them under any circumstances.

Three days later Rosslyn authorised an interview with an unnamed friend of Lord Loughborough, which appeared in the *Evening Standard* newspaper. The friend described the earl's actions as "a father's kind thought, drastic though it may appear, to protect a charming young man from the temptations which are besetting all young army officers at this moment". The friend went on: "His allowance is ample, but advantage has been taken of him more than once."

The hypocrisy of the earl's declaration, and the damage it was likely to do to his son's reputation, was not lost on others. The novelist Marguerite Cunliffe-Owen, writing under the nom de plume of La Marquise de Fontenoy, published a scathing article, which questioned the earl's own character and motives. She concluded:

> While it is possible that Lord Loughborough may be somewhat extravagant, the warning published in the papers comes with singular ill-grace from his father, Lord Rosslyn, who has been twice divorced, thrice married and repeatedly bankrupted—so many times that it is difficult to consider seriously for one moment the idea that he could ever make himself responsible for anyone else's debts. In fact, the warning would seem to partake rather of a bit of paternal irritation, not to say spite, than a fatherly care for a cherished son.

It was a well-directed barb, particularly as this public announcement of his son's waywardness only made it more embarrassing and difficult for Loughie to establish himself back in London.

And Sheila had more news—she was pregnant.

As much as Harry Rosslyn was an infamous, frivolous scoundrel, his sisters would become famous for being significant contributors to the social, political and philanthropic work of English society. Beautiful, rich and famous, all of them married important men and lived in splendour, but Frances and Millicent in particular, and Blanche and Angela to a lesser extent, were also tireless wartime volunteers, politically active and driven social activists who would have an impact on the life of Sheila Loughborough.

Frances, or "Daisy" as she was always known, was the eldest and the most prominent. Curvaceous enough to pose for Rodin, she was wilful enough to refuse when Queen Victoria picked her as an appropriate wife for her son, Prince Leopold, and she married instead Francis Greville, Lord Brooke, who was heir to a much greater title: the Earl of Warwick, which he inherited in 1893. By then they had five children, and his wife, after earlier rejecting Leopold, was in the midst of a long-standing—and socially acceptable—affair with his older brother Edward ("Bertie"), Prince of Wales before he became king.

As the Countess of Warwick, she was one of the leading "Professional Beauties" at a time when a new celebrity culture was taking hold, and was the inspiration for one of the most popular music hall songs, "Daisy Bell (Bicycle Built for Two)". But after an obscure newspaper, the *Clarion*, dared criticise the pomp and ceremony of her husband's celebrations when the family moved into Warwick Castle as "a vulgar saturnalia of gaudy pride", she stormed to London and confronted the editor. Instead of extracting an apology, she emerged an advocate of socialism—a rarity among the aristocratic classes.

It was her outspoken criticism of the wealthy, and her decision to champion the poor and embrace socialism, that would ultimately make her life politically notable. Daisy developed several charitable socialist organisations, became friends with socialists like George Bernard Shaw, HG Wells and Gustav Holst and stood for parliament as a Labour Party candidate, addressing political gatherings in her furs and jewels. But she didn't abandon society altogether. She continued to live at Warwick Castle and another family property, Easton Lodge in Essex, where she threw society parties to raise funds for her charities.

Daisy's younger half-sister Millicent, six years her junior, led a less controversial but equally progressive and famous life. In 1884, on her seventeenth birthday, she married Cromartie Sutherland-Leveson-Gower, a man almost twice her age from one of England's wealthiest families, which controlled more than 500 hectares of land across England and Ireland. He was heir to the title of Duke of Sutherland and a clutch of other peerages; when he inherited the title in 1892, he became one of the most senior peers in the House of Lords. The duke and duchess would have four children before his death in 1913.

While Daisy became increasingly more political, "Millie" embraced her role as one of the leading society hostesses of her day, a member of the so-called Marlborough House Group who clustered around the Prince of Wales and were credited with beginning the breakdown of social barriers by admitting outsiders, such as Americans and Jews. She was also among a lesser-known group of society figures, called the Souls because they met to discuss humanitarian issues rather than politics.

But it was her philanthropic work which created a mystique around the Duchess of Sutherland. She travelled to Europe during the Great War to help provide medical relief for wounded soldiers, for which she was awarded the Belgian Royal Red Cross, the British Red Cross and the Croix de Guerre, one of France's highest military honours. Back in England, she followed her older sister's example. On top of supporting numerous charities, she used her own funds to establish several of her own, as well as lobbying the government to tackle industrial issues, such as the problem of lead poisoning in potteries.

Another sister, Blanche, widow of the Duke of Richmond, also found her niche with the nursing corps during the Great War and took her daughter, Ivy, to France, where they managed a series of "rest clubs" created to provide nurses with a safe haven as they moved through the war zone. She would later be invested as a Dame Commander, Order of the British Empire, as well as Dame of Grace, Order of St John of Jerusalem.

The youngest sibling, Angela, was a divorced mother of two by the time war broke out. Lady Forbes, as she was known, volunteered at a hospital in Paris where, untrained, she took notes for surgeons in operating theatres. But her enduring role began after she saw trainloads of wounded being delivered from the Front and left for hours without food or water at a rural railway station. She opened a canteen for soldiers in the station waiting room and this subsequently expanded into a series of canteens, which became known as "Angelinas", and recreation huts. She became known as the "Forces' Sweetheart"—a title later bestowed on Dame Vera Lynn in World War II.

But Angela's canteens would end in controversy in 1917 because of a disagreement with senior military commanders who accused her of unseemly conduct—she had been heard to say "damn" and seen to wash her hair in public! Undaunted, she set up training schemes for disabled soldiers after the war. Years later she reminisced about the impact of war on women:

> Looking back, the social life of the late Victorian and Edwardian era seems to have consisted of a round of amusements, which went to make up the rather futile existence of the bulk of society. What a wrong impression of our latent capabilities the public would have if they were to judge them by looking at this. But the war proved most conclusively that these butterflies were really made of sterner stuff, and with hardly one exception, they rose to the most unexpected heights of capability. When I went to France I could hardly make a cup of tea, and in three months I felt I could run Lyons!

"Lady Loughborough gave birth to a son yesterday morning. Both are doing well." The notice in *The Times* "Court Circular" column on May 18, 1917 was simple but prominent. No elaboration was needed for either the title or the woman who now carried it. Sheila had captured media attention since her arrival in London, with magazines such as *Tatler* and *The Sketch* already taking an interest in the strangely beautiful new peeress, despite the contretemps between her troubled husband and his father, or perhaps because of it.

Then there was the Australian connection: she was perceived as a frontierswoman from the land of the wattle, who could ride a horse and sing like an angel. The colonies were no longer outposts but allies, and now one of Australia's most beautiful women was mother to a future peer—Anthony Hugh Francis Harry St Clair-Erskine.

But as self-assured as she appeared, privately Sheila was struggling like many women expecting their first baby, as she wrote to Anne Douglas, a childhood friend back in Australia, six days before the birth: "I am waiting impatiently for the babe to arrive. I really can't believe it; it seems so queer and the whole time I feel it's not happening to me at all, but to someone else."

Amid the joy and apprehension of motherhood there was also fear from overhead, as she would recount in her memoir: "The air raids were horrible and, of course, I thought every bomb was aimed at Tony. I adored him. He was the beautiful bouncing boy that Loughie always wanted."

London's social scene had retreated from its pre-war grandeur into mostly private parties and the occasional dance—the carefree fun of the 1914 Season was now a distant memory as war slipped into a third year. Buckingham Palace had closed its doors to the summer presentation of debutantes; feathers and tiaras had disappeared from formal attire; the dull sheen of pearls had replaced the glitter of diamonds around the throats and wrists of the ladies who kept up appearances. Occasionally, even among the newspaper columns that daily listed the dead and injured, there would be small items lamenting the loss of splendour and wistfully expressing the hope that it all might someday return, such as this from the *Daily Express* of July 15, 1917:

> Somebody murmured "Goodwood" at lunch yesterday, and that reminded us all that next week would in other times have marked the end of the London season and tomorrow have set a rush to the country of jaded society with the famous Sussex race meeting and Cowes a few days ahead. Then one of our party—a man whom we have always called a pessimist, and a man who hears more than most of us and says less—offered a wager of five to one that there would be a Goodwood meeting next year. I took it, and I hope I lose.

There was still the theatre, as well as frequent events to raise funds for the troops and to ease the financial burden of a nation spending an estimated £8 million a day to fund a war that was killing its young men in their tens of thousands. And this was where Sheila would make her mark in the world of society philanthropy as the "pretty Australian wife of Lord Loughborough, winning praise for her work on stage", at a charity performance of the Swinburne Ballet, for example.

The *Daily Mirror* reported her reappearance into society less than a month after giving birth: "The Lyric Theatre stage yesterday morning was in a state of bustle and movement. It was the final rehearsal for to-day's great 'Swinburne Ballet'. Gorgeous indeed were the gowns; in a lovely rosy gown was the girlish-looking Lady Loughborough, whose first public appearance it was for some little time past."

A few weeks later she was highlighted again, this time for being stylish alongside friend Diana Manners who, as Lady Diana Cooper, would become one of the most famed beauties of her time: "Veiling or chaining the throat seems popular. Lady Loughborough came with a blue film draped nun-wise around the oval of her face; Lady Diana Manners 'wimpled' like a medi-aeval abbess in white under a vast pale blue hat; her attractive young friend Miss Phyllis Boyd, had ribbons under her chin."

Loughie's aunt, Millicent, now the Dowager Duchess of Sutherland, had also returned from France and took the young mother under her wing, first at a society wedding at Westmin-ster and then for an extended stay at historic Dunrobin Castle, the Sutherland estate in Scotland. Sheila had met her son George, the new duke whom Sheila would always call Geordie, in Egypt and had also formed a close friendship with his wife Eileen, the duchess, who had also been a nurse and had now become Mistress of the Robes to Queen Mary, a senior court title responsible for the Queen's clothes and jewellery.

Sheila became a committed participant in the social work championed by the St Clair-Erskine sisters, particularly the plight of Belgian and French children orphaned by the conflict. Her involvement was even being noticed abroad. A column titled "With Women of Today" appeared in a New York news-paper and was effusive in its praise:

Eminent and esteemed writers, cartoonists and woman-haters have long made fun of women and their pet philanthropies or uplift work. The woman who has been interested in "social work" has been satirized in books, in newspapers and on the stage but it has not dampened her ardour any. And now with reclamation work to be done abroad there is a new and fertile field opened for the woman who "wants to do some good in the world". Lady Loughborough is an Australian woman engaged in such work. She is organizing a society to care for and educate the Belgian and French orphans. The organization plans to teach the orphans some trade or profession which will fit them to be self-supporting and good citizens. Lady Loughborough is called "Mother of the Orphans".

It was a title that contrasted sharply with her private role as a new mother.

5

"CALL THEM SIR AND TREAT THEM LIKE DIRT"

February 16, 1918: It was just after 10.30 p.m. as the crowds emerged from the plush warmth of the latest West End play and Leicester Square musical into the ice cold, late winter streets. Three years of war in Europe had not dulled Londoners' thirst for night-time entertainment, particularly now there was a sense that the fighting might soon be over. Debates about a new curfew and a crackdown on whistling for taxi cabs raged alongside warnings of rationing and the horrors of the Front—"a wonderful people, unwearied by war work", as one editorial noted of the nation's populace.

But the dangers were far from over and, as the streets quickly emptied, air-raid sirens began to wail, forcing stragglers to scurry. Five German Zeppelin-Staaken bombers had taken off from a base in Belgium, thundered across the channel and managed to avoid coastal air defences as they followed the

Thames to their ultimate target. Sorties by British aircraft had failed to stop the winged monsters, each capable of carrying 2000 kilograms of bombs. Dover had been hit and now the capital was under threat.

Among those making their way home was Mrs Freda Dudley Ward, wife of prominent MP, William Dudley Ward. Having dined with friends, she had shunned a cab in favour of walking back to the Belgravia home she shared with her estranged husband and their two young daughters. As the sirens sounded, she and a fellow diner who had offered to walk her home ducked into the doorway of a home unknown to them both; they were unsure how close the aerial threat was. By chance there was a dinner dance at this house that night; despite the blackened windows and hooded lamplight, its vigilant staff noticed the couple standing on the porch. The two of them were invited inside to wait out the sirens in the cellar with the others, including the guest of honour, the flamboyant Edward Prince of Wales.

Three of the bombers reached the city soon after and dropped their payload, one bomb hitting the Chelsea Hospital and killing five patients. The man-made thunder could be heard across the inner city, including by those in the Belgravia cellar; they couldn't discern from which direction the noise was coming, nor how close the bombers might be. It was a nervous although cheerful wait, something to which the city had become accustomed in a war that had dragged on far longer than most had anticipated.

When the danger had passed and the sirens were finally

silenced, the Belgravia party resumed and Mrs Dudley Ward's life had changed forever. Instead of continuing home, she bade farewell to her escort and stayed to dance the night away with the smitten prince, who had spent his time in the cellar chatting to the petite, pretty interloper. The music stopped at 3 a.m. and, before he went to bed that night, Edward scrawled in his diary that he'd "just met the world's most beautiful and marvellous creature!!!!!!!!!!" The next day he wrote to Mrs Dudley Ward, inviting another meeting, and an affair began that would last fifteen years.

The prince was on leave from his duties with the army, which largely consisted of morale-boosting visits to the troops, a role he despised. London's wealthy and titled mothers were falling over themselves to invite the handsome dandy to parties and dances where their daughters might catch his eye. The writer Lady Cynthia Asquith would note: "No girl is allowed to leave London—and every mother's heart beats high."

The previous year his father, King George V, had accepted a significant change in royal protocol, not only adopting the family surname Windsor, but also allowing his sons to take a British wife instead of the tradition of a union with the royal houses of Europe. That decision had been driven by the war, which had significantly reduced the number of potential partners, given that so many royal brides had previously been drawn from the German court.

But the prince was not particularly interested in marriage, having only lost his virginity at the age of twenty-four, in late 1916, to a French prostitute named Paulette. Since then he'd become obsessed with pursuing women and exploring sex ("I don't think of anything but women now," he wrote in his diary) and the notion of settling with one woman appeared a distant objective. He also had a penchant for married women, having previously courted Lady Marion Coke, a mother of four and wife of the 4th Earl of Leicester.

He had been linked with half a dozen or more noblewomen, mostly casual friendships or innocent dalliances, but all this appeared to change in a moment the night he met Freda. Edward showered her with attention over the next fortnight, writing almost daily, seeking opportunities to meet and even dining at her marital home on March 2, the night before travelling to Glasgow to tour shipyards. He was anxious to see her again when he returned three days later, although pleading with her to find a rendezvous other than her Lowndes Square marital home—"which I must confess, rather terrifies me!! But of course it is up to you to say whatever you wish me to do!"

On March 7 he tried telephoning, but missed her, so he penned a note and had it couriered from Buckingham Palace barely a kilometre away. There was a dinner dance that night to which both had been invited, although Edward was reluctant. He would much rather be alone with Freda so they could organise details of a getaway the following weekend: "Now about this dance this evening? You didn't seem very keen to go last night (or rather this morning) & I can't say I am really unless it's the only chance of seeing you!! ... Could you send me a message to the Bath Club to say Yes or No as I shall be there after 6 p.m."

Freda said yes, excited by the attentions of her royal admirer in the face of what had become a loveless marriage to a man sixteen years her senior. She was already fighting off a clutch of admirers who gathered around her at parties—she would call them "barrages"—but the attentions of the heir to the throne would prove irresistible. However, it would have to be discreet.

Her husband, William Dudley Ward, was serving as a lieutenant commander in the Royal Navy Volunteer Reserve. He was also the Liberal MP for Southampton and had been appointed the previous year as vice-chamberlain to the royal household, a 400-year-old senior political position which required him to write daily reports to the reigning monarch, detailing the proceedings in the House of Commons. "Duddie" was also known as a prominent sportsman, having rowed for Cambridge and competed in yachting at the 1908 Summer Olympics—a "kind, jolly and vague" man, as a friend would describe him, whose marriage had foundered and now existed in name only.

There was another reason Freda was keen to attend the dance that night. The event was being hosted by one of London's most prominent socialites, Lady Eileen Duchess of Sutherland, which meant her close friend Sheila Loughborough, the duchess's cousin by marriage, would be there. The pair had met socially and found a kinship in being young mothers of about the same age who were both in failing marriages and struggling against social norms that restricted women to a background role. Both were intelligent and strong-willed, and determined to have a voice besides being a wife and mother.

Freda regarded Sheila as the most beautiful girl she had ever seen, and Sheila had a similar opinion of her friend: "She was absolutely fascinating to look at," she would recall years later. More importantly, she said of Freda, "She had a good mind, a tremendous character, great loyalty and a wonderful sense of humour. She built one up and made one feel amusing and attractive. She had a strong influence on us all."

Sheila had been spending most of her time at Winchester, an hour's train ride south-west of London, near where Loughie was now stationed, having been granted the rank of captain with the King's Royal Rifle Corps, serving as adjutant to the colonel-in-chief of the rifle depot. A medical examination had concluded that he was unfit for active service and recommended that he be placed permanently in a desk job, where he continued until the war ended. Although this guaranteed his safety, the assessment did nothing for the self-esteem of a man who desperately needed a sense of purpose in his life.

They had even rented a large Gothic manor house called Lankhills in the wooded countryside on the outskirts of the city where Sheila was expected to play social hostess for the colonel, who was unwed. The responsibility had its benefits, taking some pressure off the marriage and opening up social opportunities as guests began appearing including a young English lord who, like many of the royals, had recently anglicised his German name, Battenberg. Lord Louis Mountbatten would become a lifelong friend.

There was a constant stream of visitors. Another was an American named Carroll Carstairs who, by some quirk, was serving with the Grenadier Guards. Carstairs would become known as an art dealer after the war but would also write one of the celebrated books of the Great War, *A Generation Missing*. After the book was published in 1930, Carstairs told Sheila he had been writing about her when his leading character had described his desire for a beautiful but untouchable woman: "When I look in your eyes I want to cry. When I look at your nose I want to laugh and when I look at your mouth I want to kiss it."

The compliments only highlighted the struggle to hold together a marriage with a man who seemed unable to contain his own demons. The marriage may have appeared stable, but in truth it was held together by the birth of Tony, who was now nine months old.

A few weeks before the Sutherland party they had been photographed together to promote an amateur stage production to raise funds for the King's Rifles at the Guildhall. Their body language made the strains obvious—Loughie posed stiff and awkward in uniform while Sheila, demure against his height, stared up worriedly at her husband, her hand pushed against his shoulder as if keeping him at bay.

Behind closed doors it was worse. He could be charming and amusing, particularly in company and playing games like charades. His favourite word was "depot", for which he gave clues in two parts: the first "fishing in the River Dee" and the second when he reappeared wearing a chamber pot on his head. Sheila laughed every time.

But his mood changed with too much alcohol and there were times when his behaviour became threatening. One night he threw Sheila's dog, Billy, into the fire (the dog was unharmed) and on another occasion he fired a gun at her kitten, claiming it had stalked his chickens. "I begged him not to drink. I knew it was the root of all his troubles but when we discussed it he would promise to give it up and then, in the next breath, refuse to admit that he drank too much, which was bewildering."

Sheila attended the March 7 dance alone, dressed in a golden ball gown (lent to her by Eileen) and wide-eyed at the grandeur of the occasion, attended by powdered footmen in rooms full of paintings that belonged in museums. It was held in Stafford House which was considered, and certainly taxed, as the most valuable house in London. Near St James's Palace, its rococo interior and state rooms were so grand that Queen Victoria, when she attended a dinner there many years before, had remarked on arrival: "I have come from my house to your palace."

Edward, his social calendar overflowing with requests and expectations, had to attend an earlier event on this particular evening; he arrived at the dance just after 6 p.m. with his younger brother, Albert (or "Bertie" as he was affectionately known), in tow. Discretion overcame desire and the prince avoided making a beeline for Freda, instead circling the room as he and Albert were introduced to guests.

Eventually the two princes reached the group of women in which Freda had positioned herself; it included Lady Rosemary Leveson-Gower, the Duke of Sutherland's younger sister, who had been one of the objects of Edward's attentions in recent months. The pair had, it was said, even discussed marriage, but rumour was that his mother, Queen Mary, had been against the union because of possible "defects" in the duchess's family line. The reference here was interpreted as doubts about the dowager duchess's brother and Sheila's father-in-law, the Earl of Rosslyn, whose gambling and womanising may have been greeted with some amusement and even lauded in some circles, but not by the King and Queen.

Having acknowledged Lady Rosemary, Edward's attention turned to the woman next to her, dressed in a golden gown. They had not met before but, as with many other men, he fell for Sheila Loughborough's wide eyes and insisted on a dance. Neither of them realised that their chance meeting would lead to a lifelong friendship, full of secrets. The prince referred to the meeting several months later in a letter to Freda, after he had resumed his duties in Europe: "I've only met Sheila once, I had a dance with her at one of the parties in March although I can't remember which & she certainly seemed a 'divine woman' though we didn't have a long talk: Rosemary introduced me to her!!!!"

Sheila would also recall their meeting. As the princes approached, she had asked Lady Rosemary what she should do and say when introduced to the royal brothers: "Curtsey to the ground, call them sir and treat them like dirt," Rosemary replied quietly.

Neither Edward nor Sheila made mention immediately afterwards of the fact that she also met Prince Albert that night, his presence hidden behind shyness and the magnetism of his older brother. Sheila danced several times with both princes.

She would note in her memoir: "It was an enjoyable evening, and I told them my grandmother was a kangaroo!"

———————

Sheila was hiding another piece of news that night, or perhaps she wasn't yet sure herself—she was pregnant again. It would be two months before she announced the news to Freda, who passed it on to the prince in one of her almost daily exchanges with him after he had returned to Italy in late March. He wrote back on July 18: "So Sheila is going to have a war baby & I can well imagine someone wanting to get away from Loughie for a bit as, although I don't know him, I've heard the kind of fellow he is & he must be trying to live with!! He was sacked from the RN College, Osborne, my 1st term there in the summer of 1907."

Edward's views, harsh as they appear here, were shared by many in London's social circles, where Sheila's marital difficulties were already being acknowledged, but the realisation that he was about to become a father for a second time did not slow down the young lord. In fact, the end of the war soon revealed the fragility of his personality as London went into a freewheeling celebration after Armistice Day on November 11, 1918.

Some of his antics could almost be amusing, like the day he and his friend Noel Francis climbed onto a roof of the Francis house in Grosvenor Square dressed in hunting tweeds with their guns and shooting sticks, where they hid behind chimney pots and shot down promotional Selfridges balloons as they drifted across the city. The police were called but the butler managed to convince the officers that the gunfire had come from another house. Sheila and Noel's wife, "Poots", revelled in the antics of their husbands: "Our husbands were such a crazy couple; we never could guess what they were going to do next," Sheila would recall.

More seriously though, he would soon be lured back into heavy gambling.

By contrast, Sheila was attracting more and more media attention. In early September 1917 she had been photographed for the prominent magazine *The Sketch*; a dark, romantic image of her accompanied an article that repeated details of her wedding two years before and mentioned the birth of her elder son, Anthony.

Eight months later the magazine returned to photograph her, and this time her pose was demure, with her strong hands folded on her lap, gazing up past the camera and dressed in a crocheted top and a single string of pearls. Yet behind her almost coy exterior, the photographer had captured a hint of steel. The heading across the top of the page was dramatic—"From the land of the wattle: a beautiful peeress".

The prince commented on it in a letter to Freda a few days later: "I see that photo of Sheila in last week's *Sketch* ... she does look so good doesn't she & has such a babyish face though a very pretty one."

As it turned out, babyish was an appropriate term, at least in terms of her mindset. Sheila wrote to her friend Anne Douglas in early October as she waited impatiently for the birth of her second child, this time with a sense of delight helped by the expected end to the war: "By the time you get this letter I hope my new baby will have arrived safely. I go to London on the 16th, I think, as I expect it any time after that. Tony gets sweeter every day and trots about everywhere now. He will be 17 months this month, so there won't be much time wasted between them! I feel I am rather like the proverbial rabbit!!!!"

On October 30, 1918, she gave birth to another boy, Peter George Alexander St Clair-Erskine. The Earl of Rosslyn came to visit—"to inspect his grandchild"—and promptly paid a £50 bet he'd had with Sheila that she wouldn't bear another son: "How clever of you m'dear," he quipped. Despite his failings, Sheila had a fondness for Harry.

A fortnight later the war was over. That night Sheila lay in bed at the Ritz with her infant son, listening to the sounds of euphoria. It reminded her of the cheers the night the war had been declared four years before. It seemed so long ago: "Thank God it was all over. Tony and Peter were safe; Loughie and my brothers had survived. Of all the people I loved, only Lionel was dead. I often thought of him. Anyhow, I decided there can never be another war. This war must end all wars—no one could ever be so stupid again."

As the armistice guns boomed across the city there was a scream. Her maid had fainted, mistaking the celebration for an air raid.

"Later Loughie fought his way into the Ritz. He told me the generals were almost hugged to death. Everyone seemed crazy. He walked around the streets most of the night, jammed in the crowd. How exciting and thrilling—strangers embraced one another, people were cheering and singing and dancing. London had gone mad. What a happy madness!"

6

THE 4 DO'S

Britain emerged from the winter shroud of 1918 to tally the loss of life and wrestle with post-war survival. The wild celebrations of Armistice Day, when thousands ignored the damp drizzle to sing and cheer the Empire, and lit bonfires beneath Nelson's Column in Trafalgar Square "as if to rob the night of some of its darkness", as noted by *The Times*, had given way to a realisation that the economy was devastated and employment scarce. The country may have won the war but it was on its knees financially and the New Year ushered in widespread civil unrest as the government struggled to cope with an orderly demobbing of its shattered troops.

It would be five months later, as the winter turned slowly to spring, that a glimpse emerged of a future free of the bloodshed and daily casualty lists. No section of society had escaped unscathed from the conflict. For both rich and poor there would be fewer husbands for a generation; war had rendered the nation's gender balance lopsided. Even so, there was a belief that Britain should return quickly to the social traditions that had been suspended since the war began, in particular the Court Season. There were 12,000 young women waiting "to make their bow to the King and Queen", as an editorial in *The Times* described the occasion.

But things would never be quite the same. The pre-war grandeur of London social life with its Edwardian stuffiness was giving way to lights and glimmer and fizz in this celebration of a rebirth. And accepted behaviour followed the trend. Life, it seemed, was too short to play by rules created in another century. The pre-war struggles of the suffragettes began to bear fruit, with women over the age of thirty being able to vote for the first time in the 1918 general election.

The royal family, having changed its name and accepted commoners as prospective wives for their sons, now signalled that its rules of social engagement had softened. Actors and actresses could now be presented to the court, provided they were "ladies and gentlemen of irreproachable character", as the change was interpreted by *The Times*. The rest of society followed the royal lead. It wasn't an era of loose morals, but a realignment of life and expectations—for commoner, aristocrat and royal alike, as Sheila Loughborough highlighted in her memoir: "The years 1919 and 1920 were gay. We danced and enjoyed ourselves. We didn't think seriously about world affairs. We did not feel guilty about not being serious. We had already been serious all the war years, and now we had won the war to end all wars."

The Prince of Wales was determined, when not constrained by royal duties, to make hay. His relationship with Freda Dudley Ward, already consummated, had now become all-consuming; they found ways of being together almost every day or, if they could not manage that, they would scrawl gushing, embarrassing love notes to each other. At least Edward did. His language suggested immaturity and selfishness, but his ardent desire for independence and to exert his right of choice in his conflict with his domineering father, King George V, also suggested an iron will and strength of character that would emerge publicly in another two decades when he chose love for American divorcee Wallis Simpson over the crown.

And Bertie—quiet, hesitant and inflicted with a crippling stammer—was shadowing his older brother, including losing his virginity to a Parisian prostitute when the war had neared its end the previous October. His older brother revealed this in a letter to Freda: "He didn't sleep at the Embassy as, in his own words, 'the deed was done', though he gave no details & perhaps just as well!! But you see darling, *c'etait le premier fois car il etait vierge*, which is why it amuses & interests me so much!! I long to see him & hear all about it."

It was not surprising then that Bertie and Sheila morphed into a private social unit with Edward and Freda as if brought together by sheer loyalty to the others. There were similarities with Sheila's experience as a teenager when, because of a relationship between her brother Roy and best friend Mollee, she was drawn into a support role with Roy's friend Lionel.

But that's where the similarities ended. She was now a

married woman, albeit in a problematic union. She also had two young children although, like in most privileged London households, children were tended day-to-day by nannies until they were aged eight, when they were then sent off to boarding school. Besides, the two men who wanted her attention were royal princes. It was hard to resist, particularly with Freda encouraging her participation:

"Freda had become my greatest friend," Sheila would write. "She and I went everywhere together. The Prince of Wales admired her, and he and his brother Prince Bertie were often with us. We danced with them a great deal at all the balls, which annoyed some of the dowagers. However, we didn't care. We knew that no party was complete without us—and them!"

They called themselves the "4 Do's", apparently a nickname dreamed up by Edward which gently mocked his brother's stutter, and perhaps as a rebellion against being told what they *couldn't* do—a secret club within their very public existence, marked with a teddy bear on the dashboard of Bertie's car given to him by Sheila. They were dangerous liaisons but that made it all the more exciting—two young princes challenging social expectation and exploring their independence with two unhappily married women.

The 4 Do's attended the theatre and music halls; they arranged dinners with select friends who knew of, or suspected, the liaisons, and mingled carefully in public at dances and parties in the grand homes and ballrooms of West London.

Sheila was no longer the wide-eyed debutante, now very much at home in London society. Reflecting on the period three decades later, Sheila quoted from the lines of a 1927 song by the playwright Noël Coward, a close friend, to describe her mindset: "Dance, dance, dance little lady, youth is fleeting."

"There were balls every night in London and parties every weekend in the large country houses, few of which exist today," Sheila would write. "Balls for the King of Spain at Eresby House where the Ancasters lived, at Holland House and Lancaster House, Crewe House, Derby House, houses in Carlton House Terrace where Lord and Lady Curzon lived and where the Duke and Duchess of Marlborough and Lady Cunard lived. Lord Farquhar gave wonderful parties at his house in Grosvenor Square. So did Mrs Ronnie Greville. We went to them all, sometimes two or three in one evening."

There were also weekend trips, either with Edward at his residence in Sandwich or as guests of people like politician and businessman Sir Philip Sassoon on one of his two lavish estates on the outskirts of London, Trent Park and Lympne near Folkestone, where they once watched him walk away after crashing his own plane, extricating himself from the debris to declare, nonchalantly, "Look, I've smashed it up into tiny pieces, like confetti."

"We often stayed with Philip . . . He was a wonderful host and raconteur and he entertained on a lavish scale . . . The princes sometimes stayed with him." Edward and Bertie even stole time at Freda and Sheila's homes, sometimes under the noses of their husbands who were either unaware of or ignored their wives' indiscretions. The frenetic pace of their trysts can be sensed in some of the short notes Edward shot off to Freda as the spring of 1919 turned into summer:

Sheila

May 12: We lunched and dined with Rosemary and Eric at Fleet yesterday & brought Loughie back in my car afterwards . . . I've been slumming all afternoon & have just had a game of squash with Do No.2 who is writing to Sheila, which won't surprise you . . .

May 14: Do No.2 left for Winchester about 3.00 in my car as he crashed his this morning; he's having marvellous weather for it & I don't expect to see him tonight!!

May 23: What big babies we 2 Do's are & I think the other 2 Do's are even bigger babies than we are!! What marvellous fun we 4 Do's have, don't we angel & fuck the rest of the world, though guess TOI et MOI are the 'bear leaders' (perhaps too much so sometimes!!) & anyway we look on life more seriously & are so different to the other 2 Do's!!

May 31: Bertie has gone to see Sheila. I hope it's all right, though I expect you know they fixed it up on the telephone this morning.

Sheila's relationship with the gentle Bertie had clearly developed beyond mere friendship. There was a mutual attraction and, from Sheila's perspective, a welcome distraction as her marriage continued to disintegrate. In the last days of May, she had waved goodbye to her mother Margaret who had finally returned to Sydney after five years abroad. Sheila was now alone with two children under the age of two, her family a six-week ship journey away on the other side of the world.

Even though they still had access to the house at Winchester,

Loughie and Sheila had moved most of their belongings back to London where they had sold Stanhope Place and bought the lease of a much larger house in Hyde Park Terrace, which looked over the park. But behind the impressive front door there was only sadness.

Loughie was disappearing into the clubs of Soho more frequently, staying with friends or running up unpaid accounts in hotels. He and Sheila argued when he was home: "He still drank too much and gambled high," she would recall. "It was like living on the edge of a volcano. I feared his debts were enormous. Then finally the crash came. He sat by my bed all one night waving a loaded revolver, pointing it first at me and then at himself. He said it would be much simpler if we were both dead, as he owed so much money. Luckily, I managed to remain calm and eventually persuaded him to give me the revolver, which I carefully unloaded and locked away in a drawer."

This was an extraordinary diary entry, a moment which says as much about Sheila as a woman as it does about the times she lived in. How could a young woman, mother of two small children, respond with such calm to a man—any man, let alone her husband—waving a gun in her face and threatening to kill her? Surely, she would have confided her despair, shared her terror with someone?

But no, Sheila was imbued not just with the familial loyalty that came with her Australian origins but had adopted the fierce codes of discretion required of marriage into the British aristocracy. As a mother and wife, she had become de-sensitised, inured to the danger inherent in her husband's miscreant ways. Sheila, like so many women who came before and after her, was blinded by the hope that love and family would curb the violence.

In the first days of June, Sheila penned a letter to her father-in-law, the Earl of Rosslyn, who had been helping her search for a bigger house in London where she could move with her two children—Tony, who had just turned two, and Peter, who was seven months and beginning to crawl. They had found a four-bedroom townhouse just north of Hyde Park, but it was her marriage which was the main concern: "Loughie and I have had another awful scene. I am so worried and unhappy. I want your advice. I hear you are coming back next week so I must see you. I can't explain in a letter as it is so long, but it is more serious than it has ever been. Everything seems so hopeless."

But even in her anger and despair, Sheila recognised her husband's human struggle. "Darling Harry", as she referred to the earl, had been kind to her since she had arrived back in London in 1916, but the truth was that he had been a poor parental role model, virtually abandoning his children when his marriage to their mother had ended in 1896. It was little wonder that his son, having grown up watching his father's infamous gambling exploits from afar, had fallen into the same hole.

Loughie had struggled with self-esteem since being forced to resign his military commission the previous December. A letter to the War Office secretary concluded: "Lord Loughborough has been unfit for general service for over 18 months and it is regretted that there is no alternative but to gazette him as relinquishing his commission on account of ill-health. He will be granted the rank of Captain but such a grant does not confer the right to wear the uniform, except on ceremonial occasions of a military nature."

The reality of civilian life had struck him hard. The ruling class were no longer able to rely on income from their vast estates, particularly in the aftermath of war. If anything, their land assets were becoming liabilities, as the cost of maintenance outstripped income from the rent of agricultural land. Instead, the new generation of young lords were being forced to sell up and move into the workforce. Some relished the challenge but others, like the playboy Loughborough, found it impossible.

He was given a desk job in the Pensions Department, among the maze of offices along Whitehall, but it was boring work and merely presented an opportunity for him to escape to the nearest club, where he would spend afternoons, evenings and even nights gambling and carousing. The situation had now become desperate.

The earl responded to Sheila's distress quickly, demanding that his son explain himself. A trustees' meeting was arranged for June 5, to assess the financial damage of his exploits and what might be done to save his marriage. On June 4, the day before the meeting, Loughie wrote back to his father in a short but grovelling letter written from a friend's house in London where he was staying:

Dear father,
No words of mine can express what I feel about your letter. I wouldn't have minded blame and being given hell for it, instead of which you write a kind letter which has made me feel a worm. Whether

anything can be done for me or not tomorrow I swear I will be a credit to you in the future. I'm miserable and my only happiness is that Sheila is sticking to me through it all which is more than I deserve. Please forgive me if you can and I hope in time to make you forget my past life. I have been a disgrace to you and everybody.

Your devoted son,

Loughborough

PS: I will be at the trustees meeting at 12 o'clock. I may not be able to face lunch but if so I will be back immediately. I will tell <u>the whole truth</u> this time and <u>keep</u> straight, not <u>try</u> to, in the future.

The meeting was short and sharp. The earl, as trustee and using money in a fund set up by his first wife—Loughie's mother, Violet—from her own family's fortune, would consider bailing him out of the financial mess, but only after he came clean about how much was owed. The trustees would then limit his finances to a £1-per-day stipend; this, on top of the £2000 a year income Sheila received from her family, was expected to allow the couple to live comfortably. In return, Loughie had to agree to give up gambling. With that in mind, he and his wife should consider leaving England and heading overseas for a period, to escape the clutches of the gaming houses and try to rekindle the marriage.

On June 7 Bertie telephoned Sheila, his brother recording the call in a letter to Freda written later the same day:

Bertie rang Sheilie up this morning & fixed up for us both to go on to "Rankhills" tomorrow after we have played golf. I suppose I shall have to try & amuse Loughie so that they can have a talk though I'll do anything for their sakes, poor darlings . . . But enough about Loughie as I'm very fed up with him, as you are darling; he's cramped our style somewhat lately, hasn't he, curse him, & I hate him though I'm so fond of poor little Sheilie.

Edward and Bertie arrived late in the afternoon and had tea on the veranda, after which Edward insisted on visiting the local golf course with Loughie to play a few more holes. It was a ruse "to give Sheilie a chance of being alone with Bertie". A reluctant Loughie could not refuse the heir to the throne and, with Sheila staying behind with the younger prince, the two set off only to find that the course was closed. Rather than head back to the house, Edward insisted on going for a walk around the course, later congratulating himself as "a little Master Clever".

He repeated the ruse after dinner, taking Loughie out of the room to give his brother more time with Sheila. Their conversation centred on the plan concocted by the earl to keep his son out of the clubs and gambling dens of the city. Edward listened quietly as Loughie detailed the plan for a world tour and withheld his opinion until later that night. After returning to London, he penned a note to Freda lamenting the decision and particularly what it would mean for the relationship between his brother and Sheila:

Sheila

What a tragic life poor little Sheilie's is & I'm afraid that a trip round the world isn't going to make it any better; Loughie's trustees must be mad giving him £300 a year & to say that he isn't to work; it's just asking for trouble!! How poor little Sheilie is dreading it, it's so pathetic, though I think Loughie realises all right; it's all so sordid though I think today has been good propaganda & I'm sure Loughie doesn't suspect Bertie at all! He was really quite nice today & I couldn't help feeling sorry for him, though I hate him!!

The princes returned to Lankhills the following Sunday, a guest book kept by Sheila recording their names, signed simply "Edward" and "Albert", on June 15. The trip had been arranged hastily, spurred probably by Loughie's absence and the fact that Freda was staying with Sheila for the weekend. The coast was clear!

Photographs of the visit would show a rare moment of relaxation for the royal brothers. In one, they're perched on top of a fence in a field behind the house, the girls on either side. Freda and Edward are happy and smiling brazenly at the camera, but Sheila and Bertie seem less certain about the attention. In another, they have swapped places on the fence. This time it is Edward and Freda who look pensive and Bertie is beaming, a pipe in one hand and his other arm around Sheila who smiles at the gesture of affection.

There were more photographs taken that day. In one of them, Sheila is standing against a wall of the house, between the brothers. Edward, hands thrust into his trousers, presents a figure of the utmost confidence while Bertie, hands clasped behind him, smiles shyly. Sheila, as tall as the two men, is holding a lit cigarette and stares unflinchingly ahead.

While the princes were with his wife in Winchester, Loughie was in London making promises he would have difficulty understanding, let alone keeping. On Saturday, June 14, he again wrote to his father, this time detailing the extent of his losses and reiterating his promises to reform. His wife had consented to stand by him but it was clear the marriage was all but over, held together for appearances and pity and the sake of their young sons.

Dear father,

This is a difficult letter to write. I feel you won't understand what a bloody fool I have been and after the way I have treated you I cannot expect your sympathy. Apart from the bills ... I owe £6,800 to moneylenders and £2,000 of racing and gambling debts. I have done this in the last six weeks. Sheila and I have quarrelled but she has consented to come back to me not as a wife but because I implored her to come back to give me one more chance to make her respect me and after I have proved this she will try to love me again. I have agreed to the following conditions:

1. I shall never touch a drink.

2. Never play any cards.

3. Never bet on a horse.

I have promised these three things and if I fail in any of them I am to allow her to divorce me. My promises as you well know have always been broken. I don't expect you to believe them this time till

Sheila

I have proved myself but I can truthfully say that I have at least realised what a mess I have made of my life and how badly I have behaved to you and everybody.

I want this one chance to make good. I don't know whether you can or even if you are prepared to save me going bankrupt but I will come and talk to you about it on Wednesday with Sheila. I want to avoid it if it's possible and start afresh and to bring no disgrace on Sheila by being a bankrupt. It is better to make a clean breast of everything to you. I am truly sorry and I mean it. I have learnt my lesson this time for good and all, and the future above will prove it. If you can please forgive my uncalled for attitude to you. I don't say this because I'm in trouble and want your help but I know how disgracefully I have behaved toward you.

Loughborough

But even as he was promising to turn over a new leaf, Loughie was telling close friends that he couldn't simply walk away from his share in a betting pool, as he wrote to "Jack" on the same day:

Just got your note. I've had no time to phone you. Am going to try and get round to see you about 6.45 but I'm full up with appointments. If not tonight before 11 tomorrow morning as I want to see you and hear all the news. I've got to forego the Derby—Sheila having made me make a vow not to race or touch a card again which I have done. It seems the only solution. I owe moneylenders £7000. I wish I'd told you before but I didn't so now I'm going to Harry tomorrow and see if he will help. Of course my share in the box still stands and I'll play

it as agreed. Has Jolly got my hat I wonder. Love to Nell. Just off to a
lawyer and will try and look in after.

Yours,

Loughborough

Sheila was writing too. As soon as the princes had returned to London her attention once again switched to her marriage, and she wanted to thank her father-in-law for his understanding: "Loughie is so touched by your letter to him. I know he realises now what a fool and rotter he has been and really means to make good not only to *try*. We will be there tomorrow about 12 and I do, *do* hope so much something can be done. All love, Sheila"

On August 12, a small item appeared in the "Court Circular" column in *The Times*. It read: "Lord and Lady Loughborough have gone abroad for an indefinite period." The trip would last less than two months and achieve nothing but a delay to the inevitable. By October 1919 they were back in London and unhappy.

7

A DUKEDOM FOR A SHEILA

Lady Maud Cunard was a woman with whom to be reckoned; a legendary, biting matriarch of society who decided later in life that she loathed Alfred Lord Tennyson's poem "Come into the Garden, Maud" and so changed her name to Emerald, simply because she liked them. She was American, married the elderly grandson of the businessman who had founded the Cunard shipping line, bore a daughter before leaving him on his country estate, and set up home alone in London where she took a series of lovers and became a patron of the arts.

Dinner parties at her sumptuous house in Grosvenor Place were as elaborate as her character, as the writer and hostess Elsa Maxwell, another American, once wrote:

Such was the way of the woman who, shortly before the turn of the century, brought London society to its collective knee and kept it there for close to fifty years. Lady Cunard loved to gather her lions together, lash them with the whip of her tongue, and watch them fight to the blood. By pitting them one against another she sought to make her guests more interesting to herself, to each other, and, not at all incidentally, to exploit her own acid wit.

As Sheila wrestled with her future and wondered at her improbable relationship with the second in line to the British throne, Lady Cunard invited her to lunch. It was an intimate affair, held at Kenwood, a great house on Hampstead Heath owned by the Guinness family, its walls lined with works of the masters, among them Rembrandt, Vermeer, Turner, Reynolds, Gainsborough and Constable.

"I distinctly remember the drive to Kenwood," Sheila would write of the day. "Emerald had called for me in her car and we arrived to find a party of eight. I sat opposite Serge Obolensky. He only had to look at a woman for her to fall in love with him. He looked at me. My heart stood still. He was the most attractive man I had ever seen, and he had just escaped from Russia with a price on his head."

A week or so later, the handsome Russian still in her head, Sheila and Loughie tried to rekindle their marriage by going to Scotland for a month to stay with Eileen and Geordie Sutherland at Dunrobin, "their dream castle by the sea", where the guests included Winston and Clementine Churchill. "We played golf and stalked and shot and fished and invented some terrible practical jokes," she wrote, before adding sadly that even in this tranquil environment, the drinking and the quarrels continued: "My love for Loughie was dying painfully, if not already dead."

As they returned to London, Sheila's thoughts again turned to Serge Obolensky. Bertie had been sent by his father to study history, economics and civics at Trinity College, Cambridge, and was in London infrequently. The relationship was cooling and a new man found his way into her life and her heart although he was aware of his royal rival: "We met again at various parties and we danced together," she wrote. "He asked me not to dance so much with Prince Bertie. I told him it was a harmless friendship, as indeed it was. He said that when he had first arrived in England after his escape he had heard my name coupled with Prince Bertie and that we were all known as 'The Duchess of Sutherland's set'. This amused me."

Sheila was falling heavily for Serge, captivated by his swashbuckling background. He had fought in the White Army during the Russian civil war, fled disguised as a student and arrived in London just as the affair between Sheila and Albert was gaining momentum. Tall, debonair and blessed with movie-star looks, he was quick to make an impression in London society, particularly as he had studied at Oxford before the war.

Serge was married, but estranged from his wife Catherine—a union he described as "one of wartime delusion" which, like Sheila and Loughie's, would dissipate when the guns were silenced. Catherine, a niece of the Tsar, was now spending more and more time on the Continent, pursuing a singing and acting career, so Serge felt free to pursue other romantic relationships.

He wanted Sheila and regarded the troubled Loughborough marriage as an imprimatur to woo her.

Besides, he would argue, London society in the immediate post-war years was much more innocent than its risqué reputation suggested. As he wrote in his autobiography: "Contrary to reports of that time and the impression that it seems to have left with succeeding generations, it was not an era of loose morality, devil-may-careness or anything of the sort. Rumours that one slept with anybody one wished to . . . could not have been further from the truth. People were just so damned happy . . . that they set about their various pursuits of happiness in as constructive a manner as was afforded them. In general, they had a whale of a time, were keenly appreciative of a good party, refused to be bored by anything and consumed quantities of good cheer."

One of the places they frequently met was the Kensington home of his cousin, Prince Felix Youssoupoff, another exiled Russian aristocrat with a background more colourful than his own. Felix had once been heir to the biggest private fortune in Russia, with a life of opulence and excess that outstripped even the tsars. The Moika Palace in St Petersburg, where he was born in 1887, one of four palaces owned by the family in the city, had originally been a gift from Catherine the Great and the family's main home in Moscow, one of three there, had been built by Ivan the Terrible. The family's holiday home in the Crimea had a zoo and was just one of their thirty-seven estates stretching across Russia, bought with a fortune created from coal, iron ore and oil fields on the Caspian Sea.

And he was as flamboyant as his heritage. Felix often dressed as a woman in public, sometimes performing and singing in drag at a high-class nightclub, and yet he was married to a beautiful Romanoff princess, with whom he had a daughter, and they remained happily together for more than fifty years.

But the prince's biggest claim to fame was that he had been the man who had led the assassination of the mystic Grigori Rasputin. Felix considered himself a hero—the man who rid Russia of a monster who had an almost satanic influence over Tsar Nicholas II and his wife, Alexandra, which was destroying Russia and killing its people as it struggled to hold off the German war machine. As it turned out, Rasputin's murder was the precursor to a revolution that would ultimately lead to the assassination of the tsar and his family and scatter the surviving Russian aristocracy across the globe, leaving their vast fortunes and palaces behind.

After escaping prosecution, Felix, his wife Irina and their daughter fled the turmoil. To fund their life in exile, he smuggled out of the palace two rolled-up Rembrandt paintings—*Man in a Large Hat* and *Woman with a Fan*—and a clutch of diamonds. They made their way through the Crimea and Europe, eventually arriving in London in 1919 with other members of the now-exiled royal family.

The family quickly settled in Knightsbridge and began to hold court; they hosted flamboyant, bohemian affairs attended by growing numbers of exiled Russian aristocrats, even the ballerina Anna Pavlova, who mingled with an eager crowd of young, titled and wealthy Londoners. It was a time when all things Russian were popular in London. The wild music, played on semistrunka guitars, and the flowing brightly coloured silks and furs were a fresh and exotic distraction alongside the staid decorum of English ballrooms. The Youssoupoffs even held séance sessions.

Among those who frequented the apartment along the southern border of Hyde Park, where Felix would tell and retell his Rasputin story, were the princes Edward and Albert and their Do's, Sheila Loughborough and Freda Dudley Ward. Here the glamorous quartet found a degree of freedom among a crowd of mostly their own generation.

But the English princes weren't the only admirers of the two young women. Titled European men crowded around them at parties: Serge called them "cavaliers". Sheila, dark-eyed and slender, looked languid as she stood alongside Freda's tiny and fragile prettiness. Serge wrote: "I came to realise what close friends Sheila and Freda were. They were truly inseparable. Whenever [they] got together, a literal panic of laughter always ensued. I was smitten by Lady Loughborough almost immediately. The competition, however, was frightful!"

Freda "had tremendous steadiness and a will of iron, tempered by humour. She reminded me of an exquisite little bird, so sharp and quick were her features and her movements."

Sheila, by contrast, was "a lazy lady": "Her entire appearance was languorous. Her every gesture was dreamlike, as placid as an inland sea. She had flowing hair that swayed gently as she walked, and she had the most beautiful skin I think I've ever seen. She dressed softly and with simplicity, and one could hardly suspect the fertile imagination that was always bubbling within. For underneath, Sheila was pixyish. As [Russian artist Savely] Sorine once said to me: 'You know, I'd just love to paint her, but I can't . . . She's Puck. She's got one of those beautiful but incredible putty faces—impossible to put on canvas.'"

As well as mixing with the Russians, Sheila's social calendar was becoming more and more full. Her marriage, and particularly her connection to Geordie and Eileen, the Duke and Duchess of Sutherland, had provided entry into this exclusive world, but she was now becoming a woman who could command the attention of the wealthy and powerful, all the way to the royal family. Her wartime fundraising experience and growing connections were establishing her as one of the new faces of society affairs.

For instance, Sheila was on the organising committee of the "Find the Slipper Ball", a lavish Mardi Gras held at the Savoy Hotel in mid-January 1920, the proceeds from which were going to workshops for disabled soldiers. At midnight young men in pink emerged with hunting horns to signal a treasure hunt by guests for a jewel slipper stuffed with gold and silver coins.

The New Year had ushered in a swirl of glamorous events as London society brought out their feathers and diamonds and began to cast off the shackles of post-war reserve. The events were limited only by the organisers' imaginations; they were customarily justified by a noble charitable cause.

There were also shooting weekends in the spring and the autumn—"so that one knew what one was doing"—and she was on familiar terms with "Bendor", the Duke of Westminster, and Violet, the second of his four wives, as well as the Duke and Duchess of Marlborough, the Mountbattens and Lord Curzon, former Viceroy of India, about whom the country's first prime minister, Jawaharlal Nehru, would say: "After every other viceroy has been forgotten, Curzon will be remembered because he restored all that was beautiful in India."

An incident that took place around this time is a good demonstration of the lavish world Sheila was living in. Just a few days before the "Slipper Ball" Sheila reported the theft of more than £11,000 worth of her jewellery from a flat in Duke Street where she was staying with friends.

Scotland Yard believed the thief had used a false key to get into the flat, where he had ignored everything but a black leather jewel case among Sheila's luggage in an upstairs bedroom. The description of the loss was glittering—a dress ring with one large diamond in platinum surrounded by brilliants, a long platinum brooch set with thirteen pearls, a ring with a sapphire the size of a sixpenny piece, another sapphire ring surrounded by rose diamonds and two strings of pearls, along with three books of war bonds and her marriage certificate.

The press made much of the robbery and interviewed Lady Loughborough on her doorstep: "I regret the loss very much, especially one or two favourite ornaments which I prized exceedingly, but I can give you no further information, as I have no idea how they disappeared," she told one reporter. The crime would never be solved.

But for all the glamour, her financial situation was actually quite grim. The Rosslyn estate trustees had taken care of

Loughie's latest debts, but the imposed financial regime of £1 per day was tight.

And Sheila's private life continued to be in turmoil. As often as not, she was attending social events on her own, or arriving as a fifth wheel to another couple. It was a statement of the obvious—that her marriage was on the rocks—and it was being noted.

Even though Sheila's relationship with Prince Albert was cooling as her attentions swung to Serge, they continued to see each other when he was in London. And despite their efforts at secrecy it was only a matter of time before it and the affair between Prince Edward and Freda Dudley Ward were reported back to Buckingham Palace. After all, it was now being discussed openly in society circles and by April 1920 the activities of Edward and Albert had reached the ears of King George and Queen Mary.

In early April 1920 King George decided to confront his errant sons. The issue was far more serious with the Prince of Wales, given that he was heir to the throne, but he was on the way to Australia and New Zealand for an official tour so that battle would have to wait until "David", as he was known in family circles, returned in September.

But Albert's dalliance was another matter. The King summoned his second son on April 7 and offered a tantalising inducement, as Bertie then told his brother in a letter, written the next morning: "He is going to make me Duke of York on his birthday provided that he hears nothing more about Sheila & me!!!!"

But it would be six weeks—the middle of May—before the letter reached the older prince and he was made aware of the battle now raging. Edward had five letters—two from Freda and three from Bertie—waiting for him when he boarded HMS *Renown* in the port town of Lyttelton on New Zealand's South Island, and he read them as the battleship headed out across the Tasman Sea in gale-force winds, bound for Melbourne. His initial response to Freda was written in two parts; at first there was his joy at receiving her letters, and then this outburst when he had read his brother's laments:

May 22. 11pm. At sea

Christ! How I loathe & despise my bloody family as Bertie has written me 3 long sad letters in which he tells me he's getting it in the neck about his friendship with poor little Sheilie & that TOI ET MOI came in for it too!! But if HM thinks he's going to alter me by insulting you he's making just about the biggest mistake of his silly useless life; all he has done is infuriate me & make me despise him & put me completely against him & I'll never forgive him for insulting you as he has!!

God damn him! Though in a way he's done me good, sweetheart, by his extra display of foulness to Bertie & me as it's cured me of any weakness that was left in me!! Christ! I'll be firm with him when I get back & tell him to go to hell & leave me alone as regards my friends; I'll have whatever friends I wish & what is more I won't have them insulted or I'll bloody well insult him! Poor old Bertie seems to be having a rather warm time just now though I'll discuss him later; I only hope to God he'll keep his head for our sakes, yours & mine sweetie!!

Edward, who would stand by his word and reject his father's demands for an end to the relationship with Freda, had calmed down two days later when he penned a second, longer letter. He and Freda had known about the relationship that had developed between "Sheilie and Ob" for several months—even that Sheila had used her house to see Serge, as she had with Bertie—so his initial indignation on Bertie's behalf had tempered considerably by his second letter.

May 24

Now as regards Old Bertie & Sheilie; B talks a lot of hot air about HM making him a duke on condition that his name ceases to be more or less coupled with Sheilie's though it certainly need not have been ever since January anyway—if not earlier!!

You & I both happen to know that they neither of them really mean anything to each other at all, do they sweetheart? . . . so that personally I'm all ready for their really breaking apart properly & cutting out the camouflage love stunt!!

From what he tells me S&L are living on top of a hotter volcano than ever & anyone in love with her is sitting on top with them! We both of us know she really loves Ob so surely it would be better for Bertie to drift away from it all & just be one of Sheilie's friends . . . we've discussed the other 2 Do's so often recently & I think we came to this conclusion though naturally I've kept Sheilie's secret re Ob so so faithfully & Bertie knows absolutely nothing & never will from me!!

It is so hopeless trying to discuss letters six weeks old & Bertie may be a Duke now for all I know. Of course if he really loved Sheilie he wouldn't care a dick about dukes or anything else.

You haven't felt comfy having either Ob or Bertie in your house for Sheilie to play with lately ... If only you could talk to Bertie sweetheart & warn him against being too thick with Sheilie, though it seems a hard thing to ask you to do when we know they can be happy together in their own way!!

Do talk to B. Fredie darling, as I know he would listen to you. And I feel that it would help TOI et MOI so much beloved as we've long felt the weight of them on our hands & it's been growing heavier anyway for you whose house they invariably use for their—-, shall we call them causeries!!

Edward seemed to be saying that Sheila and Bertie would be able to become platonic friends without too much personal hardship. But there could be little doubt about the intimacy of their earlier relationship. The diplomat, poet and later High Commissioner to Australia Sir Charles Hepburn Johnston was a frequent visitor to Buckingham Palace; in his private diaries he wrote of an evening at Buckingham Palace soon after World War II when Sheila and Bertie, who had become King George VI, were discussing their former friendship:

Then there was Sheila Loughborough's story. The K. was talking to her about the old times before he got married and what fun they all had. Sheila saw the Q. listening and thought it prudent to damp this down a bit.

Sheila: "And when you think, Sir, how innocent it all was ..."

K (red with fury): "Innocent? I don't know what the devil you mean."

But in May 1920 their relationship was about to end. Albert knew that he had to obey his father, who had already made concessions about the women he and his brothers could marry. Sheila was a married woman and, even if she left Loughie, it was doubtful that his parents would approve of marriage to a divorced woman.

It would come to a head on the night of June 2, when King George hosted his traditional pre-Derby, male-only dinner at Buckingham Palace for members of the Jockey Club. The next day was his fifty-fifth birthday, when he intended to appoint his second son as Duke of York. That evening Bertie, who had travelled down from Cambridge, wrote his father a note in which he said he was proud to accept the title and hoped he would live up to it, adding, "I can tell you I fulfilled your conditions to the letter and that nothing more will come of it."

His father read the letter the next day and replied immediately:

Dearest Bertie,

I was delighted to get your letter this morning, & to know that you appreciate that I have given you that fine old title of Duke of York, which I bore for more than 9 years & is the oldest Dukedom in this country. I know that you have behaved very well, in a difficult situation for a young man & that you have done what I asked you to do. I feel that this splendid old title will be safe in your hands & that you will never do anything, which could in any way tarnish it. I hope that you will always look upon me as yr. best friend & always tell me everything & you will find me ever ready to help you & give you good advice.

Looking forward to seeing you tomorrow,
Ever my dear boy,
Yr. very devoted Papa

The letter's subtext was that Albert had to stay away from Sheila or any other woman like her. Even though the prince would complain to his older brother about being spied on every time he went out during that summer, there would be one last dance with his former lover. After signing his acceptance letter, Bertie went off to dinner at the palatial home of Lord and Lady Farquhar with his mother, Queen Mary, his sister Princess Mary and his younger brothers George and Henry. Here seventy-six guests sat at three tables decorated with sweet peas to celebrate the Farquhars' silver wedding anniversary. They were joined after dinner by a further 150 guests, among them Sheila Loughborough, as the evening turned to dancing.

Despite the presence of his mother and his commitment to his father to end the relationship, Bertie could not resist dancing with the woman he had agreed to avoid. As they took their turn around the dance floor, they both noticed a young woman standing in the doorway. She seemed young, and vulnerable—a debutante alone in a room filled with society veterans. Sheila later asked the name of the young woman. She was nineteen-year-old Elizabeth Bowes-Lyon.

8

MOLLEE AND THE PRINCE

When Edward Prince of Wales had been preparing for his goodwill tour of Australia and New Zealand he had asked Sheila Loughborough if there was anyone interesting he should meet when he arrived in Sydney besides her parents, Harry and Margaret Chisholm.

Yes, Sheila had replied, he should meet a young woman by the name of Mollee Little, who danced divinely and could hold a lively, interesting conversation in any company. Mollee was a year older than Sheila but the pair might have been sisters, not just in their dark smouldering beauty but in their fun-loving demeanour, which many found infectious.

In the years since Sheila's departure, they had exchanged letters frequently and there were few, if any, secrets they did not share about their lives. And now she was not just a great friend but potentially her sister-in-law, the sweetheart of her brother

Roy, who had married on a whim during the Great War but divorced soon afterwards. She seemed to be the perfect dancing partner for the prince who, Sheila suspected, would need some fun after the boredom and irritation of constant public appearances, speeches and dinners.

Sheila had anticipated the prince's needs accurately, as his regular letters to Freda would show. There would be twenty-three letters during his visit, written almost daily during the east coast leg of his trip and sent in batches of up to ten at a time. They frequently laid bare his fears as a shy and self-conscious man despite his public assuredness. They also displayed a lack of self-awareness, both in the impact of his behaviour on others and his often-disparaging views of those around him.

The practical aspects of being Prince of Wales bored him senseless and he arrived in Sydney Harbour on June 16, unhappy at the prospect of "yet another terrible & pompous carriage ride through the streets"; however he was surprised and delighted at being greeted instead by a flotilla on "a marvellous harbour". His mood lightened further that night when he met Mollee Little, as he wrote to Freda when he got back to the ship at 1 a.m., misspelling her name:

Finally we went to a vast ball . . . & there I met Sheilie's great friend Molly Little & had 2 dances with her & of course we talked about S the whole time!! S writes to her a lot & so she's heard about you & Bertie . . . though I hope to meet her again at other parties & make her tell me more! She seems a nice girl & she dances well & she certainly has a look of Sheilie, particularly about her mouth!!

The attraction between the couple built over the next week in Sydney, firstly as a means of escaping the "ghastly" dinners and "pompous boobs" who, realising the prince's instant infatuation with Mollee, deliberately left her off their invitation lists until he insisted that she be reinstated.

Edward seemed to forget sometimes that he was writing to the woman he loved about another woman, as if Freda would understand a platonic attraction: "Molly Little & I laughed till it hurt, my beloved!! God! She's so like Sheilie, I can't help saying it again & she gets the hysterics just like Sheilie does!!" He confided how he had managed to reconfigure seating lists: "I've managed to get Molly Little asked to dinner here tonight sweetie & fixed it up that she should sit next to me so that's something & she'll be able to help me through another desperate evening here."

He took an overnight trip to see the site for the new capital at Canberra but couldn't wait to get back to see Mollee:

> *I got back from the up-country trip at 10.30pm beloved but was enticed to a party by Mollee Little (she spells her name Mollee) though I wasn't there 2 hours & didn't get in more than 7 dances . . . however I got 3 with her . . . I wanted some exercise after a ghastly political sort of day in the new federal district or area called Canberra which is the site of the new Commonwealth capital!!!*

There seemed to be a ball almost every night, glittering occasions with the diminutive prince the centre of attention, along with his favourite dance partner, as *The Sydney Morning Herald*

reported from a dance to celebrate his twenty-sixth birthday on
June 23:

Soon the Prince was lost sight of in the maze of whirling figures,
but occasionally an exclamation, "There he is," caused all heads
to be turned, in the direction indicated. For his next dance the
Prince chose his already favoured partner, Miss Mollee Little, who
looked charming in a frock of pale pink, with trimmings of crystal
beads. The frocks of the women were of unsurpassed beauty. In
the midst of the orgy of colour, black easily held its own, and most
of the matrons' frocks were of black and gold, or finely jetted black
cloth. Feather fans in exquisite colourings . . . were in great vogue.
If one of the stately dancers of the old time minuet could visit the
modern ballroom she would probably be speechless with horror
and agonised amazement. Last night's crowd is probably under
the impression that it danced, but to the onlooker it seemed as if
there were hundreds of couples jog-trotting, stepping in stilted
fashion, strutting, eliding, waddling, whirling, rolling, dipping,
stamping and shuffling.

The next night, as he prepared to leave Sydney to travel
across the continent, he realised his behaviour was getting out
of hand:

I'm in absolute disgrace & so, so terribly ashamed to appear so gay
sweetie but the fact is the old Davidsons insisted on organising a
mild form of birthday party for me tonight. They asked a few bits to
dinner (ML being one of them) . . . it's really lucky it's our last night

in Sydney Fredie darling as life here is too strenuous for everybody &
we are all BF's for having sat up so late so often & for nothing too!!

As he left Mollee behind in Sydney and travelled across the continent, Edward turned his attention to Sheila's plight. He had been told that Lord Loughborough "was willing" to be divorced, as he wrote to Freda in a letter on July 1:

It is the only way out for poor little Sheilie although I wonder what her plans are now. I suppose Ob and Alb [Albert] are clear of trouble. I hope so, and that it will all happen quietly. Poor old Loughie. One can't help feeling a teeny bit sorry for him as he will sink now that the only thing keeping him just on the surface—Sheilie—will be gone, though he is such a miserable rotter and I am so glad for her sake!! Bertie didn't quit what I called the volcano any too soon, did he angel?

Edward returned to Sydney after six weeks in Western Australia and South Australia for one last round of visits and ceremonies before his return to England, but his mind was focussed only on seeing Mollee again. At 1.30 a.m. on August 15 he began writing a letter to Freda from his cabin on the *Renown*, while a private dinner was still underway:

We went out to the races at Randwick this afternoon (a special meeting they had organised for me sweetheart). I saw Mrs Chisholm and Mollee Little in the grandstand & had a yarn with them, I need hardly add mostly about Sheilie!! Mrs C is a sweet woman & I've planned to have another yarn with her & I was glad to see Mollee again & she's been onboard for a slight private dinner & jazz party I've given tonight angel!!

Journalists had begun to notice that the prince's car was often parked outside Brooksby House and that he had even gone there to dinner, and had taken Mollee out for drives through the city. In his letters, in between declaring his love for Freda and lamenting the strain of the royal tour, he waxed lyrical about Mollee—about her laughter and about monopolising her at parties. He joked about her being his "bit":

I think Dickie [Mountbatten] is rather smitten with Moll, though he doesn't often get her to himself as she is really my little "bit" or rather friend, as I've only got one "bit" my Fredie & so I couldn't have another. Moll is just crazy to meet you & I'm sure you would love her Fredie darling as she has so much in her that is of our atmosphere & ideas or rather I should say of those in our little "set" meaning Sheilie, Poots etc etc. Dickie & I monopolise her at parties here.

Even as he left on August 19, the prince couldn't resist one last "stunt", inviting a dozen or so women, including Mollee, on board as the *Renown* headed out to Sydney Heads, where they anchored to wait for the mail ship to ferry out any late correspondence:

There was Grace & Archie & and then of course Mollee Little & 8 or 9 other girls, all bits belonging to & asked for by various members of the staff & ships' officers & they lunched onboard & didn't leave the ship till about 5pm. We danced for 1hr after lunch & then everyone took his bit into his cabin, except for me angel, who only took Mollee for a final talk as she isn't my bit at all!!

I've got a terrible haunting feeling that all I've said about Moll & seeing so much of her these last 5 days might make you thulky, sweetie but if only you understand that I merely look on her as a second edition of Sheilie & that I've made great friends with her & taken special trouble with her merely because she is your greatest friend's greatest friend!!!

I'm also quite fond of her for herself Fredie darling just as I'm fond of Sheilie & Poots 'mais c'est tout'!! But for you I shouldn't probably have got to know Sheilie & the same is the case with Moll; & although we may have got ourselves talked about a little in Sydney beloved everyone knows it's because of 'Sheila Chisholm' & consequently because of Fredie!!

This is no kind of apology mon amour because I have such an absolutely clear conscience about it all; the only thing I fear is giving you a false impression of it all though I don't think I have really!! Moll & I had a final yarn about Sheilie who I'm afraid I'm going to miss by a whole month as she sails in the middle of September.

Moll is the only woman I've got to know at all well on this trip. As a matter of fact I think Mollee is rather fond of Roy Chisholm, Sheilie's youngest brother, a nice fellow & good looking & he's certainly fond of her. But enough about Mollee angel; she shoved off with the rest of the women & we sailed at 9pm.

The prince and his retinue might have left Australia's shores, but tongues had begun to wag and would do so for decades. Mollee and Roy Chisholm (who, according to his sister, had been unhappy about the prince dancing so often with his girlfriend) were engaged four months later and married the following year, settling first at Roy's property "Khan Yunis" (named after one of the Anzac battles in Turkey during the Great War) at Braidwood in southern New South Wales and, a few years later, in Macleay Street, Potts Point, when Roy came to work for his father at the bloodstock agency.

But each time her name appeared in a newspaper, often because of her heightened profile, there would be the reminder that she had been "the favoured dancing partner of the prince", the articles regurgitating details of Prince Edward's private trips to Brooksby House, their walks along the beach and his passion for jam sandwiches. On the surface these appeared innocent reminders, perhaps out of admiration for a local girl who had struck up such a special friendship with a prince, but there was also the subtle implication of something more to the relationship.

In early October 1923 Roy and Mollee had a son. David Anthony Chisholm was named after the Prince of Wales, "David" being the last of the prince's seven Christian names. It was a very personal statement of the friendship, confirmed a few days later with a snippet in *The Sydney Morning Herald*: "Mr Roy Chisholm announces that the Prince of Wales has consented to be god-father to his baby son, born on Wednesday. Mrs Chisholm will be remembered as Miss Mollee Little, a favourite dancing partner of the Prince of Wales during his visit to New South Wales."

Sheila

The fact that the birth occurred three years after Edward had left Australia would not prevent the gossips from insisting that David Chisholm, who would always be known by his middle name, Tony, was actually the illegitimate son of Mollee and the Prince of Wales, particularly as he had the softer features of the refined Edward rather than the robust darkness of Roy, whom Sheila reckoned looked like Rhett Butler. The ensuing controversy would remain undiminished more than eighty years later.

9

NO MAN IS WORTH LEAVING ONE'S CHILDREN

Mollee Little and Roy Chisholm might have been headed toward the altar but back in London, Sheila was desperately trying to find a way to hold her marriage together. Her dalliances with Prince Albert and Serge Obolensky aside, she was resisting reasons to leave her husband, for the sake of her children, now aged three and two.

In July 1920 Loughie had confessed again to gambling and running up debts with bookmakers and moneylenders but wouldn't say how much he owed. Despite Sheila's renewed pleas with her father-in-law, the earl had washed his hands of his son, suggesting that they leave England and start a new life in a country like Canada. The prospect seemed bleak: "I was in despair. We talked it over. I thought Australia a much more sensible idea. I felt my brothers would be a good influence. It might really help Loughie and also, I could escape from the temptation of my secret love for Serge."

Loughie finally agreed to go with his wife and children to Australia, but only for a year as a trial. And he wanted to go ahead, by himself, to spend time in India while Sheila packed up the house. "He said I could easily cope with the boys as we were taking two nurses and my maid and he would join our ship in Bombay. I pleaded and begged him not to go before us but I could not explain why. I hardly dared admit even to myself that my feelings for Serge were growing stronger all the time."

Loughie insisted and fled, leaving his family and his White-hall desk job behind and heading to India for what would turn out to be a six-month shooting and social safari where he cut a notable figure—a rare aristocrat among the ranks of military officers and well-to-do commoners. His appearances at society fancy dress balls were reported widely, alongside descriptions of the new gaming tables of baccarat and roulette, which were beginning to appear in Calcutta. Instead of moving away from gambling, he was simply shifting to another location, beyond the gaze of his financiers.

Back in London his family described it as a business trip "visiting governors and officials" but the alibi fell through when a London bookmaking firm launched a lawsuit for non-payment of a £444 debt. Loughie did not deny that he owed the money but, when the trustees of the fund set up by his mother realised it was for gambling losses, they refused to pay up. Before he left for India, Loughie had pleaded with the bookmaker to be patient: "Apart from your firm I owe the ring roughly £1700," he wrote at the time. "I am not in a position now to pay one penny. I am trying to get one man to take over the whole lot and let me pay him back in instalments as I intend to meet them in full."

Loughie and the bookmaker had then met over lunch to discuss a scheme in which the troubled young peer would bring clients—some of his gambling friends—to do their betting with the firm. In exchange, he wanted "an interest" in the operation and more gambling credit. The bookie refused until he had cleared the initial debt, so Loughie wrote the cheque even though he knew it would bounce. The bookie, stupidly as it turned out, extended more credit and Loughie promptly lost another £200 in quick time.

It was then that the bookie decided to sue, but he would lose when it finally got to court, several months after Loughie's departure. The debt was real and acknowledged but it was a gambling debt and, so, was illegal and invalid. The judge accepted the argument and threw out the case; it was the second time Loughie had escaped conviction because of a technicality.

Sheila sailed from London with the children a month before the case went to court and became public. Before leaving she said her goodbyes to Serge: "I at last admitted to myself that I was in love with Serge but eventually the moment came when I had to say goodbye to him forever, and we chose Freda's house. After he had gone she sat up with me all the rest of the night, trying to comfort me. She saw me off the next morning from Tilbury Docks."

It took a week to reach Marseilles, where a cable was waiting. It was from Serge: "Vickers has given me a job in Australia. Coming overland to join Malwa. Get me a cabin somehow."

Sheila

Sheila was in shock—"an Alice in Wonderland situation to say the least of it". Ignoring her previous decision, she rushed off to find the ship's purser. Every cabin was taken but there was a single bed, in a downstairs cabin with two priests, that was spare if the passenger who'd made the booking didn't front by the time the ship sailed.

Serge arrived by train: "I felt so bewildered that I didn't know if I was pleased or sorry to see him," Sheila later wrote.

Fate would dictate what happened next as they waited to see if the mystery passenger turned up to take his bed. He didn't and the ship sailed with Serge Obolensky aboard.

On the evening of October 3, 1920, the *Malwa* arrived at Port Said in Egypt, the northern terminus of the Suez Canal, on its first London–Sydney run since being requisitioned as a troop ship during the Great War. There would be an overnight stop to take on coal before making the 190-kilometre run through the man-made canal, which linked Europe and Asia. It was a messy undertaking, the coal being carried in small baskets by a small army of workers dressed only in loincloths and covered in coal dust.

To avoid the dust invading the luxury interiors, the ship was sealed and its portholes locked. Many of the passengers—a mix of Australian businessmen, merchants, wool buyers and engineers, plus Indian civil servants and British army officers on their way to the sub-continent—chose to go ashore for the evening, returning late in the hope of avoiding the mess.

Sheila and Serge joined those going ashore, riding in an open carriage through the wide streets to a restaurant by the beach where they whiled away the hours beneath a full moon, brilliant against the black Egyptian night and the peace of the man-made sea. "The sense of the past and the mystery of the future," Serge would later recall, "made the night memorable beyond any I have ever known."

On their way back, Serge had his fortune read on the beach. The fortune teller made scratches in the sand and allowed the fine white grains to trickle through his fingers before declaring that Serge would be returning through Port Said within a year.

"It was very late when Sheila and I returned to the ship. We reached the gangway but then realised that the heat on board was going to be unbearable because all the portholes would be closed. So we decided to spend the night wandering through the city until daylight came and with it the time for the ship to sail. We watched the dawn come up upon the shimmering harbour and I realised I was in love. We watched the Oriental sunrise and then returned sadly to the ship."

After she arrived in Sydney Sheila would get letters from friends asking if it was true that she and Serge had eloped. She denied it because it wasn't true, but although unexpected and uncomfortable, his presence on board was not unwelcome. She even accepted his flimsy excuse that he had seen a business opportunity. He already worked for Vickers, which manufactured harvesting equipment, and Australia's vast agricultural industry offered opportunities for machinery sales. It would also give him the chance of a clean break from his marriage, which was in name only as his wife continued to pursue her singing career across France.

He didn't need to say the obvious: that he was besotted with Sheila and was chasing her across the world in the mad hope that she would see sense and leave Loughie. Divorce seemed out of the question for Sheila, driven by social expectations that wives should remain loyal to errant husbands if only for the sake of their children, although she freely admitted to herself that she was in love with another man: "We both knew we were in love, but not a word of love was spoken," she would write. "The urgent clasp of hands told us what we knew. But I was married—so was he."

On board ship they were treated as a couple and invited to the captain's table, dancing and eating together while discussing the "thin film of white control over the Eastern abyss" and how the world was changing post-war. They posed together for photographs and slept on deck with other passengers, listening to the chatter of jackals in the dunes as the ship slipped silently along the canal. They marvelled at the red-sailed feluccas on Aden harbour and wandered the narrow streets of Jeddah, exploring bazaars and mosques.

Serge watched with delight, as a husband might watch his wife, when Sheila pranked fellow passengers by pinning a notice to the bulletin board announcing that the ship would heave-to at noon so passengers could bathe in the Red Sea—gentlemen to the starboard and ladies to the port. Bathing suits could be rented from pursers. This was all in character—an idiosyncratic Australian character—for a woman he found irresistible but who remained just beyond his reach because she loved her children and didn't want to abandon their fragile father.

Loughie was waiting at the docks when the *Malwa* reached Bombay a week later for a one-night layover. Sheila had cabled ahead so he was expecting Serge and seemed unperturbed. His reunion with Sheila and the children appeared happy, if stilted. Serge watched on with mixed emotions. In Loughie he saw a man who was clearly a drunk and a gambler who was at times verbally abusive to his wife, but who struggled with post-war life and seemed resigned to failing, lacking the self-control or will to avoid self-destruction. It seemed only a question of whether he would take his family with him.

The Loughboroughs stayed at the Taj Mahal Palace Hotel and dined at the Royal Bombay Yacht Club; the colonial grandeur hid the awkwardness of the reunion, which resolved nothing. He had donated a gold cup—the Loughborough Cup—for a race meeting and, instead of joining his family for the onward voyage to Australia, wanted to stay and see who won. Sheila, saddened, took it to be yet another excuse. The following morning Loughie stood at the end of the pier, bareheaded in the blazing sun, watching the boat carrying his family until it was out of sight.

Sheila was subdued for the next few days, regret and worry etched across her face. But by the time they reached Ceylon, Loughie seemed to be forgotten as Serge and she explored the city in rickshaws. As they passed through tropical woodlands and rice paddies straddling mountains, they marvelled at the sight of elephants by the roadside and ancient temples engulfed by sweet-scented foliage.

They made their first Australian landfall in Perth, where the local media interviewed them as they stepped ashore together. It was breathlessly reported that Prince Obolensky was "more than ordinarily tall with a charming personality and thorough grip of the English language". But it was Lady Loughborough, an Australian girl who had made good, who held most interest: "Her ladyship was formerly Miss Chisholm, daughter of Mr and Mrs Harry Chisholm of Sydney, and is journeying to visit her parents after seven years' absence in England. During a short chat Lady Loughborough said that residence in England had been full of interest, particularly during the war period, but that she was more than delighted to come to Australia—as it was still her home".

They steamed across the Bight, reaching Melbourne on November 1. The timing seemed almost magical and was certainly fortuitous; they were met there by Harry and Margaret Chisholm, who had travelled down from Sydney for the Melbourne Cup. The next day Serge and Sheila watched the wonder horse, Poitrel, carry an unprecedented 10 stone to win the Cup; they had backed the winner at 8 to 1. Australia appeared to be a land of sunshine, joy and millionaires.

The entrance to Sydney Harbour a few days later only confirmed Serge's impression that he had arrived in a place of wonder and opportunity. He was seen by the media as an exotic—"a bona fide Russian prince," boomed *The Bulletin*, "who discourses on the Bolshevik horror which robbed him of the family wealth and sent him out to look for work."

Harry and Margaret, who had accompanied them on the

Harry "Chissie" Chisholm, Sheila's beloved father, who established one of Australia's earliest bloodstock agencies

Margaret "Ag" Chisholm, Sheila's mother, who spent most of the Great War tending wounded Anzac and British soldiers convalescing in Egypt

Sheila, aged four, photographed in 1899 between her brothers Jack (left) aged eleven, and Roy, aged eight. The brothers would not get on, forcing her father to sell the family property, Wollogorang.

Roy Chisholm, whose childhood love affair with Mollee Little eventually ended in marriage

Mollee Little, Sheila's best childhood friend and sometimes mistaken for her sister, was described by Sheila as "fascinating, with golden brown hair, a retrousse nose and the biggest blue eyes I have ever seen".

Sheila, aged sixteen, at Wollogorang in 1912 as her family prepared to sell the property and move to Sydney.

Mollee (left) and Sheila dressed in their swimming costumes in the summer of 1914. Much of Sydney's eastern suburbs was still semi-rural. The girls used to swim out past the men to be brave.

John "Jack" Chisholm, Sheila's oldest brother, at camp in Cairo before heading to Gallipoli. He was the reason that Sheila and her mother diverted to Egypt instead of going home.

Sheila in Egypt in 1915,
dressed to attend one of
the rare social occasions,
probably on the eve of the
Gallipoli campaign

Sheila in her uniform as a volunteer nurse in Cairo during the Great War, alongside
two trained colleagues

Freda Dudley Ward, Sheila's best friend during her early years in London and the mistress of Edward Prince of Wales for fifteen years. Like Wallis Simpson after her, Freda would be a mature, steady influence on the dandy prince.

A rare moment of complete ease for the royal princes. The "4 Do's" in 1919 sit on a fence, Prince Bertie smiling with his arm around Sheila, during a visit to Sheila's Winchester home, Lankhills (seen in the background). From left: Edward, Freda, Bertie, Sheila and Edward's equerry, Edward "Fruity" Metcalfe.

FROM THE LAND OF THE WATTLE : A BEAUTIFUL PEERESS.

LORD ROSSLYN'S DAUGHTER-IN-LAW : LADY LOUGHBOROUGH.

Lady Loughborough is the wife of Lord Loughborough, eldest son of the Earl of Rosslyn. Before her marriage, in 1915, she was Miss Margaret Sheila Mackellar Chisholm, daughter of Mr. Harry Chisholm, of Sydney. She has two little boys, Anthony and Peter, the elder of whom is two years old. The younger was born last year.—[Photograph by Sarony and Co.]

The heading on this photograph, published by *The Sketch* magazine in 1919, sums up the media response to Sheila's arrival in London. Little did they know that she was having an affair with the second in line to the throne.

Sheila stands smoking a cigarette between the two princes and future kings of England.

Prince Serge Obolensky and Sheila pose as a couple during the voyage aboard the *Malwa* to Australia in 1920. They fell in love during the trip.

Malwa, accepted his presence because (according to Freda Dudley Ward) Sheila had kept her latest marital woes and subsequent infidelity from her parents, so Prince Obolensky appeared to be a gallant escort rather than the insistent suitor he had actually become. Harry Chisholm, white-haired and ruddy-cheeked, even arranged introductions to businessmen for him and membership at the Union Club in Bligh Street, where he took up residence.

It was a new world, with many of the trappings of London but few of its formalities—an increasingly independent nation that was about to begin its own airline, admit women to parliament and thrash England 5–nil in the 1920–21 Ashes series: "People did what they wanted," he later reflected. "They weren't concerned with self-conscious European attitudes at all."

There was also a frontier aspect to its way of doing business as Serge was about to find out, dragged from his bed at 6.30 one morning by a young associate and driven to Bondi Beach: "It was completely wild, that beach. The only structures were towers from which lookouts watched for sharks. But the beach was packed with people. Beyond the expanse of white sand, all of Sydney it seemed was riding in the early-morning surf. This was the way the business day began, with a swim in that tremendous surf before breakfast. It was also where I first learned to shoot the breakers."

Sheila and the children settled back into the family home, now at Double Bay. But she and Serge continued to see each other. They attended society events, race meetings and parties; he was introduced to everyone as simply a close friend of hers who was exploring business leads in Australia. And, to give him his due, that's exactly what he did.

She accompanied Serge and one of her cousins when they drove out to explore the farmland along the spine of the Blue Mountains and the opportunities for selling farm machinery there and in the towns beyond—places like Bathurst and Quandialla. They then headed south to Goulburn and the old Chisholm homestead, Wollogorang, and continued on to the city of Canberra, which was now slowly emerging, before heading further south. In Melbourne they stayed with Dame Nellie Melba at her home, where the diva sang ballads in the evening accompanying herself on piano, and they took to the grass courts with the tennis greats Sir Norman Brookes and Gerald Patterson.

Photos would show a relaxed and happy period without the physical trappings of their glamorous world, Sheila helping to paint a fence at the Melba house, Coombe Cottage, and Serge, in boots and jodhpurs as a "jackaroo", leaning casually on the railings of a stockyard.

But there was always the shadow of Loughie. Sheila had half-expected that he might not come on to Australia, and return to England instead, but he cabled in early January to say he was boarding the steamship *Morea* and would be arriving in Sydney within a week.

"Loughie's coming to Sydney. I've to decide," she announced to Serge one night, making it clear that she was on the cusp of abandoning her troubled marriage. They had just returned from a visit to the station owned by her brother Roy, who had split with his first wife, Constance Coldham, and had now announced his engagement to childhood sweetheart Mollee Little.

Sheila was under pressure. Her family desperately wanted her to try to save the marriage but Serge decided to speak his mind, as she would recall in her memoir: "Serge said that I must run away with him. We would go to Hollywood and make our fortunes on the movies. Loughie would, of course, divorce me and Catherine would divorce him. This was our only hope of happiness."

Sheila was torn. Finally, she confided in her mother: "She was horrified and gave me a terrible lecture. She said I would lose my sons; that the Rosslyns would take them and I would not be allowed to keep them. In my heart I knew she was right because my love for Tony and Peter was stronger and no man on earth was worth leaving one's children."

Sheila tearfully told Serge of her decision. Serge could only stand back and wait: "Sheila's husband then arrived from India. He was greatly better, and while I knew what it would probably mean, I consoled myself by thinking of his and Sheila's happiness and that of their beautiful children. She intimated that she was going to give it another try, and she was right; but thereby my closest friendship in Australia would be broken off. Deep in my heart I knew I would be losing someone who would mean something to me for the rest of my life."

On his arrival, Loughie told the local media that he expected to be in New South Wales and Queensland for three months, before heading back to London. For Serge, suddenly the hardships of Australia appeared very real: the unsealed dirt roads and grim economy and the narrowness of the rural conversations, which offered little but an argument about the price of wool and the struggle to sell machinery. City life seemed easy, but the rigours of the bush were wearing. This was a country of extremes. Isolated, Serge suddenly felt lonely and Europe beckoned: "It was then that I realised that I had been living in Australia for the sake of a dream. I had no idea until then just how great a part of that dream Sheila had represented. I was lonely and loneliness is always worse when one feels that one really isn't proving anything."

Within a fortnight of Loughie's arrival, Serge was on his way back to London. Sheila watched him go: "I wondered if my heart was broken. Mummy said that I must devote at least a year to Loughie and try in every possible way to help him. This I did."

Serge boarded wistfully: "As suddenly as I had decided to leave for Australia, I returned in spirit to the Old World. This time it was a long journey back."

10

EVER YOURS SINCERELY, ALBERT

A letter addressed to Sheila arrived on the same boat that had brought her errant husband to Sydney. It was delivered to their rented Potts Point home as the couple sat down to discuss the future. Sheila knew from the envelope stamped with the royal seal that it was yet another complication in her life. She opened it carefully, a missive to be treasured whatever it said, and later to be folded carefully and stored among her most precious belongings, like the others that would follow:

Buckingham Palace
December 20
My dear Sheila,
I have got so much to tell you that I don't know where to begin. Do forgive me for my terribly long silence.

I have been meaning to write to you for ages but something has always cropped up to prevent me at the last moment and I have been frightfully busy and this letter has never been written.

So much has happened of late. It seems ages and ages since you left here although it has only been 2 months and I feel London altogether a different place without you.

Whenever I go into a ballroom I always look around the room hoping to see you, as I know there is somebody missing, and it is so so sad not seeing you, and I do so miss you.

But we hope that it will not be long before you are back among us again. I have no idea where you are now but hope you have reached Australia safely and found all your family well.

I expect that you must be very glad to be at your old home after the years here away. But I do hope you will come back again after the 6 months have elapsed. I shall look forward to the day when you return and I hope to be able to welcome you back once more.

My very best love for you Sheila.

Yours ever sincerely,

Albert

Bertie had promised to give up Sheila Loughborough, but this letter made it clear he was struggling to forget her. There seemed to be a longing and regret that they could never be together and that their affair had been cut short, not by them but by his father's demands. He'd been worried that he would be spied upon and reported back to the palace if he socialised with her, and he had said as much to his brother after he accepted the title of Duke of York, lamenting to Edward in a letter: "Oh! If only one could live one's own life occasionally."

During the summer of 1920 they had continued to see each other at dances and parties, even though Sheila was also being wooed by Serge Obolensky. Much to the annoyance of Edward, who viewed their relationship as a threat to his own dalliance, Bertie had continued referring to the 4 Do's. But the tryst was over, despite rumours that her divorce from Loughie was imminent, and her departure in September had left a void Bertie hadn't been able to fill, at least not yet.

He had already begun to show an interest in Elizabeth Bowes-Lyon, the lonely debutante Sheila had noticed on the night of the Farquhars' party. They had danced at an RAF Ball in July and he had accepted an invitation in September to stay at her family home, Glamis Castle in Scotland, where he had tentatively held her hand in front of others. And the week before writing to Sheila, Bertie and Elizabeth had sat together at a party given to celebrate his twenty-fifth birthday.

He was clearly attracted to the young woman, someone who would be approved as a suitable wife, but he was not yet over Sheila. The prince mentioned none of this in his letter and neither would he when he wrote again in April 1921, let alone revealing that he had proposed to Elizabeth on February 28. She had refused, apologising and asking for forgiveness before asking: "We can be good friends, can't we?"

He made sure to confirm his single status when he wrote to Sheila again at the end of August.

Sheila

Balmoral Castle

August 21st, 1921

My dearest Sheila,

Thank you ever so much for your letter of 16th June. I am so glad you received mine safely. David, I know, has written to you and you would have got it now. I arrived here yesterday. I was very glad to get away from London at last because I have been there all the time since the last I wrote to you in April.

The season started very late this year, not till after Ascot week owing to the coal strike but when it did start it was pretty hectic and I suppose, went to a dance four nights a week besides having a lot of work as well, so I am pretty tired especially mentally. Change is what I want.

No, I am not engaged or married yet!! Does it surprise you at all? I don't think I ever shall be, anyhow not for some long time to come.

It is all so difficult and tricky these days here and there seems to be more and more gossiping old women than before. I have seen very little of Freda lately who has been out of London and away for some time. David is much better now since he has had a rest. You know he overworked himself in July and nearly broke down completely.

I am so sorry to hear you say you have no plans for returning to England yet. We are all waiting patiently for you!! I do hope things are going easier for now and that you are not so worried as before.

I often think of the old days in 1919; they seem a very, very long way away now, but hold many memories. Your baby bear mascot is still on the car guiding me straight as before!!

Do please write again soon and tell me more about yourself, as you know how I want to know.

Again, so very many thanks for your letter,

Ever yours very sincerely,

Albert

In fact, Edward had not yet written, but he would do so in November, to "my dear little Sheila"—a rambling six-page letter in which he moaned about his royal duties and in particular a planned tour of India. He asked about her family and "sweet" Mollee:

I expect Moll has forgotten all about me by now though she and I got quite a lot of amusement out of some of the Sydney stunts last year and laughed a good deal!! She is so sweet, and tell her I hope she's forgiven me about the photograph incident on board Renown out at the Heads the day we sailed. Is she still more or less engaged to your brother Roy?

Then there was the sore point of her husband:

I won't ask news of Loughie. I expect it's better not, though it would be wonderful to hear he had really pulled himself together and was reformed!!

He can be so charming and on the other hand sometimes makes me want never to see him again!!

Please burn this when read as it's much safer isn't it?

Bertie drifts along much as usual and hasn't made any progress towards matrimony though he wants to get married and was trying fairly hard a few months ago!!! I've seen a good deal of him this last year . . . The life and atmosphere of London has changed a good deal and for the worst since you left and Fredie and I hardly ever go to parties nowadays.

Edward was right not to ask about Loughie. Little, if anything, had changed. In February 1921, within a month of his arrival in Australia and having moved his family into a sprawling home in Bay Street, Double Bay, he had left Sydney and headed north to Queensland, where he used his father-in-law's contacts to ingratiate himself into the racing community. His name would appear sporadically in Brisbane's social pages—"also noticed" and "among the crowd". It hardly seemed the behaviour of a man who had just been separated from his family for four months and who claimed to desperately want to reconcile with his wife. She meantime was attending similar functions in Sydney, often with her parents, and gaining attention as magazines clamoured to publish exclusive photographs of her as a visiting celebrity.

Loughie finally made his way back to Sydney, but there seemed to be little to keep him amused. The social calendar was limited, compared to London, and he was not interested in a career, so it was inevitable that he would quickly become bored. England beckoned, as Sheila told Bertie in a long letter. He replied immediately:

Buckingham Palace
December 8th, 1921
My dear Sheila,
Thank you so very much for your letter of October 16th, which I received safely. It is so nice to hear you say that you hope to return to England during the next year. You will find things a bit changed, I expect, but I understand that you have still got your house in London at 18 Hyde Park Terrace.

Tony and Peter are quite big now I suppose and I shall not recognise them again. I don't think I have changed. Anyhow, I don't think I've got a long white beard!!!! as you suggest. And I don't feel very old.

Thank you so much for your good wishes for my birthday. It is coming next week.

David left for India on October 26th, very sad and depressed at the thought of being away for eight months and missing for the hunting etc of the season. From what I have heard his tour has been triumph after triumph. He is wonderful, isn't he at these world tours and he does take much infinite trouble about them all.

I try to do my best in keeping the front at home but I can never equal him in the amount of work he does in all things. <u>Anyhow, I have a very fine example to copy in how things should be done</u>.

I am fairly busy now in doing functions most weeks but I am able to get away for weekends. I have had four days hunting this season. But at the moment the man I was hunting with has suddenly gone sick and will not be able to hunt again this season. This has rather upset my arrangements for the moment but, no doubt, I will be able to settle it all soon.

Everything is different enough already without worries of this sort as well. Greig is still with me and we get on splendidly. James Stewart has left and I have got a man named Waterhouse who is both private secretary and equerry. He is most useful because he knows everyone and everybody, which makes my life easier.

I am surprised to hear Freda has never written to you as you were such friends. I have quite lost touch with her too, and see her very occasionally at parties. There are very few parties going on now as no one seems to be in London, which makes it a very dull place, and I am never there unless I am obliged to be. We had a wonderful time at Dunrobin. What a marvellous place and we had some good grouse shooting and stalking.

So you were thinking of going on the cinema. Have you got a cinema face or whatever is needed for it? It must be very hard work I should think but, as you say, it would bring in some money.

We are all nearly broke here but I have heard now that the Irish government has signed, the income tax will drop a shilling or two. How I hope this is true, don't you? I hope you get this letter safely and with it I send every good wish for Christmas and the New Year and hoping to see you back here at no very distant date.

Ever yours sincerely,

Albert

The "cinema" reference was almost certainly the idea put in her head by Serge that they should run away together to Hollywood. She had dreamed about flying to America in her childhood and now, in her continuing unhappiness, the notion of a magical escape remained powerful. Little did she know that both she and Serge would end up there in later years, one as an influential member of society and the other as a frequent and feted visitor.

It would take another year for the Loughboroughs to pack up and head back to Europe, not as a reconciled and happy couple with a young family as she'd hoped, but disenchanted and together only for appearances and the sake of their children. Loughie took little responsibility for his behaviour. Instead he blamed Australia's climate for being disagreeable.

Although her own marriage was crumbling, there were two unions forged at this time which would have been important to Sheila. The first was the marriage of her brother Roy to her best friend Mollee Little on April 24, 1922, which drew coverage from *The Sydney Morning Herald*:

The bride wore a dainty frock of sand coloured georgette with a gold embroidered girdle and a fine lace hat of the same colour as her dress with ribbons of blue, and a wreath of hand-made flowers round the back of the crown. She carried a sheaf of blue delphiniums. Mrs Harry Chisholm wore a grey stockinette gown with touches of pale blue and a large black hat with deep ivory feathers. Lady Loughborough wore a simple gown of cream jersey cloth with a large black hat. Her two little sons were present in white silk suits. A small and intimate reunion of relatives of the bride and bridegroom took place after the ceremony. Many very beautiful presents were received. Mr and Mrs Chisholm departed Sydney later in the day for their honeymoon, the bride going away in a grey tweed coat and skirt.

She did not attend the second wedding, which happened twelve months later and half a world away. Prince Albert had written once more in late 1922, his letter more distant than the previous three—"dull", as he described it:

York Cottage, Sandringham
December 22, 1922
My Dear Sheila,
I was so glad to receive your letter of November 8th this morning. I was just going to write to you to tell you how very glad I am to hear that you are definitely coming home this next April with all your family which means, I suppose, that you are coming for good. Freda told me at a dance the other night all about it and it will be nice seeing you again after all this time—two years, as you say.

Yes, I think things are more or less unchanged here and we all do the same things as we did before. But I have not seen much of David and Freda lately as we are moving and hunting in different places and the days do not always fit in. Life is just as strenuous, plenty of work. We fit in hunting between stunts when we can, which is a good life and every moment is occupied.

I am down here with the family for a few days for Christmas, after which I hope to get a good month hunting. I have given David your love and he sends his. Please forgive this very dull letter. I shall be looking forward to your return with great expectation.

Best wishes to you for Christmas and the New Year.
Ever yours sincerely,
Albert

He missed one piece of news, perhaps because of a continuing longing he held for Sheila or simply because it was too personal. Albert had proposed a second time to Elizabeth Bowes-Lyon who, yet again, rejected him because she regarded their relationship as a friendship rather than intimate. He would try once more in February, 1923. This time Elizabeth accepted and they were married on April 26.

Two weeks later Sheila Loughborough arrived back in London with her husband and their two sons, Tony, who was about to turn six years old, and Peter, aged four, after a voyage that went via the Cape of Good Hope and the west coast of Africa rather than the Suez Canal and the Mediterranean. One of their maids had photographed husband and wife about to board the *Nestor* as it weighed anchor in Sydney, covered with streamers as they said goodbye to the party of well-wishers, including Chissie and Ag. Sheila looked pensive, the goodbyes difficult. Loughie was beaming.

Sheila summed up their time in Australia succinctly and sadly: "We remained in Australia for nearly two and a half years and Loughie did not change at all."

On May 22 the new Duchess of York recorded in her diary how Prince Edward had come to dinner where they were staying at Windsor and suggested they drive to London for an evening of dancing at the Embassy Club: "So we dashed up to London in his car & joined Paul's party there. Among Prince Paul's guests were the Prince of Wales' friend Freda Dudley Ward, Sheila Loughborough, Alice Astor, Prince Serge Obolensky and Lord Cranborne. Danced hard till 2.30. David sent us back in his car. Very tired & enjoyed it awfully."

Sheila also made mention of the evening in her memoir, but from a different perspective: "The Prince of Wales was with us and Freda, of course, also the Duke and Duchess of York. Prince Bertie, now the Duke of York, had married the little debutante we had seen in the doorway . . . three years before, Elizabeth Bowes-Lyon."

11

AN EXTRAVAGANT PEER

May 15, 1923

Lord and Lady Loughborough, who have returned from a long visit to the latter's parents in Australia, have taken Lady Cynthia Asquith's house in Regents Park. Lady Loughborough is a remarkably pretty woman and when she first came to London created something of a sensation.

The *Daily Mirror* was one of a number of media outlets that noted the return of the Loughboroughs as they swept back into London society, reinstated onto party and dance lists for the summer, nights at the theatre, weekends away in Scottish castles and holidaying among the social and political elite at Frinton-on-Sea.

On the surface the marriage appeared solid—the two years away from the temptations of London a success—but the public welcome and acknowledgement hid their private despair. All was not well. Within months Loughie was gambling again— worse than ever before it seemed. Aimless, with no job or purpose, he was back in his old haunts, sitting night after night in the smoky haze of places like the 43 Club in Gerrard Street, Soho, where, once inside the doors, you might have been in a Chicago speakeasy with its tinny piano and dubious clientele.

The 43 Club's owner, the infamous Kate Meyrick, noticed and pitied him. She would later recall him as being young, handsome and yet fragile, often sitting with her staff as if he were part of the furniture, greeting guests and friends alike and brushing off the inevitable ribbing about his precarious financial position, which had been made public on numerous occasions: "He displayed many of the symptoms of a manic depressive, with wild swings of emotion," she would write in her memoir, which was considered scandalous when published in 1933, a few weeks after her death. "But Lord Loughborough always seemed to remain in the gayest spirits no matter how unmercifully he was chaffed, taking everyone's jokes with complete good humour."

Increasingly, Sheila was going her own way socially. London was completing its transformation from hesitant post-war cele- brations into an era of economic and social prosperity. Life was changing on the gender front too: women were admitted to the bar for the first time in 1922 and one young woman, identified only as Miss Drummond, had created headlines as a successful marine engineer. Barbara Cartland, until then a newspaper gossip columnist, published her first novel, *Jig-saw*, a risqué society thriller that quickly became a bestseller; Agatha Christie was also beginning her career, although initially with somewhat less success. On a broader social front, parliament had also recognised equal rights for women in divorce cases, making it possible for wives to divorce their husbands for adultery.

If Sheila looked beyond her marriage pall, life seemed wonderfully exciting. As much as she missed Australia, she knew that her future lay in London and mainland Europe. It was the centre of the world and she was happy back in its bosom. There were new cafes, fashions and dances. The theatre scene, always vibrant, was now a thriving jumble of music and dance and comedy; there were two evening sessions every night, in theatres stretching from Covent Garden to Stepney, Finsbury Park and south across the Thames. George Robey was at the peak of his comedic popularity and Gracie Fields was on the verge of singing stardom.

There was opera at the Lyric and the Savoy, musical comedy at Daly's and the Winter Garden and plays at the Apollo, Globe and Ambassador. At the bottom of St Martin's Lane, the Coliseum was the city's flagship variety theatre venue. Hundreds would line up each night outside it, perched on camp stools and wrapped in blankets as they waited for its ticket office to open. Hawkers would wander up and down the lines selling hot tea and sandwiches, and street musicians, singers and conjurers would entertain the crowd before passing around the hat.

The wealthy "smart crowd" flocked to clubs like the Embassy in Old Bond Street and the Hotel Metropole on the fringe of Mayfair, happy to pay the cover charge of 1 guinea for men and 10 shillings for women to watch the revue *Midnight Follies*, dance the Shimmy and Heebie-Jeebie to the new jazz bands, and swill champagne and cocktails until 2 a.m.

The spectacular Hippodrome Theatre, on the corner of Charing Cross Road and Leicester Square, built to host circus and aquatic shows at the end of the 19th century, had been revamped for music hall and variety theatre as audience demands changed. Charlie Chaplin had been one of the first performers there, but now it began to host American jazz as entertainers ventured across the Atlantic in great numbers, with the vaudeville industry in the United States starting to buckle under the onslaught of the movies.

The foreigners had mixed success, just as many English acts struggled on Broadway. The four Marx Brothers had played to small audiences at the Coliseum but Sophie Tucker, "The Last of the Red Hot Mamas" as she became known, had wowed them at the Hippodrome and packed out the 5000-seat Rivoli theatre in Whitechapel.

Brother-and-sister routine Fred and Adele Astaire were struggling to win audience support for their dance musical *Stop Flirting*. They'd had a short season at the Queen's Theatre in Shaftesbury Avenue and were about to close. But that all changed the night the Prince of Wales and a group of friends, including Sheila Loughborough, attended. Rave reviews followed and the Astaires went on to play over 400 performances.

Lady Alexandra Curzon later recalled that particular evening:

I was with the Prince of Wales, and we went to see *Stop Flirting* at the Queen's Theatre. He sent his equerry "Fruity" Metcalfe, who would later become my husband, backstage between acts to say that the Prince of Wales and his party would like them to join us for dinner at the Riviera Club ... The place was packed. Prince Edward, Prince Bertie, Prince Henry and Prince George; they were all there ... Who were all his English friends? Well, I suppose they were all from our world, the circle in which we all moved—Edwina Mountbatten, Sheila Loughborough, Freda Dudley Ward. That was his age group, and that was the world that went to parties, and from nightclub to nightclub, and then away for weekends. One always went away from Friday to Monday to some delicious country house nearby.

Sheila would recall her friendship with the famous siblings: "I had known the fascinating Adele for years. She and her brother, Fred Astaire, had come into our lives in the early twenties. They came to all our parties."

⚬⚬⚬

Sheila often left a lasting impression on those she met, like the writer Frances Donaldson who, in her autobiography *A Twentieth-Century Life*, said she had been inspired by Sheila's frankness at a dinner party in 1924:

Today, the insensitivity, sometimes vulgarity, which often accompanies a sense of superiority is out of fashion, but on the night when I first dined with the Nortons I fell in love. Walking up the stairs after dinner, Jean [Norton] said to Sheila Loughborough: "This is the dress I bought in Paris. Do you like it?" and Sheila replied: "Well I would if it wasn't for that tarty bit of ribbon round the neck." No one I had ever met before would have given that answer. Asked the question, my mother or friends would have replied: "Yes, I think it's lovely," and given their real opinion to someone else. This speech had a dramatic effect on me, suggesting unimagined freedoms.

Sheila Loughborough not only attended the great balls and intimate dinners but hosted her own: "The Prince of Wales was there, the Duke and Duchess of York, Prince Henry and Prince George . . . and many of our fiends. [The jazz star] Aileen Stanley sang for us. My butler got drunk! He had elongated the dining room table and forgotten to put in the leaves. He then appeared with plates of eggs and bacon, which naturally fell through on the floor. All he said was: 'There goes another one.'"

Although her public persona was that of an independent and feisty woman, Sheila continued to be shackled to her marriage until January 1924 when, finally, she decided that she'd had enough. With the financial backing of the Rosslyn estate trustees, Sheila and the boys moved into a house at 19 Talbot Square while Loughie took a nearby apartment, but only after one last plea to Loughie for him to play an active role in the raising of his young family. Later discovered among her personal records was a letter sent, but apparently never received, which read in part:

Darling,
I know I'm wasting my time as your mind is made up that you are going to Trent to enjoy yourself and Tony, Peter and myself are going

to be neglected again for your pleasure—why I write this is purely to say that if your attitude is going to be the same as it is now and was in the past, you had far better not come to Hyde Park Terrace but leave my Trustees and myself to bring up Tony and Peter in a school which does not believe in the mother neglecting her husband and children night after night and day after day as you have done to Tony, Peter and myself. As Tony said tonight, he's forgotten what you look like and you can't blame him when you go every afternoon either to have your face washed, watch football, nails manicured, golf at Trent, in fact anything except seeing our children.

She had plenty of evidence, although much of it was as tragic as it was infuriating. Any number of friends could have told her of Loughie's indiscretions—Diana Cooper and Helen Azalea "Poppy" Baring among them who were aware of an encounter between Loughie, his friend Noel Francis and a society actress named Lois Sturt. In mid-January Sheila had been out of London for a weekend and her husband had gone to stay with Noel, the pal with whom he had shot down the Selfridges balloons. Both had alcohol problems and the result was toxic, as Lady Cooper described in a letter to her husband Alfred Duff Cooper:

Poor Loughie, who had just come out of an inebriates' home, and Noel, who had been tee-totalling for months under a vow, celebrated the occasion by getting gloriously drunk together. They were joined by Lois Sturt and an orgy that would have made Nero and Caligula turn in their graves appears to have taken place.

"The scandal", as Lady Cooper referred to the incident, was the last straw for Sheila and news of the estrangement quickly swept Mayfair, echoed by coverage in the social pages over the following months, which mentioned her frequently, and always alone.

For example:

April 6, 1924

The Prince of Wales and [his younger brother] Prince George and the gay young set which includes the pretty Australian countess of Loughborough . . . were all dancing indefatigably at the ball given at Sir Philip Sassoon's house in Park Lane last week. Flowers were in almost pre-war luxuriance and the whole hall was ablaze with blue and mauve hyacinth.

June 14, 1924

Lady Cunard entertained a large party to dinner and a dance at the Ritz Hotel last night. The guests included the Duchess of Sutherland, Lady Betty Butler, the Earl and Countess of Carlisle, the Duchess of Rutland, Mr and Lady Diana Duff Cooper, Sir Frederick and Lady Ponsonby, the Viscount and Viscountess of Maidstone, Lady Loughborough, Lady Sarah Wilson, Sir John Milbanke and the Honourable Mrs Cochrane Baillie.

July 15, 1924

A cabaret ball in aid of the children's country holiday fund has been arranged for Tuesday next at the Hotel Cecil. Among the organising committee is the Duchess of Westminster, Lady Louis Mountbatten, the Countess of Brecknock and Lady

Loughborough. This fund provides a fortnight's holiday for the poorest London children. They stay in the country or seaside cottages and learn often for the first time what country life means.

While Sheila seems to have had London in her thrall, Loughie had fallen further, if that was possible; a transient shifting between friends and hotels around London, running up accounts that would never be paid. But his credit eventually ran out and in June he was forced to apply for bankruptcy, revealing that his debts were now £18,000, the modern equivalent of A$1.5 million. Most of this was owed to Indian moneylenders, who had ignored all Lord Rosslyn's appeals and continued to lend to his son.

Far from protecting Loughie from temptation, the six months he'd spent on the sub-continent on the way to Australia three years earlier had merely given him unfettered access to money without oversight. In 1920, the morning after his father had allowed the trust to clear an £11,000 debt, the same book-maker had simply ignored every paternal plea and offered him more money, a drip-feed of cash that was destroying him as he emulated his father and flung money around, wildly betting on cards and horseracing. Added to the £9000 debt he had racked up in 1916, it showed the depths of his descent.

Inevitably, he was forced to make his appearance before the bankruptcy court, where his weaknesses were judged harshly. No account was taken of the greed and incompetence around him, perhaps because he was still blaming others, insisting that his title had been a "handicap" in seeking a career. This time his pleas fell on deaf ears. It was a case of gross extravagance, the bankruptcy registrar declared, refusing to discharge the bankruptcy for three years. More embarrassing was the wide public exposure as the courts examined his finances. *The Times* was among a number of papers which laid bare his useless life in an article under the heading "An Extravagant Peer. Wife Supporting Household", which detailed how it had been Sheila's money that had been keeping their home running.

A few weeks after the court declaration the Earl of Rosslyn wrote to his son:

My dear Loughborough,

I know it is useless but I write you my last word before completely giving you up. We parted somewhere about September 15—you with the expressed anxiety to get back to your farm. Neither Cumber nor Slouch know where you are and believe you're with me, and letters there are returned through the dead letter office.

Surely you must realise you are ruining your last chance of salvation ie: peace and happiness with your wife and children. It is little use reciting the reasons for your separation by agreement—suffice it the terms were "Give up all drink and learn to manage affairs".

You have practically made no effort, and what effort can you expect your wife to make? You profess your love for your children. How can you imagine you will be allowed their guardianship under present conditions?

As a man of the world I know all you are doing. Your whining to Tommy and then Denise, how sympathetic each of them is and how you love their advice, only to break completely away from it and go to the devil.

How may I ask can you live in London hotels without borrowing . . .
You should not leave the farm again till you can go to your wife and
say "I am clean again both as regards women and drink".
   Rosslyn

The earl's anger had not diminished four years later, when he published his autobiography, *My Gamble with Life*, which concentrated on his own fraught relationship with money. It included little about his personal life or the fallout from his disasters and there were only two brief references to his son, whom he called Loughborough.

The first was a passing reference to his birth in 1892: "That year, besides squandering a terrible amount of money, I found time for some formal duties at home, and the Duke of Cambridge was staying with us at Dysart for his annual tour of garrison inspection, when a second child—a son this time—was born to us."

His memoir provided no subsequent sense of his fatherhood, let alone any love he had for the son he had rarely seen in childhood and influenced only through his own wayward actions. Nor was there any recognition that his own weakness and lack of interest might have contributed to his son's difficulties.

Instead, Rosslyn's second reference to Loughie, as brief as it was amid his self-serving tale, was a reference to their estrangement: "I pass over the vagaries, to use a generous word, of my eldest son, Loughborough, in the hope that he will someday shed the dust with which he has so freely covered himself."

As she sought solace from her marital nightmare Sheila might have considered fleeing into the arms of Serge Obolensky, who was now working at a city brokerage, but it seemed their paths were destined never again to cross romantically.

While she had been in Sydney, trying vainly to make her marriage work, Serge had formally ended his marriage with Princess Catherine. And a few months before Sheila returned to London Serge had found a new love in the much younger American real estate heiress, Alice Astor.

Serge's attention had been sparked by stories about the young woman's interest in the occult, and in particular that she had been one of the first people to descend into King Tutankhamun's tomb when it was opened by the archaeologist Howard Carter. Alice was twenty years old, beautiful and rich; Serge was aged thirty-two, handsome and, in his own words, "impoverished". She was a commoner with the political power of new money (her aunt, Lady Nancy Astor, had just become the first woman to be elected to the House of Commons) and he was an aristocrat with the social power of old titles.

Serge was bewitched by Alice's youth while she probably viewed him as the father figure she'd lost during a tumultuous childhood. Her father, the fabulously wealthy and creative real estate investor and inventor Colonel John Jacob Astor, had divorced his wife Ava in 1909, when Alice was seven. The family was further split two years later, when Ava married an English aristocrat, became Lady Ribblesdale and moved to London, taking Alice with her but leaving her son, Vincent, who was older, in America with his father.

Worse was to follow. On April 15, 1912, JJ Astor was one of the 1502 passengers who drowned aboard the RMS *Titanic* on its way to New York. The tycoon's body was found a week later, identified by the initials *JJA* inside the collar of his shirt. He wore gold and diamond cufflinks and had £225 in English banknotes and $2440 in US currency in his trouser pockets (the modern-day equivalent of A$400,000).

His death, after the earlier family upheavals, clearly had an impact on Alice, who came across as a quiet, serious and shy young woman. Her engagement to Serge would cause yet another family rift because Lady Ribblesdale, in particular, was opposed to the union, not just because of the age difference but because of her desire that Alice should find a moneyed English peer.

Serge and Alice ignored the doubters and weathered Lady Ribblesdale's opposition. The young woman was forced to run the gauntlet of suitors proposed by her mother and the pair would have to wait another year, until Alice turned twenty-one, before she was free to make her own marriage choice.

Serge would later recall how Vincent Astor had wanted to buy his sister, as a unique wedding present, a pair of diamond earrings. They'd once belonged to Marie Antoinette, who had sewn them into her corsage as she fled Paris in 1793 during the French Revolution, before she was ultimately caught and beheaded. Strangely, the earrings had been retained by the French royal family and sold almost a century later to Serge's aunt, the mother of Felix Youssoupoff, but she, in turn, had had to leave them behind when the family fled the Russian Revolution. "I begged Vincent not to buy them," Serge wrote later. "I am superstitious in some respects, and those jewels were associated in my mind with bloodshed and tragedy. The earrings seemed to bring tragedy to whoever owned them." Vincent bought the couple an estate in New York instead.

Sheila Loughborough was among the guests when Serge and Alice finally wed on July 24, 1924. She went with Loughie even though they were now formally estranged. It would be the last public event they attended together and a firm statement that Sheila had drawn a line under both relationships—her marriage to Loughie and her love affair with Serge.

Sheila would later reflect on the finality she felt on that day: "My love for Serge was luckily and obviously dead, and to me there is nothing so dead as dead love."

12

A STRANGE SEX ANTAGONISM

The crowd was baying, fifty deep in places around the room, enjoying the theatre of the absurd playing out in front of them. In the ring, set up in the centre of the first-floor auditorium of the grand public town hall at Canning Town, the two combatants were slugging it out in a four-round amateur contest, each giving as good as they copped.

But it was more than the sheer physical encounter that made the spectacle so special. Brawls were frequently seen here in the poverty-riddled streets of East London, but rarely in this hall, which was normally reserved for rowdy trade union meetings. Here the humanist and Nobel Prize–winning writer Bertrand Russell had spoken out against imperialism; here Sylvia Pankhurst had held meetings to rouse support for the suffragette movement, but never could either of them have imagined this becoming the venue for a boxing match between a serving police officer and a member of the British aristocracy.

The jostling and cheering crowd should have taken delight that these two men, representing sections of society they would normally despise, were beating each other up, but there was something heroic about this contest and its venue. Instead of despising the two participants, the crowd was adoring and encouraging them. Detective Black was known to many of them, as either a reassuring face or an irritating presence; he was a senior officer at the nearby West Ham station and an accomplished fighter with a semi-professional "pug" career behind him.

His opponent couldn't have been operating further out of his comfort zone. Even his rather soufflé schoolboy nickname "Buffles" indicated he was in the wrong part of town but Sir John Milbanke was a man who could hold his own in any company. At twenty-three years old and a titled baronet from the Yorkshire Dales, he had been a better-than-average footballer at Cambridge, a star polo player in the annual match against rival university Oxford and even a jockey in the amateur steeplechase events.

But boxing was his passion. The "Boxing Baronet", as the papers had dubbed him, was championing a revival in the popularity of the sport by setting up amateur bouts around London, often fighting his close friend, another aristocrat named Raymond Vincent de Trafford. Their contests in halls around the city attracted big crowds, who flouted the anti-gambling regulations by betting on their favourite toff. The two pugilists always wore well-padded gloves, "twice the weight of those used by the professional pugs and which do not impair the usual dinner party festivities after the bout", one newspaper account quipped.

Still, Buffles took the sport seriously enough to be trained by former Commonwealth light- and welterweight champion Johnny Summers, and he was distraught when threatened with the loss of his amateur status in late 1924 when he was accused of gambling in the lead-up to another planned fight against a policeman, AJ Clifford. He pleaded ignorance to the bets, made by de Trafford, and was let off with a week's suspension. It was enough to lose the bout but not his treasured status.

The young peer was equally at home and aggressive with a pen in his hand as a glove. In a lengthy column published in *The London Evening News* he lamented the decline of what he called "the art" and prescribed boxing not only for physical wellbeing but for common good and decency. His piece read in part:

There is nothing which keeps a man so fit and gives him such a splendid sense of well being; and as a game it has the great merit of requiring only two to play it. Boxing can be enjoyed all the way round in evenings and in the very heart of London or one can indulge in half an hour's brisk practice in the early morning before starting the day's work. The value of boxing does not lie only in the fact that it is good exercise or that it enables one to defend oneself in an emergency. There is nothing that fosters the sporting spirit quite so admirably; and after all, it is the sporting spirit of the English as a race that is the essence of what historians are so fond of calling their "political and administrative genius".

To be able to take blows in good part, and to return them without malice—how much would not many a foreigner give to acquire that gift for himself and for his people . . . Let the nation as a whole take to the sport—employers and employed, bishops and bottle washers, princes and profiteers—and I think we should find a speedy return for the effort expended in increased dignity, self-respect and sense of proportion, and a lessening of industrial unrest and class hatred.

So there he was standing toe-to-toe against a member of the constabulary, far from the clubs of Mayfair and Soho, and in a part of the city that his type would never normally frequent unless by accident. He was not expected to win, but the contest was worth watching. The first two rounds were fairly even as the fighters warily circled each other, the detective marginally on top on points as the bout reached the halfway point.

The match exploded in the third round when Sir John was caught in the face by Black's straight left. He staggered under the blow but recovered his feet and then struck back, retaliating with a right hook which caught the detective flush on the jaw and sent him to the floor. Now it was Black's turn to recover but, when the bout entered the last round, his size and experience came to the fore as he gradually wore down the baronet. The next morning an excited journalist from the *Western Daily Press* newspaper reported:

Every blow of Sir John's was applauded, and at one time he appeared to be an easy winner, for paying little respect to the arm of the law, he sent Black down for the count in the third round. No champion could have landed such a blow with better judgment. But Black got to his feet to defeat the count and though he had to spend most of the time beating off the attacks of Sir John, he retained a slight lead and was awarded the verdict on points.

John Charles Peniston Milbanke looked like a boy, but he acted as if he was every inch a man. In 1920, even as a skinny eighteen year old, when photographed with his arms crossed for a picture that would be archived by the National Portrait Gallery, he commanded attention: tall, handsome, square-jawed and with eyes that challenged the cameraman to capture his confidence.

His lineage suggested a reason to be confident about his place in life, boasting generations of leaders: high sheriffs, politicians, the cupbearer for Mary Queen of Scots, even Lady Anne Milbanke, the brilliant wife of Lord Byron, and her daughter by the poet, Ada, the Countess of Lovelace, the gifted mathematician recognised as the world's first computer programmer. The Milbankes had been granted a baronetage by James I in 1616 after which they built a great house at Halnaby, in the county Durham, and created a dynasty although, like so many aristocratic families, their lands and country houses would be sold or abandoned within the first few years of the 20th century.

The Boxing Baronet's father, Sir John Peniston Milbanke, was the 10th Baronet and a war hero—a schoolboy friend of Sir Winston Churchill who was awarded the Victoria Cross at the age of twenty-seven for gallantry in the second Boer War. His citation read:

> On the 5th January, 1900, during a reconnaissance near Colesberg, Sir John Milbanke, when retiring under fire with a small patrol of the 10th Hussars, notwithstanding the fact that he had just been severely wounded in the thigh, rode back to the assistance of one of the men whose pony was exhausted, and who was under fire from some Boers who had dismounted. Sir John Milbanke took the man up on his own horse under a most galling fire and brought him safely back to camp.

Fifteen years later, Milbanke Sr took heroism a step further, re-enlisting at the age of forty-two to fight the Great War and then dying on the battlefield of Gallipoli, walking into the teeth of enemy fire at the head of his troops and swinging his swagger cane. Here his remains would lie forever, never individually identified among the carnage of the August 1915 landing. His son, at the age of thirteen, had lost a father and become the 11th Baronet.

In a strange way then, the present Sir John Milbanke and Lord Loughborough both followed the same course in their lives. Each of them tried to live up to a reputation: for Loughie, the romance of a life of audacity and swaggering bravado; for Sir John, the reality of a life of swashbuckling bravery and daring. Both men would achieve their aim, one in self-destruction and the other as a man to be reckoned with.

And both men would become infatuated with Sheila Chisholm.

Sheila had met Buffles in the summer of 1923, not long after the Loughboroughs returned to London from Australia, when he arrived at her house one day in company with Freda Dudley Ward and a hairdresser. Freda had been pestering Sheila about cutting her hair, which she insisted was dowdy and too long: "Everyone has short hair," she declared as Buffles, whose presence and nickname were never explained, sat and watched Sheila being clipped like a sheep in the sheds at Wollogorang. "I almost cried when I saw my hair lying on the floor. Tony and Peter seemed quite frightened; they didn't know what was happening to me and wanted my hair put on again. Buffles told me years later that he fell in love with me at that moment."

Freda was the conduit the second time they met as well, at a polo game in which Buffles starred for Cambridge against Oxford—just another admirer, albeit somewhat younger than the others, who saw a pretty young mother whose marriage was on the rocks.

But there was something different about him, which emerged not in charm and polite conversation but the antagonism of mutual attraction. This became apparent the third time they met, during a social outing with mutual friends when Sheila objected to him smoking a pipe inside the clubrooms: "I felt furious and said: 'I am accustomed to young men removing their pipes and brushing their hair before speaking to me.' He glared at me and left the room."

Later in the evening there was another confrontation: "We all decided to play tennis. Buffles appeared in the hall, near the cloakroom. To my amazement and rage I suddenly found myself pushed inside and the door being locked behind me. I kicked the door and yelled for help but it was a waste of energy and breath. He had the key in his pocket and no one could induce him to let me out for over an hour. I could have killed him!!"

Even when she split from Loughie she was reluctant to become too involved with Buffles. She had plenty of admirers and the last thing she needed was to commit to another relationship. Estranged was not divorced and there were certain standards to maintain, at least publicly.

Privately though, she was searching for the elusive sense of love that the words of Baudelaire, that she used to read in the orchard beneath the pear trees back at Wollogorang, captured.

There was another poet, an Englishwoman named Christina Rossetti, whose words haunted her, particularly a verse called "A Pause of Thought", which dealt with the search for love and, despite its futile nature, the unwillingness of youth to give up or stop loving:

> I looked for that which is not, nor can be,
> And hope deferred made my heart sick in truth:
> But years must pass before a hope of youth
> Is resigned utterly.
>
> I watched and waited with a steadfast will:
> And though the object seemed to flee away
> That I so longed for, ever day by day
> I watched and waited still.

Sometimes I said: "This thing shall be no more;
My expectation wearies and shall cease;
I will resign it now and be at peace":
Yet never gave it o'er.

Sometimes I said: "It is an empty name
I long for; to a name why should I give
The peace of all the days I have to live?"—
Yet gave it all the same.

Alas, thou foolish one! alike unfit
For healthy joy and salutary pain:
Thou knowest the chase useless, and again
Turnest to follow it.

Buffles Milbanke embodied that search even though Sheila couldn't really explain this attraction, even years later: "He was arrogant and yet shy, an attractive mixture," she would recall. "I loved him but he annoyed me. We seemed to have a strange sex antagonism."

They both had Alsatians—his bitch named Mova and hers a male named Mr Fang—and both loved to ride horses. And they were both competitive, riding for hours in Richmond Park on summer evenings in 1924: "He had several polo ponies and we would race each other for miles, galloping into the sunset, with the two dogs following us. They never seemed to tire. We were competitive with our dogs and our ponies."

It was as if their relationship embodied her desire to

challenge the dominance of the men around her while enjoying the power of being a desirable woman among them: "I thought I could do anything he could do—I often couldn't."

The first public indication of a friendship was in June 1924 when the *Daily Express* reported on a dinner and dance at the Ritz hosted by Emerald Cunard who, curiously, had hosted the lunch years before when Sheila had met Serge Obolensky. The guest list was described as large in the column but only fifteen were mentioned, including Sheila Loughborough and Sir John Milbanke.

Three months later Sir John gave his own dinner party at the Ritz. It was one of a dozen parties, dinners and dances held across London that night but a brief mention somehow found its way into *The Times* "Court Circular" column which noted: "Sir John Milbanke gave a dinner party at the Ritz Hotel on Tuesday when his guests included the Earl and Countess of Brecknock and Lady Loughborough." There appeared to be special intent in its publication and brevity. Few readers who actively followed the social meanderings of the elite would have missed the revelation that Sheila Loughborough, estranged wife of Lord Loughborough, was attending a dinner on the arm of a young aristocrat named Sir John Milbanke. In a world in which the wife was routinely much younger than her husband, here was a coupling in which the woman was seven years older than her beau.

Despite her attraction to Buffles, Sheila remained unconvinced about a more serious relationship. Her father came to visit in the spring of 1925 and tried to persuade her to divorce Loughie. And he liked Buffles: "He said our separation was neither one thing nor the other, that I was too young to live alone and asked what sort of a position I would be in if I fell in love and wanted to marry again etc. I told him I would never marry again, to which he replied: 'Nonsense.'"

Having Chissie in London was important for Sheila. Ag came every year, staying several months each time, but her father always remained at home. He had been abroad once before, but as the ship steamed back into Sydney Harbour he hurled his top hat into the waters and declared: "Australia is good enough for me", vowing to never again leave her shores.

But his daughter's new life had changed that and now he was in London, conceding that the "old country" was not as bad as he'd thought. Sheila loved showing him off to her friends at the Embassy Club, hosting a party attended by "the princes" and organising a visit to Paris where he was feted by members of the French Jockey Club. But it was over too soon and Sheila waved him goodbye before the end of summer not realising that it would be the last time she would ever see her father.

13

PALM BEACH NIGHTS

The club was humming and May Meyrick, owner and manageress, checked her watch. 1 a.m., as she would recount some years later in a first-person account published in an American newspaper, the *Milwaukee Sentinel*, still a few hours before she would consider closing for the night. Outside, the temperature had plunged to near freezing as November became December and autumn turned to winter, but here, in the warmth of a room draped with gold curtains and giant gargoyle-like masks staring from the walls, the city's elite celebrated the end of 1925 with carefree gusto.

There was no need to close while they were still spending money, she decided. May and her mother, Kate, had long flouted the licensing laws to keep their nightclubs open for business well into the morning hours. The rich and powerful, including the lawmakers and peers, were among their clients, so they feared little other than the occasional crackdown. This club, called Jade's, tucked away at the back of Golden Square behind Piccadilly Circus, had been quietly acquired the year before from a wealthy peer who had fallen out with his business partners. It was a simple operation compared to the Meyricks' notorious Soho premises, the 43 Club, which focussed on gambling rather than dancing.

The sound of chat and laughter rose and fell as the band played, the lighting dulled by the haze of cigarettes while waiters scurried back and forth to refill champagne buckets. Downstairs the "breakfast room" was also filled with guests crowding onto wooden benches, after helping themselves to warming plates piled with kippers, eggs and bacon, which soaked up some of the alcohol they'd previously consumed. Then they returned to the dance floor to resume their excess.

May looked on, scanning the room for any potential problems, but there were none, save the nightly adulterous pantomime played out among the women competing for male attention. There appeared to be a truce tonight but May didn't expect it to last long.

As she pondered how and where the skirmishes might begin, May was called to the front door by the porter. A taxi had pulled up outside and there were four guests who wanted to come inside. May personally screened all the guests. Exclusivity was essential for business. Dress code of evening gown and dinner suit was expected, of course, but wealth, beyond being able to pay the bar tab, was not an actual prerequisite. To gain entry, you had to be known.

She walked up the short passageway, lifted the flap that covered the spy hole in the front door, and assessed the man outside. Undoubtedly a foreigner, she thought, and probably Italian or Spanish, judging by his handsome swarthy features. The sombrero felt hat was also a giveaway. He was probably a waiter from a nearby restaurant, still in his dinner jacket and trying to bluff his way inside. The spy hole swung shut. "No," she said firmly to the porter and began walking back toward her desk, which served as a partition between the hall and the main room. She wanted to see how the expected catfight was developing.

Behind her, someone was knocking again at the door, apparently unhappy at their rejection. The porter peered out again. "Lady Loughborough is one of the party," he called out to her. May stopped. She hadn't seen past the foreigner. Lady Loughborough was a regular and welcome guest—one of the most prominent of London's society women, with connections to the palace. May walked back to open the door herself, hoping to immediately mend the error.

Sheila Loughborough was with Poppy Baring, daughter of the millionaire banker and long-time MP Godfrey Baring, and one of London's so-called "Bright Young Things". There were two men with them, standing behind the women. May didn't recognise either of them.

Lady Loughborough was clearly irritated by the initial refusal, not just as a personal slight but because it would have looked bad in front of her guests. "I want to sign some friends in," she said, an expectation rather than a request as she swept past May in a swirl of gold, her lavish evening coat seemingly made of tissue.

She went straight to the book on May's desk, signed for each of her party, paid the entry fee and was shown to the best unoccupied table in the room. May glanced at the book to see who her male companions were. She read only the first name—Rudolph Valentino.

Valentino had arrived in London a week earlier for the release of his new film, *The Eagle*. The movie, which opened at Marble Arch on November 22, may have received mixed reviews from the critics, but Valentino caused a sensation wherever he went and tonight the most famous movie star in the world was in May's club. She scurried through to inform the staff, but there was no need. She could hear his name being whispered at almost every table already.

"Rudy" was in the house and every woman was staring, their own conquest plans forgotten in a collective moment of adoration. The band too was abandoned—the dance floor was cleared in seconds as the women returned to their seats to stare. Valentino seemed not to notice the whispered commotion around him, probably used to the reaction and determined not to respond in case it encouraged the horde. Neither did Lady Loughborough seem to notice; she was ordering champagne and omelettes, coolly aware of her coup.

May chuckled to herself—the immediate threat of an unseemly, glittered catfight had evaporated. All the other men, until a few minutes ago the centre of attention, were now ignored. In fact, if they had all quietly left, none of the women would have noticed. As their female companions gawked, the men glowered, resentful of Valentino's presence. May could hear the same resentful comment being muttered everywhere around the room: "I don't see what you see in him."

May knew the peaceful standoff could not last, of course. It was only a matter of time before one of the huntresses made a move. It was a question of who had the most audacity and what might follow. Valentino knew it too, clearly apprehensive behind the impassive mask.

As the champagne arrived at his table, it happened. May, who had moved closer to ensure the service was perfect, was almost knocked over by one of the older women in the room, clutching a small memorandum book in her bejewelled, liver-spotted hand. Her request was pitiful: "Oh please, Mr Valentino. I've been so longing to have your autograph."

Rudy looked up, one eyebrow raised. The woman repeated her request and announced who she was, as if it mattered. He might have said no and asked to be left alone, but movie stars could not afford such solitude. Instead he sighed and reached into his jacket, pulled out a small gold fountain pen and signed the notebook with a flourish. It was like a starting gun, the green light for the stampede as a dozen or more women—duchesses and ladies, actresses and MPs' wives—grabbed menu cards and wine lists and rushed forward, etiquette and dignity forgotten as they jostled for attention.

Valentino, his smooth countenance now creased, gave in and began signing the cards shoved at him for a few minutes before putting his hands up. He'd had enough: "No, I won't sign any more."

May Meyrick was forced to step in and save her famous

guest: "Please now ladies, I'm sure Mr Valentino wishes to be left in peace to dance." The women moved away, grumbling at missing out where their rivals had not, and went back to their disgruntled men. Valentino smiled in gratitude at her. The room quietened and then the band struck up. Couples began returning to the floor as Valentino turned his attention to Sheila. The omelettes now arrived and his table forgot the rest of the room while they tucked in.

May still watched, not swooning like the others but studying his face to try to discern signs of the sex appeal that had captivated the legion of his female admirers, but he remained impassive. In contrast to his on-screen presence, he was reserved, even wooden. As though he was wearing a mask.

It was only when he finally got up to dance that May saw the sensuous Rudy appear. He danced sublimely. Sheila Loughborough was acknowledged as one of the most beautiful women in London and, as the beautiful pair moved gracefully together across the floor, the room seemed to stand still for a second time. May could hear the gasped exclamations: "How divinely he dances. Isn't it wonderful!" The floor all but cleared as women pulled their partners from the floor, so they could sit and watch. The men who tried to invite their women companions to dance were met with an indignant, "No, no. I want to watch Rudolph. Sit down!"

Later Valentino sought May out and asked her to dance. "I'm very much obliged to you for having stopped that stampede," he said quietly as they moved across the floor. His voice was a surprise—"educated but not cultured," as she would later recall.

His manners, like his dancing, were exquisite: "Thank you very much for the pleasure," he said at the end of the song, bowing deeply from the waist, as if on the screen.

Her curiosity satisfied, May's natural business instincts took over. She went upstairs and telephoned a friend who she knew would be at a nearby rival club: "I thought you might be interested to know that we have Rudolph Valentino here," she said when her friend came to the phone. "Feel free to come along, but do so now."

The first cab pulled up outside fifteen minutes later, followed by several more. The porter was flustered: "There are about a dozen taxis drawn up outside. What am I to do? Are they all coming in?"

"Let them all in," May nodded. The woman she had phoned was first through the door. Another thirty followed, filling the club within minutes. Word had spread quickly; women were eager to see their screen idol: "Where is he? Has he gone yet? Let's hurry."

Another autograph stampede threatened, but was quietly quelled. Instead, the latecomers joined the throng watching from afar as Valentino and Sheila lingered until 3 a.m. Within ten minutes of their departure, the club had all but cleared. The night was over, but the gossip was only just beginning.

Rudolph Valentino was in Europe not only to publicise his movies. His private life was as tumultuous as his looks were silken; his first marriage, to co-star Jean Acker, had failed and his second, to actress Natacha Rambova, was now on the rocks. He had decided to spend Christmas in London with his brother, Alberto, and sister, Maria, while he waited for his divorce to come through from the French courts.

His friendship with Sheila Loughborough would only complicate matters further, particularly when his girlfriend, Pola Negri, became aware of rumours that he was courting the glamorous socialite. Not only had Sheila and he been the centre of attention at Jade's, but she also hosted a private dinner party for him the following week, at which some of the cream of London society was present.

However innocent her actions may have been and however turbulent her private life undoubtedly was, the fact remained that Sheila was still a married, if estranged, woman who was entertaining Hollywood's most famous screen heart-throb. Tongues wagged furiously as Sheila hired one of the West End's most popular music duos to entertain him at the dinner party.

The combination of Sheila and Rudy provided great fodder for the gossip columns, which meant it was only a matter of time before news drifted across the Atlantic to Pola Negri. Incensed, she cabled him from the United States to call off their relationship, but then she relented when he responded immediately, denying there was anything untoward and pleading with her to reconsider. He was still in London on January 19 when Ms Rambova, whose real name was Winifred Hudnut, was granted a divorce, citing abandonment by Valentino as the cause. Satisfied, he sailed for New York two days later.

One week later Sheila also sailed for the United States, with her close friend Poppy Baring in tow. It was sheer coincidence, she would claim. A friend named Ali MacIntosh had cabled earlier that month saying: "Why sit in a London fog when you could be in Florida sunshine? The Cosdens and Rod Wanamaker want you to come and stay with them at Palm Beach. Do. Ali"

Sheila had met Ali, the son of a Scottish wine merchant, at a weekend party in 1917 and his relationship with her would be enduring, not as a suitor but a social connection that spanned two countries. The decision to accept Ali's invitation in the winter of 1926 would change her life.

Ali was about to be married to silent-screen star Constance Talmadge although it would not last. Neither would his second marriage to Lela Emery, heiress to a leather fortune. Instead, Ali would become a fixture on the Palm Beach circuit as the city grew from a small resort town into the winter escape for America's social royalty.

Ali owned the Alibi Bar and was a debonair social host frequently photographed with beautiful women arriving at a fashionable restaurant, shopping trips, golf courses and night-clubs. He was described in a *Life* magazine feature, in which he was pictured with thirteen different women, as "spinning through the Palm Beach social season like a whirling top".

"I find it quite difficult to describe Ali," Sheila wrote. "He was witty, kind and generous to a fault. His power of exagger-ation was fantastic. He always made me laugh even more than Loughie, which is saying a good deal."

The "Cosdens" were oil magnate Joshua Cosden and his wife

Nell who made a fortune in oil, lost it in wheat futures and regained it in the Texas oil boom. He owned reputedly the largest private home ever built in Palm Beach. Rod Wanamaker was a businessman and philanthropist who sponsored golf tournaments, cross-Atlantic flights and even explorations to chronicle the life of Native American Indians through photographs.

Sheila accepted the invitation, excited by the chance to go to America and by a new endowment sent by her father with a note—"you seem to have a champagne appetite, my darling". Freda Dudley Ward would watch over Tony and Peter while she and Poppy were away.

Like Sheila and Freda, Poppy Baring would capture the roving eyes of the House of Windsor's princes; she was as exotic as Sheila but a petite version: "She was tiny and very slim with enormous dark eyes and a wide red mouth," Sheila would describe her. In his desperate search for a wife after being forced to dump Sheila, Bertie had proposed marriage to Poppy. A few years later Bertie's younger brother, Prince George, also asked for her hand. Both proposals were rejected—not by Poppy, but by their mother, Queen Mary, who considered her not good enough for her sons.

Sheila would never explain the shift in companions from one best friend to another, from Freda to Poppy, but it coincided with her return to London and subsequent shift away from the two princes. The younger woman was also more willing to explore new adventures overseas.

The log of the SS *Olympic* which left Southampton on January 26 would show that Sheila fudged her birth date by two years, perhaps unwilling to admit to having turned thirty years old the previous September. She gave her intended address in New York as the Carlton Club, but wrote that she also had plans to stay with a friend, Mrs Cosden of Palm Beach, Florida.

The crossing was horrendous, described by the captain as he finally sailed past the Statue of Liberty a week later as one of the worst crossings by the White Star Line, with snow storms and ice fields, fierce winds, and 14-metre-high waves smashing over the crow's nest and destroying deck railing. But Sheila's memoir does not reflect the danger, rather the excitement. One night, unable to sleep, she and Poppy sat in their shared cabin playing ukuleles, "singing a rather blasphemous song about the *Titanic*".

When their ship finally berthed on February 3, Serge Obolensky was among those waiting on the docks. He was now living in New York with his wife and young child, and recalled the arrival in his biography, describing it as "much talked-about, ever-impending".

"There was a whole host of gallant New York gentlemen anxiously awaiting their arrival," he wrote, naming Carroll Carstairs, adventurer Charles Suydam Cutting, and realtor and socialite Lytle Hull, among others who wanted to meet her. Carstairs had organised a welcome party—dinner and the theatre—for the pair on the day they arrived and Cutting was sent off to meet the women, steer them through Customs and get them safely to the dinner party. He came back with Sheila and Poppy, shaking his head. "Too damn many beaux," he grumbled, revealing that there had been another group of men at the docks to meet the pair, who then insisted that two of them be invited to the party.

The arrival of Sheila and Poppy coincided with two blizzards within a week of one another, which swept across the east coast accompanied by 100-kilometre-per-hour winds, plunging temperatures in New York to below zero, halting transport systems and killing more than two dozen people. They sheltered in their hotel until the worst had passed and eventually travelled south to Florida, where they were soon in the midst of the social whirl, among a group of society women who joined the chorus line of Florenz Ziegfeld's production *Palm Beach Nights* at the Club de Montmartre theatre-restaurant, which he had created for his shows.

That night's "billion dollar audience", as it was described, included names like Randolph Hearst, Gloria Vanderbilt, Rod Wanamaker and Joseph Pulitzer, who cheered as Sheila and others popped balloons as they performed with Ziegfeld Follies star Polly Walker. It was a charity event in aid of a local hospital and a glamorous introduction for Sheila to the elite of US society, launching her as a new star on the other side of the Atlantic. *Palm Beach Nights* would reopen as a Ziegfeld Follies production on Broadway the following year.

Later, at a private supper party, Sheila was introduced to Vincent Astor, one of America's richest men and brother of Serge Obolensky's wife Alice. Vincent, sternly handsome, was something of an enigma. When his father JJ Astor, by all accounts an arrogant and disliked man who largely ignored his son, died aboard the *Titanic* in 1912 the then 21 year old inherited a business empire worth an extraordinary $US87 million, made up mostly of great swathes of Manhattan property stretching at one stage several kilometres from Broadway to 150th Street.

But the young man belied his appearance. He had a highly developed social conscience and was horrified at the family reputation for being slumlords, selling off land cheaply to the newly formed Municipal Housing Authority to provide affordable housing. Despite this charitable move, Vincent still managed to double the value of the family business over the next 50 years. When he died in 1959, childless because of mumps, he willed the vast bulk of his fortune to a private foundation to "alleviate human misery".

But on this balmy night in 1926 Vincent, despite being married albeit unhappily, was only interested in Sheila Loughborough and began to shower her with attention—a "rush", as her American hosts later told her.

During the night someone began singing the production's title song, *No Foolin'*, with substituted lyrics naming Sheila and Poppy:

> *No foolin', wedding bells are all bunk,*
> *Don't get married, stay drunk, no foolin',*
> *No foolin' with dear little Pop,*
> *She'll tell you to stop, no foolin',*
> *No foolin' with Lady Loughboro',*
> *Or away from you she'll go, no foolin'.*

Sheila may have been wary of Vincent's eagerness but it didn't stop her from staying for a week at his Long Island mansion, where his attentions continued. On the first morning, about

11 a.m., Vincent sent a male friend to her room: "Vincent has sent me to tell you that he is waiting for you to play tennis," he announced after tapping on the door.

"I am reading and will not be down for an hour," Sheila replied.

The man sounded shocked: "Did you hear what I said? Vincent is waiting for you to play tennis."

"Let him wait," she replied, and kept on reading her book.

In her memoir, she would recall: "Vincent continued to give me the 'rush'. I was flattered and it was most entertaining but I liked to be asked, not told."

The arrival of the two women in California in early April immediately sparked great interest; they were greeted almost as visiting royalty by the *Los Angeles Times*, which sent a reporter to interview them in their suite at the Ambassador Hotel and published a lengthy interview.

"We came to America primarily to visit Palm Beach," Sheila told them. "It's a beautiful place and has a wonderful climate, but we felt our American visit wouldn't be complete unless we saw California. And now that we are here, we find it far more charming than Florida. The scenery here is lovely. Everybody has shown us utmost courtesy. And we like the American manner of speech so much. We are trying to learn it. Don't you think we have made some progress?"

She added: "One thing I like about Americans is their lack of reserve that makes it so hard for Britons to get acquainted. I don't know why the British are so shy. I guess it is self-consciousness."

But Sheila had another reason to be in California. Tucked away in the bedroom desk drawer at her home in London was a plain linen white unsealed envelope. Inside was a small white card, embossed with the name of its sender—"RUDOLPH VALENTINO, Hollywood"—and scrawled on it was a short, hand-written message in green ink, which read: "Love and kisses from 'the girl friend.'" The meaning of this cryptic message can only be guessed at, but whatever its purpose, the card was something she would keep among her most treasured possessions for the rest of her life.

Valentino had just begun production of what would end up being his last movie. *The Son of the Sheik*, sequel to his 1922 film *The Sheik*, would be filmed mostly on the United Artists lot off the Santa Monica Boulevard; later they would shift to the Arizona desert for the outside shots. He invited Sheila to visit him on the set, something his agent, George Ullman, later remembered because she was the lone "non-film" guest he entertained among the legends of the silent screen. He later wrote:

> I think that Rudy had a better time during the filming of *The Son of the Sheik* than in any other of his pictures. He used to have his lunches brought down from home, and there gathered in the dining room of his suite at the studio Constance Talmadge, Ronald Colman, Vilma Banky, George Fitzmaurice, Alistair MacIntosh, Louella Parsons, Marion Davies, Lady Loughborough, Eugene Brewster, Corliss Palmer, and many others. All these I met at different times at Rudy's famous luncheons. Brilliant conversation was the order of the day.

Valentino also had a habit of entertaining small groups of people at his estate. Called "Falcon Lair", it was a red-tiled Spanish villa built at the end of a winding dirt track at the head of Benedict Canyon, overlooking Beverly Hills. Valentino had bought the property the previous year, to have more space for his stable of Arabian horses and his dogs, and to house the trappings of his spectacular career. It also gave him the privacy he craved: in the years before the hills became dotted with the mansions of movie stars, his only neighbours were Douglas Fairbanks and Mary Pickford. Valentino filled the house with antiques, particularly with medieval armour, which was his particular passion, and he had large petrol tanks installed, so he wouldn't have to stop and fill one of his cars in public.

A few nights after Sheila's interview with the *Los Angeles Times* was published, Valentino invited her to dinner at Falcon Lair. It would be an intimate affair with a handful of guests, among them studio boss Joe Schenck and his screen-star wife Norma Talmadge, who would find fame not only as a popular actress but as the accidental originator of a Hollywood tradition when on one occasion she stepped into wet concrete in front of Grauman's Chinese Theatre.

Suddenly Pola Negri arrived unannounced at this small dinner party and the sparks began to fly. She was unaware that Sheila was in the United States, let alone at her lover's house, and to discover Sheila standing next to Valentino at the front door, greeting guests as if she was the hostess, was almost unbearable. Rudy tried to make light of the moment with a casual introduction, but Pola was livid.

"I was completely taken aback," Pola would later recount. "Since his cable denying the rumours of their affair, I had forgotten all about her. And here she was in his house, her cool insolent expression seeming to mock me."

Norma Talmadge intervened, and took Pola aside to tell her that she needed to hide her emotions, because she was "too transparent". But the lull was only temporary. Pola disappeared upstairs and entered Valentino's bedroom, where she found there were two photographs on his dressing table. One was of her and the other was of Sheila.

Adela Rogers St Johns, the celebrated scriptwriter and journalist, was another who had been invited that night and she described the ensuing scene as "fireworks". The guests watched on as Pola slapped Valentino's face and stormed off.

Sheila remained unmoved throughout the ruckus and the dinner resumed: "Afterwards he danced the tango with me all evening. His girlfriend (whose name I cannot remember) was furious. She apparently smacked and scratched his face when the party was over and retired to bed for ten days, which suited me as it was the length of our stay. We saw him every day and I liked him enormously. He gave me his gold chain bracelet, which he always wore and about which I teased him. He said it was his luck. In the next few months the whole of my life changed for the better, and he died. I felt I had taken his luck."

Three weeks later—having been feted by society in New York, Palm Beach and Los Angeles for three months—Sheila and Poppy sailed for London, waved off by yet more media coverage of her trip: "Our cabins were full of flowers and farewell telegrams. I was sad to leave but longed to see Tony and Peter. I did not return to America for eleven years."

On August 15 Rudolph Valentino collapsed while staying at the Ambassador Hotel in New York. He died a week later, aged just thirty-one, from peritonitis. Despite Pola Negri's claims that they were formally engaged, Valentino never confirmed this; she would make yet another scene at his funeral, where she collapsed dramatically. Nine months later she married another man.

Despite his great fame, Valentino's private life seemed to be in constant turmoil. His first marriage, to actress Jean Acker, ended on their wedding night when, realising she was a lesbian and regretting her decision to marry, she locked him out of the bedroom. His second, to Natacha Rambova, ended bitterly and his relationship with Pola Negri was a series of dramatic scenes.

In the years after his death, it was suggested that these relationships had been "lavender marriages", intended to conceal his own sexuality, yet, in the months before his death, he had described his idea of the perfect marriage in terms that would indicate otherwise: "What I am dreaming of is to have a home where I could live in peace, with a loving wife who would not be wanting to play in film, and who would greet me, each evening, after work, with my children."

That description appeared to fit Sheila Loughborough, who arrived back at Southampton on May 4 just in time for her own marital drama.

14

"WEDDING BELLS ARE ALL BUNK"

The Hotel Somerset in Orchard Street, Marylebone, was a discreet, boutique establishment with a handful of "apartments" and breakfast if required. With wrought-iron railings and pretty baskets of spring flowers, it was tucked away from the bustle of Oxford Street—far from the grandeur of Belgravia or the splendour of the Rosslyn estate.

But it would be here in the first few days of summer 1926 that the fraught marriage of Sheila Chisholm and Francis Edward Scudamore St Clair-Erskine, Lord Loughborough, finally came to an end. The couple hadn't lived together for more than two years and had clearly established separate lives, but the divorce laws of those times, which did not accept mutual consent, made it almost impossible to end matrimonial agony and allow both parties to move on with their lives.

The grounds for divorce had been extended two years before,

and now gave women equal rights against their husbands, but the options were still limited—adultery by one but not both parties, desertion for more than three years, cruelty, habitual drunkenness, insanity or imprisonment for life.

Increasingly, couples were choosing the route of adultery, real or otherwise, but they always had to take great care to avoid the perils of perjury or being accused of "collusion to secure a divorce". The popular solution was "hotel evidence", in which the estranged husband and an uninvolved woman booked into a hotel for a weekend, usually in a seaside resort like Brighton. But far from hiding away, as an adulterous couple might, they would parade around publicly as husband and wife during their stay, even being seen in bed together by the chambermaid serving breakfast the next morning. When the case was called to court, the staff would often be called as witnesses, even though the adultery was fictitious. The stage and film actor Claude Rains was one who used the tactic in 1924, when he wanted a divorce from his wife Marie Hemingway.

And Lord Loughborough, taking pity on his long-suffering wife, followed the same route. On June 18 a hand-delivered letter arrived for Sheila from Loughie, in which he had penned an apologetic means by which she could escape: "It is a long time since we lived happily together and I know that, as far as I am concerned, you have had a difficult time in various ways. I think the fair and proper thing to do is to give you an opportunity of obtaining complete freedom from me if you want it. The enclosed will give you what you require."

Inside the envelope was an invoice and receipt from the

Hotel Somerset made out in the name of "Mr and Mrs Erskine" for accommodation and meals charged between Sunday, June 13 until Tuesday, June 15. When she checked the register at the hotel a few days later, with her solicitor in tow, Sheila confirmed that her husband's handwriting was there. She had no idea who the woman was, or if there was actually a relationship between the pair, but it should be enough for a court to end their sad farce, provided it was presented in a believable fashion. She moved swiftly.

Less than a month later, on July 14 in the Edinburgh Court of Session, Sheila was granted a divorce and custody of the two boys, Anthony and Peter, now aged nine and seven respectively. Their father did not contest the application, which was supported by evidence from "a London inquiry agent and a staff member". Lord Murray, the presiding judge, chose to ignore the obvious divorce application sham.

The inevitable media coverage the next day painted a sad summary of an eleven-year union. The *Dundee Courier* reported the proceedings at length, particularly the evidence of Lady Loughborough "quietly dressed in a grey costume with a light blue, close-fitting hat who gave her evidence with marked composure".

In fact, Sheila was nervous and had almost pulled out of the hearing: "I had waves of tenderness, remembering all the niceness of Loughie . . . and how he had always made me laugh. Freda and Poppy literally had to push me onto the train."

Her father-in-law was also furious: "I did not tell a soul . . . but unfortunately he found out . . . and hurried to Scotland to put a stop to it. He called on the judge and told him the whole thing was a collusion and said he refused to allow his son to be divorced."

Worried about the intervention, Sheila's lawyer, Sir Charles Russell, suggested she dress carefully: "I must look the part of the pathetic, ill-treated little wife. I borrowed my nursery maid's grey coat and skirt and felt hat, wore no makeup—not even lipstick—and I certainly looked pathetic."

As it turned out, there was no cause for worry. The Earl's protestations fell on deaf ears when Sheila described how the marriage soured after the first few, happy months: "My husband drank and gambled and got into terrible trouble," she said under questioning from her lawyer. "He was horrid and abusive to me and drank terribly. It seemed to get worse each year."

She told of their move to Australia in the hope that new surroundings might change him. "Did his conduct improve in Australia?" Sir Charles asked, knowing the reply would be negative.

"No, he promised not to drink and not to get into trouble but he did again," she replied. "He always blamed wherever he was, first England and then Australia."

She continued that when they returned home in 1923, things did not improve: "I had persuaded my husband to have a cure for drink, which he did, but when he came out of the home he was not better at all. Life for me was intolerable. Finally I asked the trustees and his father to meet, and they agreed that it was intolerable, and that I should have a house for myself and the children. The house in Hyde Park Terrace was sold, and I got my present small house in Talbot Square which is just big enough for me and the children. I have not lived with my husband as his wife since January, 1924."

The hearing lasted 20 minutes with only one anxious moment, when she was handed a Bible and told to remove one glove while she swore an oath: "I removed my glove as directed and, to my horror, noticed that I had forgotten to take off the red varnish from my nails, which hardly went with my pathetic and dowdy appearance." All was well, she noted, because the men in the court didn't appear to notice.

Lord Murray had little hesitation in granting the application and Sheila was on the midday train back to London. The decree nisi which arrived a few weeks later declared that Sheila was "entitled to live single or marry any free man as if she had never been married" although Sheila had no intention of making use of the second option: "I was free—what a strange feeling? I decided that never, never again would I marry anyone, and hummed to myself: 'Wedding bells are all bunk.'"

She may have felt "free" but the divorce highlighted her concerns about parenthood and her relationship with Tony and Peter. The social norms of the time meant that children of the well-to-do were mostly raised by staff, in this case a woman known as "Nannie". Sheila's role, as the mother, was to play with them and take them on holidays: feeding the ducks at Kensington Gardens, a picnic in Hyde Park and holidays by the sea with other adults who had children, like Freda, Jeanie Norton and Lady Olive Baillie who owned Leeds Castle.

Sheila struggled with the guilt of her limited role as a mother and the impact on them of a broken marriage. She was hopeless at discipline and unable to admonish them without adding: "here, have a sweet". The boys constantly sparred. Peter was the more physical of the pair, showing talent as a boxer which Buffles encouraged and honed with lessons, and once knocked his older brother out cold as they fought while waiting for a train. She comforted herself with the notion that it was just boys being boys: "They were devoted to each other but fought a great deal, which rather worried me."

Two months after the divorce, Sheila and Tony drove down to the Sussex coast to enrol him in preparatory school where he would board, returning home only for holidays. His brother would follow a year later. It was a difficult and tearful parting for both; a premature wrenching that she would still feel many years later: "We were determined to be brave and pretend we didn't mind. We have since admitted to each other that we both cried ourselves to sleep for nights. I disapprove of the English custom of tearing little boys away at the early age of eight but what could I do against tradition? (I dislike the word!) I think the American system is far more humane."

Sheila resumed her place among the royal set during the Season. She celebrated her divorce by attending a fancy dress ball thrown by the Duchess of Sutherland; she and seven others—including Freda Dudley Ward and Lady Diana Cooper—dressed as the Cambridge rowing crew, complete with boat and pale blue oars (Lady Diana's husband, Duff Cooper, was the coxswain). The King and Queen of Spain were the main guests at the ball, held at Hampden House and regarded as the event of the season; the Prince of Wales and his younger brother, Henry, turned up dressed as "Arabs" and kept changing costumes throughout the evening as "stunts".

In August Sheila was holidaying at the fashionable French seaside resort of Deauville, with its luxury hotels and casinos, where she was noted by the *Western Morning News* as one of the women wearing the latest fashion in beach wear—brightly coloured bathing wraps:

> Beach strollers who drink aperitifs at small round tables near the sands are also wearing the new coloured rubber shoes or boots. The boots are most attractive, for if not patterned in "harlequin" fashion with many different colours, they are of bright red, bound with white or perhaps blue and white, with lacings to match the piping. These front lacings over the bare legs are left open for about one inch from the instep to above the ankle, and it is said that these boots provide just the right support when playing games upon the sands. Lady Louis Mountbatten and Lady Loughborough are keen polo players and in the morning, they too adopt the bright patterned bathing robes which are as gaily flowered as any cretonne.

London had entered the Jazz Age and the American queen, Sophie Tucker, was making her return appearance to the stage and club scene at the Kit-Kat Club in the Haymarket, advertised as the most luxurious dance club in the world. Sheila, who had been among the invited first-night audience in the United States a few months before, in March when Tucker had opened her New York club, Sophie Tucker's Playground, on West 52nd Street, was at a table with Lord and Lady Mountbatten and Lord Beaverbrook.

Tucker recalled years later in her memoir:

The biggest thrill of the evening was when His Royal Highness, the Prince of Wales, came in. He sneaked in on the balcony, as he wasn't dressed and he came only to hear me sing. I kept trying to spot him up there, but I couldn't. I wondered how he was going to take one of my new songs, "I'm the one the prince came over to see" which, of course, was a play on his recent visit to the United States. The prince didn't object to it. In fact, as I learned later, he was the one who laughed the loudest.

The singer was enthralled by the London nightclub scene, which had expanded rapidly since the end of the war; it consisted mostly of small and intimate places, each with its own loyal crowd. Some, like the 43 Club, reminded her of the American speakeasy joints "decorated with women and more women and more women", but others were more glamorous, like the Kit-Kat Club or the Café de Paris in Piccadilly, which had opened in 1925 and 1924 respectively, and quickly established themselves among Europe's leading nightspots.

Tucker also took delight in the genteel summer Sunday lunches at a hotel in the village of Bray on Thames outside London, where the well-heeled sat by the river in sporting clothes beneath coloured umbrellas; after lunch they would punt and canoe, then have cocktails from 6 to 7.30 and dine at 8 on the terrace. At 10 p.m., after dinner, she would entertain them with a small orchestra while everyone sat on cushions.

The venue would become notorious seventy years later when

an MI5 document emerged that accused well-known American stage and screen actress Tallulah Bankhead, who was living in London, of being an "immoral woman" who had an orgy with five Eton boys, including "the grandson of Lord Rosslyn". The report was wrong in the sense that it almost certainly referred to Loughie's half-brother Hamish St Clair-Erskine, and therefore Lord Rosslyn's son, who was expelled for his sexual adventure.

There was also a new trend in small dinner parties, at which Sophie Tucker would be asked to perform. She later recollected the night at Sheila Loughborough's, at which she taught the Prince of Wales how to dance the Charleston:

> The smartest of all parties was also the smallest. There were only eight guests. This was the party that Lady Loughborough gave for the Prince of Wales at her house in Talbot Square. During the evening I was sent for to sing for the prince. His equerry, Captain Alastair Mackintosh, came and escorted me to Lady Loughborough's. That special intimate little party was as informal and full of fun as a party of college kids over here. I sang all the songs the prince called for. He loved playing the ukulele. He got me to teach him my song, "Ukulele Lady". That same night I taught him the Charleston, then all the rage in the United States.

Sheila's re-emergence as a single woman had coincided with one of the most exciting and rapidly changing periods in England's history. The breakdown of social barriers and the class system had begun, if subtly, as ageing estates and family fortunes began to disappear. Parliament was in heated debate about further changes to the electoral system. Women had been given the vote in 1918, provided they were aged thirty, but now the push came to lower the female voting age to twenty-one, which was greeted in some quarters as a backward step.

The Roaring Twenties brought with them radical changes in social attitudes, fashion and style. Hand in hand with jazz and the Charleston came the flapper look: exciting and reckless, it saw hemlines creep up to the knee while dresses became shapeless as hips and bustlines were eliminated. Women smoked luxuriously on long cigarette holders and dared to apply make-up in public. Chaperones were dispensed with and hairstyles followed the latest hemlines and attitudes—short and radical; bobbed, shingled and cropped.

Australian newspapers delighted in reporting:

The former Sheila Chisholm of Sydney is definitely ranked among the most interesting of London's young society women. An acknowledged leader of fashion, Lady Loughborough is credited with being one of the first to adopt the shingle, at a time when long hair and the bob were the only admissible forms of hairdressing. Lady Loughborough's shingle was said to be the closest cut in society and was so successful that her example was immediately followed by hundreds of other women. Always beautifully dressed, Lady Loughborough is a great favourite with the younger members of the Royal Family, and is often chosen to partner the Prince of Wales and his brothers at smart society functions.

Sheila

The plaudits for her kept coming—at the Embassy Club "looking lovely dancing with John Milbanke", winning applause playing Shakespeare's Beatrice in a society performance at the New Theatre, or simply being beautiful, as espoused by "The Rambler" writing the "Talk of the Town" column in the *Daily Mirror*:

> There were so many beautiful women at the Café de Paris gala last night in aid of the dockland settlements the discussion arose as to who were the reigning beauties of modern society. The three girls who came into the argument were, curiously enough, seated together at an adjoining table. They were Lady Loughborough, a beautiful Australian girl, Mrs Lionel Tennyson, Lord Glenconner's lovely sister, and Miss Poppy Baring, the strikingly handsome daughter of Sir Godfrey Baring. At a table opposite sat Prince Obolensky, and I mention him in this connection because as good looks in the sternest sex are concerned, he is regarded as possibly the most handsome man in town.

Rather than fade into the background of society as a pitied divorcee with little money, Sheila Chisholm had emerged from the sadness of her marriage to be a woman to be noticed. And she was rapidly becoming one of the most socially prominent women of her time.

Yet she seemed unaware or, at least, coyly indifferent, as she noted in her memoir about the day she was teased by the Marquesa de Casa Maury, the former Paula Gellibrand: "Paula's blonde beauty was quite unique. She had large, strange-coloured eyes and her hair was the colour of light and dark honey. She was tall and dressed to perfection. She teased me and said that I wore my clothes upside down. I knew it was useless for me to try and be chic—I just couldn't be bothered or was not the type and even later on, when dressed by Patou and Molyneux, the fittings always bored me to death."

Europe beckoned and in the spring of 1927 she travelled to Rome on a whim with Paula: "I just wanted to flaunt my freedom, I suppose. We stayed at the Grand Hotel for two weeks. I was spellbound by the beauty of Rome; it seemed a golden city. We did all the picture galleries, St Peter and the usual things. I was fascinated by the proportions of the Venus de Milo. She was about as tall as Poppy (5 foot 3 inches) and measured 45 inches around the hips (we revisited her with a measuring tape). We decided that she must have been very fat!"

They also became intrigued by the concept of "fiancées" in Italy—an affair between a married man and woman who had split from their respective spouses and begun a relationship while negotiating the difficult path of getting an annulment from the Catholic Church: "This arrangement was considered quite respectful," Sheila commented with some triumph.

Sheila's mother, Ag, was waiting when they returned to London. She had come to see her grandchildren and spend the summer. There was also a cable from Sydney with news that Chissie was ill and had to have what was regarded as a "slight" operation: "He cabled several times that we were not to worry—it was nothing serious."

15

LINDBERGH AND THE DERBY BALL

In May 1856 a young surgeon at the University College London was dismissed for unbecoming language and conduct—apparently he had used the word "bloody" and slapped a patient on the buttocks. The controversial sacking of Dr Sherard Freeman Statham would prove a blessing for the city's poor, particularly around Kings Cross, where, in the days before the National Health Service, medical facilities were all but non-existent for those who couldn't afford to pay.

Barely a month later Stratham opened, at his own expense, a sixteen-bed hospital where he offered treatment for two hours per day to the poor of north London. Within a year it had been expanded to fifty beds, boosted by funds from railway companies, whose lower-paid workers were among the thousands now receiving treatment. His hospital had also attracted the help of twenty physicians, surgeons and dentists, who embraced

Statham's altruism.

The young doctor died a year later, struck down by tuberculosis, but his vision, which now became known as the Great Northern Hospital, continued to grow over the next seventy years, shifting and adding buildings and services, and eventually responding to the heavy demand by pioneering outpatient facilities.

In 1921 it changed its name to the Royal Northern Hospital, but, despite its success and the plaudits it received, it was constantly struggling for funds to keep its doors open, mainly because of the huge growth in patients and costs after the Great War, when those who had borne the brunt of the conflict—the poor—returned to their homes to resume their lives and tend their wounds.

By 1926 the hospital was being forced to close beds even as it nurtured expansion plans to cater for a continuing population growth. By now it had 400 beds and catered for almost 5000 patients a year and another 200,000 outpatients, in a surrounding population of 1 million citizens who had little or no money for health care. Dr Statham's retort to his stuffy superiors had become the biggest general hospital within 100 square kilometres.

Because the hospital itself had no cash reserves and serious debts, its board, which included senior MPs, peers and even royals, wanted to tackle the financial problems head-on and to reduce or eliminate its debt burden. It decided to appeal to the city's wealthy directly, through a series of letters addressed to prominent individuals, hoping to strike a chord. The appeal largely fell on deaf ears but there was a second plan brewing. Fundraising was already a staple for many institutions and a favourite pursuit of the otherwise idle rich—wealthy women in particular. The Royal Northern Hospital's Ladies Association had previously run numerous events each year, but its contribution to date could only be counted in the hundreds of pounds, which was a drop in the bucket.

The hospital's treasurer, Sir Philip Sassoon, MP and Under-Secretary for Air, thought he could do better than that. The Sassoon family was among the wealthiest in London. Sir Philip's father, Edward, was Indian-born and a member of the Iraqi Sassoon family (he famously carried documents designed to prove he was a lineal descendant of Shephatiah, the fifth son of King David) and his French mother, Lady Aline, was a daughter of the Rothschild banking dynasty.

Sir Philip was private secretary to Field Marshall Sir Douglas Haig during the Great War and played the same role to the British Prime Minister David Lloyd George in the years before taking a senior cabinet role himself, helping to manage the fledgling Royal Air Force. He was probably best described as a "Bridesheadian" figure, in the mould of Evelyn Waugh's great literary creation, but as politically and financially hardheaded as he was a figure of social hedonism. "We were fond of him but he was strangely impersonal," Sheila observed.

In April 1927 Sir Philip launched his new fundraising campaign, appointing a committee to organise a new and spectacular charity ball to coincide with the biggest day on the English racing calendar, the running of the Derby. It would be bigger than anything seen in the city. The committee, in a flush of enthusiasm, booked the Albert Hall but a month later was struggling to sell the 2000 tickets it needed to fill the arena, and feared a financial disaster looming. The problem was that the ball could not be held on the night of the Derby because Lord and Lady Derby traditionally entertained society with a ball of their own.

In desperation, Sir Philip organised an "At Home" at his city residence in Park Lane to discuss alternatives. The evening was hosted by Sheila Loughborough, who had been encouraged to join the hospital's Ladies Association and was then persuaded to take responsibility for the new venture. She had been handed a disaster: "Practically no tickets had been sold. Would I take it on? I reluctantly agreed."

The gathering and its proposal was reported in the *Daily Express* on May 12: "A ball in the aid of the funds of the Royal Northern Hospital, of which the Prince of Wales is president, is to be held at the Albert Hall on Derby Eve, May 31. The ball is being supported by Lady Loughborough and promises to be one of the most brilliant functions of the season."

Not only would guests get "an unusually good all-star cabaret", but there would also be a fancy dress competition, "an excellent supper" and door prizes, including a car—a two-tone Austin 7 Swallow that, in popularity, was the English equivalent of the Model T Ford in the United States.

The plan was audacious, given that there were only a few weeks in which to organise the event; they were gambling heavily on the organising skills of Sheila and her ability to harness her society influence and burgeoning address book. The media was to become a key component of her strategy: Sheila would provide a continuous drip-feed of details about the function, aimed at whetting the appetites of the social climbers who wanted to be seen at the height of the Season.

First up came an interview with the man who would organise the cabaret, Joe Coyne, an American-born vaudeville star who had crossed the Atlantic to London with the rise of musical comedy in the 1920s and was one of the most popular leading men on the West End stage. The entertainment he outlined for the Derby Eve Ball was a series of acts that read like a musical circus. Included were: a woman dancing the Charleston on her head; an acrobatic dancing duo called Nervo and Knox, whose acts included slow-motion wrestling; a strong man, plus numerous others.

But Coyne hinted at something more—a unique mystery performance, "something you've never seen at the cabaret", which would begin after the arrival at midnight of the Prince of Wales, whose presence alone was expected to spark a ticket rush. Sheila's friendship with the prince had paved the way for the hurried rearrangement of his schedule.

Four days before the event, Joe Coyne's mystery was revealed: there was to be an exhibition boxing match between two Londoners, Teddy Baldock and Johnny Curley: "This exceptional attraction will add still further to the interest of this remarkable ball which bids fair to prove the financial and social success of the season. Nearly all the boxes have broadly been sold. A few tickets can still be obtained."

Baldock, a bantamweight aged just nineteen, had set London alight a few weeks earlier when he fought fifteen rounds against US veteran Archie Bell before a sell-out crowd at the Albert Hall and became the youngest-ever British world boxing champion. Curley, a former English lightweight champion, had been one of his sparring partners, but Baldock was the main billing because, even though his army of supporters from his East End home would crowd into a fleet of omnibuses to follow him to bouts, he had also been embraced by the elite from the West End.

The Prince of Wales had even attended one of his bouts and asked to meet him afterwards, although the young man was so shy he had to be dragged from his dressing room to shake hands with the prince. And women loved him, as the *Daily Express* noted: "Women, of whom there were more present last night than have ever been seen in an Albert Hall boxing crowd, adore him. He has large, soulful eyes and a tip-tilted nose and he is as wiry and muscled as a lusty colt."

But the evening's pièce de résistance was still to be revealed. And it was a piece of luck and Sheila's determination that clinched it. Two days before the ball, the organisers announced a surprise guest—American airman Captain Charles Lindbergh, who a week earlier had completed his historic non-stop trans-Atlantic flight from New York to Paris in his plane, the *Spirit of St Louis*. It was by chance that Lindbergh had decided to fly on to London and was due to arrive the day before the ball, but Sheila made the most of this opportunity, pestering Lord Beaverbrook who offered Lindbergh a fee to write his story for the papers and attend the ball. The coup led to a rush on tickets, as was reported by the *Daily Mirror*:

> The interesting announcement that Charles Lindbergh, the young hero of the recent transatlantic flight, will attend the ball which is being organised by Lady Loughborough at the Royal Albert Hall next Tuesday evening has immediately led to enormous demand for tickets. Nearly £5000 has already been taken and it now seems certain that all previous Albert Hall records will be surpassed. Indeed I have grave doubts whether the number of tickets will be sufficient to satisfy the demand.

He was right, although Sheila might have been forgiven for being disengaged. Two days earlier, her 69-year-old father, Harry, had been rushed to hospital back in Sydney for an operation. He had been unwell for some months but the speed of the decision to hospitalise him was distressing, exacerbated by the fact that her mother, Margaret, was with her in London for the Season. What might have been a moment of personal triumph was now tinged with worry.

Lindbergh's spectacular entrance into London on the evening of Monday, May 30, created pandemonium. Under the escort of six biplanes across the Channel, he flew up the Thames and across East London and the city before banking over Buckingham Palace and heading to Croydon, where he made his approach to land. But he was forced to abort because of the sheer size of the crowd, who had ignored the authorities and broken down picket fences in the stampede to get close to their hero. At the same time a grandstand collapsed and two people were injured in a plane crash on the edge of the airfield.

Lindbergh was forced to circle the airfield until police cleared a landing path through the estimated 150,000 people; after landing, he then had to wait for ten minutes in his plane while authorities beat a path through the well-wishers, who wanted to carry him around the airfield on their shoulders in celebration.

A photograph taken from one of his escorting planes shows the white crucifix shape of his aircraft against a swarming black sea of people, like ants invading a picnic. "Heaven help my machine," Lindbergh called out, before he was taken to the control tower where he made a speech describing the scene as astonishing. This was all manna from the heavens, in terms of publicity for Sheila's Derby Eve Ball.

Anticipation had built to fever pitch by the night of the ball and Sheila, who was feeling more relaxed with the news that her father appeared to be recovering from the operation, now faced a dilemma. Queues of people in their finery had formed at the Albert Hall, with people who hadn't booked tickets desperate to get inside and catch a glimpse of the famous guests and entertainment. The venue had never held such a crowd, but there was a problem—it was illegal to sell tickets inside the hall. In an inspired stroke, Sheila set up a kiosk in Bayswater Road, outside the gate, where she signed guests in personally while dressed in her gown—"much in the same spirit as dominates famous actresses who autograph their photographs for large sums", as one account later commented.

It was difficult to judge the size of the crowd, but it was easily the biggest event ever catered for inside London's "village hall" and the most successful charity ball ever held. Inside, a giant model of a racehorse and jockey had been suspended over the dance floor. There was also a gigantic replica of the famous 1893 painting of the Epsom Derby by William Powell Frith, which hung from the Grand Tier, the highest ring of private boxes in the auditorium. But it was Lindbergh and the Prince of Wales the crowd had come to see.

The "Mariegold in Society" column in *The Sketch* magazine a few days later summed it up:

The Derby Eve Ball was one of the most successful festivities ever held. Cheer succeeded cheer at the Albert Hall when the two most popular young men in England arrived at different times—the Prince of Wales and Captain Lindbergh; while Teddy Baldock enjoyed an ovation too, when he appeared. But before the arrival of the Prince, the airman or the boxer, there was plenty of activity and much to see, the rose-adorned Royal Box being the centre of interest. Prince Arthur of Connaught was with Princess Arthur, the latter in a frock of pink georgette and diamante; and Prince and Princess Paul of Serbia were with them. Lady Loughborough, who worked so hard to make the ball a success, flitted from box to box, a charming figure in a deep orange dress. Lady London-derry, who was wearing almost exactly the same shade, was in the above group, waving a huge orange and black fan; and so was Lady Cunard wearing black and silver. When Captain Lindbergh appeared in Sir Philip Sassoon's box next door, it was Prince

Loughie and Sheila prepare to board the ship *Nestor* in 1923 that would take them back to London after two years in Australia. Sheila's father Chissie is in the background.

The fun-loving Loughie, who carried the title Lord Loughborough as the eldest son of the Earl of Rosslyn, one of Scotland's most famous families, photographed in 1926 as he faced divorce from Sheila and financial ruin from his gambling

Sheila's house in Talbot Square was the scene of many dinner parties through the 1920s, often with a nightclub singer. This one, circa 1925, was held for the American jazz queen Sophie Tucker (centre rear). Sheila is standing to the left of Sophie. Freda Dudley Ward is in the middle of the table on the right.

The many faces of Sheila—glamorous, dishevelled or avant-garde—as seen here (third from left) dressed for a party in Florida in 1926 with friend Poppy Baring (far left). Sheila must have liked the look because she kept the photograph in her personal album.

Sheila in 1926 soon after returning from America where the film star Rudolph Valentino gave her his gold bracelet. Her fashion sense made her a society celebrity.

Buffles and Sheila relaxing with their two dogs in 1927. She would refuse his offer of marriage four times before finally agreeing.

Vincent Astor and Sheila pose casually on a windy Isle of Wight in 1927, surrounded by children, including Sheila's sons Tony and Peter. It was the only photograph of the multi-millionaire in her album despite their close friendship.

Sheila on the occasion of being presented for a second time to the King and Queen in 1928. She wore the Dudley crown but felt foolish.

A beaming Buffles and Sheila on their wedding day in 1928. The marriage celebrations were front-page news and brought traffic along the Strand in central London to a halt.

Sheila poses with sons Peter and Tony in the garden at the Milbanke family home, Mullaboden, in Ireland in 1930.

Sheila with her racehorse, Dr Strabismus, which she bought for £50 in 1931. It won its first race at odds of 50 to 1.

Sheila and Buffles at Ascot. They sat in Lord Derby's box every year, where she earned the nickname "Mascot" because she was next to the aristocrat on the day in 1932 when his horse, Hyperion, won the classic.

A caricature of Sheila and Poppy Thursby entering a nightclub in 1932, around the time they took over the management of one of London's most famous clubs, Ciro's, for a £100 bet, and turned a struggling venue into a success.

Sheila in the early 1930s at her most glamorous. She was aware of her beauty and effect on men but was often disdainful of the trappings.

Arthur who brought the occupants of the royal box to their feet to greet the airman, who gave a delightful speech to the crowd before sitting down between Lord Lonsdale and Lady Cholmondeley. The Prince of Wales arrived very late, just as Teddy Baldock and Johnny Curley were to start their exhibition match, and this was held up while HRH greeted his friends. The biggest cheer rose when the Prince put out his hand to Lindbergh and held it as the latter climbed into the royal box from Sir Philip's, so that he could be photographed by the Prince's side.

Sheila watched from a few feet away: "The Prince of Wales and Lindbergh stood together in the front of my box, shaking hands and talking. The crowd went crazy. They sang 'God Bless the Prince of Wales' and 'Old Glory'. It was very exciting!"

But as Sheila basked in the glow of her success, news filtered through by cable from Sydney that her father had taken a turn for the worse, and had died. *The Sydney Morning Herald* reported, succinctly, on June 11 that after the operation "he gradually became weaker, and for the last few days his death was expected".

Neither Sheila nor her mother could attend the funeral, which was held just two days later at Rookwood Cemetery. The *Herald*'s report listed by name more than a hundred mourners who had turned out to show their respect for a man who had helped build Australia's great bloodstock tradition and forge an international reputation. It was a reminder to Sheila of just how far she was from home and family, particularly at a time when she was rebuilding her own life as a single mother. Life wasn't just about ball gowns.

16

AN INCOMPARABLE SHEILA

As London continued its exuberant recovery from the ravages of war, a young photographer emerged who would capture many of the most celebrated images of a unique period in history. Cecil Beaton, son of a successful timber merchant, began his celebrated career by encouraging his sisters and mother to pose, using an early model folding Kodak camera to capture their image, usually at their family home in Hampstead in north London.

Beaton was a restless and precocious talent who had attended Harrow and studied art, history and architecture for a time at Cambridge but, disenchanted, left in 1925 without a degree. He lasted a week in his father's timber yard before deciding to pursue his art, based on an eye for beauty and photography and a love of the famous and fashionable. By 1927 he was being used regularly by *Vogue* magazine. In that same year he held his first exhibition at a studio in New Bond Street, offering a mixture of painting and photography. But it was the latter that really grabbed the attention of the public—a collection of society figures in strange poses and costumes, described by the *Daily Express* as "the most entertaining photographs in London for years".

The images captured the glamour and mystery of the social elite with a mixture of angles and settings. There were the Jungman sisters, Zita and Teresa, joined at the head like conjoined twins; Edith Sitwell posed as a Gothic tomb sculpture; Lady Cunard was in polka dots, Paula Gellibrand shining in foil and the actress Tallulah Bankhead in balloons.

And among them was a strange portrait of Sheila Loughborough. Far from the usual soft glamour of society magazine shoots, Beaton had used a "secret" technique to capture an image of her head inside a bell-shaped jar, as if in a trophy cabinet on a side table. Because of its ingenuity, this photograph would end up in the National Portrait Gallery. Beaton would remain a friend of Sheila throughout her life.

Beaton was one of the young elite dubbed the "Bright Young Things" by the media—the artistic, the bohemian and the spoiled who cut a swathe through London in the late 1920s. They were involved in a hedonistic search for pleasure and the exploits were closely documented by the press to provide vicarious pleasure for their readers. While some criticised their cavorting as the self-indulgence of the idle rich, others viewed them as the cutting edge of social change.

This was the generation that was too young to have fought in the Great War, but was forced to endure the guilt of their good fortune. Their answer was to live without consequence. They rebelled against the resolute conservatism of their parents, and Beaton's motto seemed to provide their mantra: "Be daring, be different, be impractical, be anything that will assert integrity of purpose and imaginative vision against the play-it-safers, the creatures of the commonplace, the slaves of the ordinary."

Sheila flittered at the edges of the Bright Young Things. She was a mother of two, now aged in her early thirties and an accepted member of the establishment set, with membership at places like the Embassy Club; but there were crossovers socially and she had younger friends like Beaton and Poppy Baring, the Mitford sisters Diana and Nancy, the writer Evelyn Waugh and the Sitwell siblings. Among their number was also Hamish St Clair-Erskine, who would become romantically involved with Nancy Mitford for a period.

The "stunts" of the Bright Young Things were frequent, entertaining, disruptive, always theatrical, but childish at times. For example, one day they formed a conga line through Selfridges, up and down the lifts, through the departments and even over the counters. They staged chases through the streets of London, and held wild and exotic parties. Theirs was a life of theatre and fancy dress, fuelled by alcohol and drugs, and sexual experimentation; they were followed by an eager press, keen to report their latest exploits with feigned horror, such as the night they organised a table of divorced women at a prominent nightclub, having learned that the former husbands—all peers—were holding a celebration, entertained by a dancer, at the same establishment on the same night.

And wherever the Bright Young Things went and whatever they explored, society inevitably seemed to follow them, even if at a discreet distance. In the summer of 1928, for example, the BYTs held what would become an infamous event they called the "Bath and Bottle" party at a swimming pool in the centre of London. Tom Driberg, then a young journalist with the *Daily Express*, was an invited guest and immediately realised the potential newsworthiness of the gathering, rushing out to file a story from a nearby telephone box to describe the scene:

Bathing costumes of the most dazzling kinds and colours were worn by the guests. Dancing took place to the strains of a Negro orchestra, and the hardy leaped later into the bath, of which the water had been slightly warmed. Great rubber horses and flowers floated about in the water, which was illuminated by coloured spotlights. Many of those present brought two or three bathing costumes, which they changed into in the course of the night's festivities. A special cocktail, christened the Bathwater Cocktail, was invented for the occasion.

Swimming dinner parties suddenly became the rage across London, as other social "sets" followed the fun. One of the first was held at Maidenhead in Berkshire on July 20. Driberg went along and wrote another account:

Lady Loughborough was one of the first to change her evening dress for an extremely becoming black and white bathing dress and to plunge into the water, and her example was rapidly followed by the honorary Imogen Grenfell whose aquatic prowess was greatly admired by everybody present. Lady Patricia Ward was another who found the attraction of the river irresistible and so did her brother, Lord Ednam, Mrs Euan Wallace and Lord Blandford. It is curious how few good swimmers there are among society women and girls.

"Gossip journalism" in British newspapers can be traced back to the late 17th century, when a sexual tryst between a lady, her maid and a mastiff was reported, although not by name. In the 18th century such weighty matters as the details of public hangings and "soup swilling" by Scottish lairds found their way into the pages of the London newspapers; authors of the calibre of Daniel Defoe got their start by writing such material as the tone changed from private to political scandal and the battle between the Whigs and the Tories hotted up. In the 19th century, Charles Dickens hired Lady Blessington to supply information for his newspaper, the *Daily News*.

The art of the "paragraph writer" had developed in the early 20th century as society hostesses themselves either fed journalistic contacts or even paid other women with contacts to provide titbits to columnists, often just a few simple sentences about their travels—"Lord and Lady Blah Blah are leaving tomorrow for the continent"—or even their health and recovery. There were numerous examples of the travels and travails of Sheila, as Lady Loughborough, being reported by *The Times* "Court Circular" in the pre- and post-war period—seemingly irrelevant snippets, which gave the subject an air of importance and attention, rather than of scandal and derision.

In the mid-1920s, the style and subject matter changed again as newspapers began employing struggling aristocrats to write about the world they inhabited. For the first time, the gossip journalist worked from inside the story. Driberg was one of the most prominent columnists of his age; a young Oxford graduate, he had begun his career as a £3-per-week journalist with the *Daily Express* where, after the Bath and Bottle scoop, he was assigned to help a senior colleague, Colonel Percy Sewell, to write the much-read "About Town" gossip column under the esoteric pseudonym of "The Dragoman", which was defined by the dictionary as an interpreter or guide in Eastern countries.

The colonel spent most of his afternoons on the golf course and wrote about the older set—"elderly aristocratic ladies and aged clubmen"—while Driberg concentrated on his Oxford contemporaries and their friends, such as the author Evelyn Waugh, whom he had met at university. His copy was usually laced with quirky observations about "green beer" and other extravagances of the ruling class, whom he often satirised because of his political views (he was a member of the Communist Party).

But Driberg was also a participant, often attending the parties he reported upon and behaving as badly as the guests he named. The art of the newspaper gossip column was changing just as society was evolving; it was becoming more daring and carefree, and eager to test the boundaries of social acceptability. Others newspapers followed the *Daily Express*, realising the value of inside information. There was Lady Eleanor Smith writing "Window in Mayfair" in the *Weekly Dispatch* and Lord Castlerosse's "Londoner's Log" in the *Sunday Express*; Lord Balfour was "Mr Gossip" in the *Daily Sketch* and Lord Donegall penned for the *Sunday News*. The author Nancy Mitford was said to provide information about her friends, as did Randolph Churchill, son of Sir Winston.

Waugh, a friend of both Mitford and Churchill, would parody this world in his novels. He despised the Bright Young Things for their privileged birthright and yet revelled in their artistic bravery. Although he insisted that the characters in his books were entirely fictional, it was clear to others that they were at least loosely based on the men and women with whom he partied and those who watched. The gossip writers in the 1930 novel *Vile Bodies* were based on Castlerosse, Donegall, Balfour and Driberg.

Sheila Loughborough seemed to sail through this period effortlessly, straddling two worlds. She was part of established, serious society and yet she was young enough and exotic enough to be considered part of the new style:

July 28, 1927
Daily Mirror
Lady Betty Butler differs from most modern girls in that she makes no attempt to appear self-assured or to entertain the guests at a dinner party by hyena-like yells and imbecile remarks. The beautiful Lady Loughborough is another . . . She is going to spend the summer in the Isle of Wight where she has taken a house with Lady Morvyth Benson.

October 12, 1927

Daily Express

I went on later to the inauguration of a new restaurant, once famous as a nightclub and found the crowd so great it was almost impossible to move. I saw the keen yachtsman Sir Duncan Lewis, who spends most of his time on the sea; the honorary Bruce Ogilvy, one of the Prince of Wales equerries, and Sir John Milbanke, the boxing baronet. Beautiful women were there in large numbers and among them I noticed Lady Ashley, Miss Poppy Baring, Miss Tallulah Bankhead, Lady Gibbons and Lady Loughborough, who has just returned from Paris and is one of the keenest supporters of the London ice club.

Sheila had indeed been in Paris, where she was already making a name for herself in the restaurants and clubs along the Champs-Élysées. Her name and her companions there were picked up not only by the British media but by the scribes of major US newspapers, particularly on the night she dined with controversial American socialite Alice de Janzé. Alice had gained international notoriety after shooting her lover, Sir John Milbanke's old boxing compatriot Raymond de Trafford, and then shooting herself on a platform at Gare du Nord railway station. Both of them survived; indeed, they would later marry (and divorce) each other in a tale immortalised in the film *White Mischief*, based on James Fox's book.

Chicago Tribune

PARIS Oct 20: For the first time since she shot her purported admirer, Raymond de Trafford, member of an aristocratic English family, and then turned the weapon on herself, the Countess de Janzé, the former Alice Silverthorne of Chicago, appeared tonight amid the bright lights of Paris. Looking well, the countess slipped back into her old place in the smart international crowd in Paris. She went to Ciro's and to the opening of the Blue Room, the French capital's newest nightclub. She was a member of the gay party, which Michael Framer gave for Grace Moore, Lady Loughborough and a number of others. It was the most brilliant opening in Paris in years.

Back in England, Sheila's activities were followed it seemed almost weekly. She appeared in society ballets and *tableaux vivants*, in which costumed participants created living static pictures; she helped organise charity functions and even competed in sporting events, like the ice hockey match organised by one of the leading members of the Bright Young Things, Lady Ponsonby, later the Duchess of Westminster. She was also among a number of society beauties, including her friend Lady Diana Cooper and the actress Lillian Gish, who were immortalised in plaster representations exhibited by the renowned Russian-American sculptor Gleb Derujinsky.

At times, the columnists didn't even require an event to discuss socialites; on one occasion simply their names were enough to justify breathless reportage, such as the *Daily Express* of August 23, 1928: "Beautiful women often have beautiful names. Look at Lady Diana Cooper—the type of all Dianas. Look at Sylvia, a bewitching incarnate of Lady Ashley. Look at Lady Loughborough, an incomparable Sheila. And I can't think of too many lovely Rosemarys, Annes or Dawns."

The notion of beauty had changed in the late 1920s; *Vogue* declared it an era of the *jolie-laide*—translated literally as "pretty-ugly". Beauty was now more than simply the physical; it was spiritual, which the magazine said perfectly described Sheila Loughborough, while Diana Cooper was "elusive ethereality", Zita Jungman "divinely fair" and Edith Sitwell a "Gothic Madonna".

Cecil Beaton expanded on this in his 1930 *Book of Beauty*:

> In the old days it was enough that a beautiful woman should be gracious and charming; the beauties were seen rather than heard. A Grecian goddess, however dumb, justified herself; but today it is more essential for a woman to be bright and attractive, and good looks do not signify unless backed up by intelligence. In this beauty-glutted age personality is more important, perhaps, than looks. The old belle is not a contemporary figure, for she is unamusing and has but a little and formal sense of humour.

Sheila was not afraid to make use of her royal connections. Victor Perosino was a struggling nightclub owner who ran a small club, appropriately called Chez Victor, in a back street of Mayfair. The club traded well into the morning hours, offering food for theatregoers and revellers who wanted to kick on after the cabaret venues had shut; it specialised in what was known as the "Bacon and Eggs Hour". Sheila was an occasional patron and had taken a liking to Victor, because he was discreet but also because he was a former waiter trying to make good.

When she asked him one night how business was doing, he

shook his head and replied: "Badly, your ladyship. Expenses are big and money is slow."

Sheila thought for a moment, then declared: "I promise you that this shall be the most successful place in London within a month."

The next night the Prince of Wales booked a table at the club. Within a year, guided by Sheila's suggestion that Victor poach from the Kit-Kat Club an American blues singer named Aileen Stanley, whom the prince liked, Chez Victor had been transformed into the favoured late-night club of London's younger blue-bloods, who clamoured for membership.

But in doing so, it had attracted the attention of the police. In late February 1928, amid a crackdown by Scotland Yard on the illegal sale of alcohol at late-night venues, Chez Victor was raided. Police created a fake traffic accident in Grafton Street outside the club, complete with a screaming woman; the doorman felt compelled to leave his post and investigate. This allowed officers, who had been waiting around the corner, to file into the club unannounced, where they examined glasses and took names and addresses of the high society clientele. The timing had been carefully arranged to ensure that the Prince of Wales would not be there and cause embarrassment to the royal family.

Lady Loughborough watched impassively from the table she often shared with the absent prince and Victor remained unperturbed, as he told a reporter the next day: "It was all done so calmly that no-one seemed disturbed and the dancing went on as usual. I don't think anyone was upset. When the police left they wished me good night in a friendly way and, so far, not a word has been heard from them officially."

Vincent Astor had continued his pursuit of Sheila, arriving in London in the early summer of 1927 to oversee construction in Germany of the world's largest private yacht, the *Nourmahal* which measured 80 metres long with eleven staterooms, a library, a dining room for 18 and a 42-man crew.

He joined Sheila who was staying on the Isle of Wight with a group of friends that included Serge Obolensky, his wife Alice and their baby son, Ivan. Buffles Milbanke, whom Sheila was keeping at arm's length romantically, was not among them perhaps because she knew the handsome American would be arriving:

"I gave Vincent a golden sovereign to put under her mast for luck," she wrote later. "I continued to sing 'Wedding bells are all bunk'. We had many arguments and Vincent returned to America rather cross with me."

It seemed that the relationship with Astor was problematic, attracted as they were to one another and yet, not unlike Sheila and Buffles, faced with a barrier that prevented a fully-fledged love. They would remain lifelong friends. She would keep photographs of them in her albums, a handful of grainy prints taken as they relaxed in their dressing gowns among a group of children, including Tony and Peter, on the windswept hills above the sea.

Vincent's fabulous riches obviously did not interest her. She was simply not ready to commit again so soon after divorcing

Loughie. Besides, he was a married man although it was a complicated relationship.

Vincent had married childhood friend Helen Huntington in 1913 but it became clear soon afterwards that they shared few common interests and they quickly drifted apart. Helen also preferred the company of her female friends, once having been described by the novelist Glenway Westcott as "a grand old lesbian". Rather than divorce, Vincent and Helen simply led separate lives until 1940 when he finally ended the marriage.

Despite her resistance to his charms, Vincent wanted to see Sheila again when he returned to London in early 1928 to collect his yacht. Before sailing it back to the US, he took the *Nourmahal* for a trial run to the Channel Islands. Other than the crew, there were only six people aboard, including Sheila and Poppy—and no Buffles. But nothing had changed with Vincent, even arguing over nationhood: "We quarrelled so often over England versus America. I told him he was anti-British. There were too many arguments. My mother always said: 'The largest yacht in the world is too small if you are in it with someone you don't really love'!"

Spurned yet again, Vincent sailed away alone across the Atlantic, a package of gramophone records chosen by Sheila his only reminder of the woman he wanted but money could not buy. When at sea he opened the parcel to find two dozen copies of "Rule Britannia", each played by a different band or orchestra. He was livid but couldn't help laughing. It was Sheila's revenge in an ongoing argument between them about the United States and Britain.

In the background was Buffles, the athletic action man who could see he had serious competition and had to make his move. He proposed marriage not long after Astor left on the *Nourmahal*, but Sheila said "no" because "I had several proposals of marriage in the next few months, but I wanted to stay free". Buffles tried again during the summer and Sheila turned him down again although she was beginning to question her lifestyle, particularly as both boys were now at boarding school, which gave her even more time. Being "free" was beginning to wear thin for a woman who still hankered for "true love".

It was when Buffles travelled to the United States for business in the autumn of 1928 that Sheila began to realise that she wanted more from life. In the summer she went to stay in the country, in Oxfordshire, where her social calendar overflowed and the events blurred and became unremarkable: "I don't remember much about 1928," she would write. "We continued to dance. Someone said: 'Life seems to be composed of picnics, parties and balls.' There were many weekend parties—I supposed it was fun?"

In September she got a cable from Buffles, who was still in America: "I am telling people we are engaged. It makes life so much easier." Sheila was shocked but admitted to her friends Freda, Poppy and Paula Gellibrand that the thought of him surrounded by American girls bothered her: "I was obviously in love with Buffles," she wrote later. "I cabled Buffles: 'Tell them anything you like.'"

When he returned a few weeks later Buffles asked her again but she stubbornly refused, the fourth time she had done so.

He'd had enough of these rejections: "If you don't marry me then I'll return to America and you will never see me again."

The dramatic declaration stopped her for a moment and forced her to rethink. He was being serious. Was she doing the right thing or would she regret it if he walked away? "What should I do? In the end I told him if Tony and Peter approved then I would marry him."

Sir John Milbanke had finally worn her down at a time when her sons needed the stability of a family. But before accepting, she needed their approval: "Do you mind if Mummy gets married again?" she asked after driving down to their school one weekend. The brothers—aged 10 and 11—looked at one another, as if expecting the question, and left the room to talk it over while their mother waited nervously.

"Does Daddy mind?" Tony asked when they returned a few minutes later.

Sheila shook her head: "No darlings. Daddy doesn't mind."

"Oh well, as it is old Buff then we don't mind either."

Sheila invited Loughie to lunch with her and Buffles the next day to tell him. He accepted the decision graciously: "He said to Buffles, 'I hope to God you can make her happy, old chap. I never could. Bless you both.' It was touching and typical of Loughie."

The engagement of Sir John Milbanke and Lady Sheila Loughborough was announced by the *Daily Express* as a front-page news story on November 3, 1928, trumpeted as a society scoop. Alongside it was a portrait of Sheila, described with equal exuberance: "Lady Loughborough is one of the prettiest and most popular of the younger women in society. She is a great friend of the Prince of Wales, and her petite figure, always exquisitely dressed, and her dark shingled head are to be seen at all fashionable parties of the season."

They were married eleven days later in what seemed to be a rushed affair, given her reticence and that Sir John had only just arrived back in London three days before. Sheila made no mention of the timing in her memoir and her account was perfunctory compared to the happy memories of the initial days of her marriage to Loughie. The initial attraction to Buffles had been instant and physical but now, five years later, it seemed to have waned, and the relationship was now about comfort and the fear of regret.

Sheila's confusion showed in her response to Loughie's request to be allowed to attend the wedding. Not surprisingly, she refused it as being inappropriate but then, inexplicably, carried a bouquet of white lilies sent by her former husband. Neither would she let her children attend: "On looking back, I can't really think why," she wrote.

News of the union was greeted by the media with odes to the bride, such as this from "The Dragoman", in his "About Town" column:

The beauty of Lady Loughborough has been sung so often in these columns that it is difficult to say anything new about so lovely a lady. Her slim figure, soft, clear voice and perfectly shingled head are frequently in evidence in the newest and smartest dance clubs and restaurants, where her infallible flair for dress, coupled with her essentially feminine charms make her always a "sight for sair een".

Sheila

They were married quietly at the registry office on November 14 and then attended a service in front of friends and family in the 400-year-old Queen's Chapel of the Savoy, which attracted hundreds of onlookers and caused a traffic snarl in the Strand. The *Daily Mirror* the next morning carried a front-page photograph of the couple at the altar while *The Sketch* devoted most of its column "Mariegold in Society" to it and declared itself delighted by the informality of the wedding invitations and the turnout of the rich and famous:

Lady Loughborough and John Milbanke's wedding "made history" from the social point of view, not only on account of the extremely informal invitations they sent out to summon their friends to the ceremony—just cards signed "Buffles" and "Sheila" and asking "Will you come to our wedding"—but also because of the very large number of well-known people who managed to tuck themselves into the limited space at the tiny Savoy Chapel, and of the many beautiful and smart young women who attended the ceremony. The Boxing Baronet was resplendent in a cutaway coat, light waistcoat, and large spotted tie of the old-fashioned Ascot type. Lady Loughborough—now Lady Milbanke—wore a sleeveless coat over her beige lace dress, and did not carry a formal bridal bouquet . . . very simple and unassuming.

Presumably all women are subscribing to the oft repeated classic belief that black is universally becoming. Lady Denman wore a black velvet suit spotted over with white dots, Lady Brecknock, who was accompanied by her husband, had a narrow roll of Astrakhan to her black suit; while Mrs Dudley Ward's dark coat was relieved by a beige suit. Lady Diana Cooper, in brown and cream flecked tweed suit, came as a relief from the general blackness, and other notes of colour were supplied by Lady Victor Padgett's beige dress and Lady Louis Mountbatten's great cluster of greeny-brown orchids.

Any amount of smart men came to the wedding. The Duke of Sutherland looking very thoughtful, strolled into the chapel wearing a blue lounge suit, and Sir Philip Sassoon was a late arrival; while the energetic dashers included Mr Channon and Mr Belleville. The distinction of being the last to arrive—next to the bride herself, of course, who was brought and given away by Captain Benson—fell to Miss Poppy Baring, Lady Loughborough's greatest friend, and a bride of the near future herself. One of the most striking figures at the church was Maharanee [sic] of Cooch Behar, whose exquisite blue and gold sari peeked out from beneath her sable coat.

Even the columns that were more slanted toward men were impressed. "A Man about Town" in the *Mail*, whose writer went under the pseudonym of "Jack Londoner", mentioned that the bride and groom had invited the media inside the church. He also liked the invitation: "I thought this was quite a refreshing change from all the long rigmarole about the bride's parents requesting the pleasure etc etc," he wrote, adding: "It is an idea which will probably be widely copied."

Even the new Lady Sheila Milbanke's wedding invitations were setting a trend.

17

A TEMPORARY UNSOUND MIND

Life as the new Lady Milbanke continued without incident into 1929, even with the change of name and title to a lesser one. After returning from a honeymoon in Paris and the south of France she was reintroduced to the court in a ceremony arranged by Eileen Sutherland and wearing the tiara of Lady Dudley: "It was made of pearls and diamonds and was so heavy it gave me a headache. The fashions at the time were ugly—my belt was around my hips, skirt to the knees, a long train hung from the shoulders and three white feathers wobbled on my head. I felt foolish and no doubt looked it."

There were friends aplenty. Sheila was now firmly at the centre of London society particularly after the success of two Derby Balls, which was already regarded as the city's premier charity fundraising ball. On May 25, as she finalised details for the third ball, Sheila joined a host of society women including

Edwina Mountbatten, Venetia Montagu, Diana Cooper and Jeanie Norton to dine with the press baron Max Beaverbrook for his fiftieth birthday.

The dinner was held in his mansion near Hyde Park. Stornoway House had fourteen bedrooms, six reception rooms and even a ballroom, a mark of the business success of this Canadian-born son of a Presbyterian minister. Lord Beaverbrook had hinted at surprises for the women, all dressed in their jewelled finery, and they sat down to find cheques for £100 each under their plates (the equivalent of £5000), as Sheila recounted two decades later: "Max had thought it over carefully and decided to give us each £100 instead of a box or something from Cartier, as he knew we would change anything he gave us the next day.

"I was about thirty and remember thinking, 'how ghastly for poor Max to be so old . . . fifty'. He didn't look it. Times have changed many things. One seldom hears the witty, carefree fascinating conversation, combined with the fun and gaiety we knew in those days. This party was almost the end of the 1920s."

In August Sheila and Buffles rented a house at Runnymede, on the banks of the Thames at Windsor near the fields in which the Magna Carta was said to have been sealed 800 years before. There they intended spending the month entertaining a parade of friends, among them the young banking heir Loel Guinness, who crash-landed his private plane in a field by the house on the day he arrived and walked away unscathed.

It was the only excitement in what was supposed to be a month of long walks, golf and tennis and lazy dinners as daylight stretched well into the night, but on the morning of August 4, as she began preparations for another big lunch party, Buffles took Sheila aside with some tragic news—Loughie was dead.

The details of his last few hours would emerge at an inquest to determine if he had fallen or jumped through an open window. Sheila would always believe the former but couldn't bear to attend the hearing. Instead, she forced herself to read the newspaper accounts, which she then hid from the boys.

The sadness wasn't just his death but the manner in which he had been living, virtually penniless and, effectively, homeless; he had recently been forced to quit a rented one-bedroom flat in Cork Street off Regent Street, an up-and-coming art-house corner of the city, but a far cry from the stately addresses he had once enjoyed.

But tragic Loughie still had many friends, among them Dr Alfred Lennane who had also been his GP for some years. Loughie had called him that morning and they'd spent most of the day together, meeting for a long lunch which stretched to dinner, perhaps discussing their joint interest in art or the doctor's recent purchase of not one, but two Stradivarius violins.

They left the restaurant about 9 p.m. and headed to a house in Holland Road, Kensington, where Loughie had been offered a bed for the weekend. Neither was drunk. In fact, Loughie had consumed very little alcohol at all during the day; instead he had sipped ginger ale, except for one brandy and soda that the doctor had prescribed for his friend to counter a coughing fit brought on, he believed, by excessive smoking.

Strangely, the previous month Loughie had been featured in a newspaper advert for Baron's cigarettes. It appeared in the *Daily Express* on June 26 and featured a photograph of the handsome thirty-seven year old, dressed in the uniform of the King's Royal Rifle Corps he had not worn for more than a decade, and declared: "LORD LOUGHBOROUGH writes 'I find the flavour of Baron's Virginia Cigarettes exactly right. Flavour, coolness, smoothness and mildness. I like them very much indeed.'"

There were three women at the Holland Road address when the two men arrived about 9.15. Miss Violet MacDonald, who would describe herself as a single woman of independent means, knew Loughie well. He had stayed at the house before and his father, the earl, had once rented her father's yacht for a social event. She had agreed to let him stay, even though she already had guests—her aunt and a friend visiting from South Africa. But there was room enough in the large house, because her parents were away in Scotland for the weekend. After introductions, they sat down to play rummy, again sans alcohol.

The mood was jovial, they would all later testify, other than during a break in play at 10 p.m., when Loughie excused himself to make a telephone call to someone in Eastbourne. Violet's aunt, a Mrs Pickthorne, thought he looked a little upset when he returned to the table, but he resumed playing, without explanation. The game continued until 11 p.m., when Dr Lennane said goodnight and caught a cab back to his home in the city, just off Pall Mall.

The doctor was still awake when the telephone jingled a

few minutes past midnight. It was Violet MacDonald, worried about the behaviour of Lord Loughborough, who was acting very strangely and threatening to leave. Would the doctor come back please, and help settle his friend. They would put the doctor up for the night if necessary. The doctor agreed and called a cab.

Miss MacDonald would later recount the strange series of events that had occurred after Dr Lennane left and before she phoned him. Loughie had decided to turn in for the night, and been put in the third-floor bedroom normally used by her mother. Miss MacDonald and her aunt stayed up a little later but, when they went upstairs, found their guest on the landing. He was clearly agitated; he said he wanted to leave and only agreed to stay if he could remove a collection of tortoiseshell hair brushes and articles on the dressing table.

The items were removed and he seemed to settle down. Miss MacDonald said goodnight and went into the next-door bedroom, which she was sharing with her aunt. But a few minutes later Loughie knocked on her door and insisted that he was in the wrong room and wanted to go. They tried to pacify the troubled man and eventually led him upstairs to another room on the fourth floor, at the top of the house. It was then Miss MacDonald decided to call the doctor. Something was desperately wrong.

It was almost 1 a.m. when Dr Lennane got back to Holland Road. He found Loughie perched on the edge of a bed in his pyjamas, with his suit folded neatly and packed in his suitcase. He was worried, he told the doctor, that he was going to "cause a disturbance to the family, which he hoped was not infectious".

"I chaffed him," the doctor recounted a few days later, "and he seemed quite all right."

The doctor went downstairs to the bed Loughie had rejected but, still concerned and puzzled, went back up three times over the next thirty minutes to make sure that he was all right. "He was in bed but he was not asleep. After that I went to bed."

Miss MacDonald, disturbed firstly by a dripping tap and then by the unmistakeable sound of one of the huge floor-to-ceiling windows being slid open, also saw him lying on his bed as she passed the room. He was awake, but quiet. Eventually the house settled, although Dr Lennane could not sleep. He decided to read with the light on and door open in case his friend, in the room overhead, called out: "I must have dropped asleep for I gradually became aware that there was some moaning, apparently from the garden."

Rather than run downstairs and check outside, the doctor ran upstairs to check on his friend. What he discovered only confirmed the worst: "I ran up to his room to see that he was all right. I was astounded to find the bed empty and window open. It was wide open. I rushed down to the garden and found he had fallen on the crazy paving."

Dr Lennane woke Miss MacDonald to call an ambulance. It was clearly serious, given that Lord Loughborough had plunged at least 10 metres onto stone. The doctor, feeling around in the darkness, could tell his friend had broken an arm and one of his legs in two places. He must also have suffered internal injuries, although they weren't immediately obvious.

The young lord was unconscious when he arrived at St Mary Abbott's Hospital in Kensington at 2.30 a.m., but he appeared to wake up as they prepared him for emergency surgery. Dr Lennane, who had gone with the ambulance, said the stricken man nodded, as if in recognition of those around him.

The doctor left the hospital to go home as Loughie was being wheeled from surgery. Soon after, the Earl of Rosslyn arrived and joined the growing number of family by the bedside. Dr Eric Macdonald, an assistant medical officer, said Loughie seemed to recover from the anaesthetic but did not speak, let alone offer any explanation about what had happened. It was a matter of waiting.

But, just as it seemed he might recover, the young lord's condition quickly deteriorated. He died just after 7.30 a.m.— already psychologically broken and now physically destroyed.

Lord Loughborough's death was front-page news, even across the Atlantic where he was viewed as a hell-raiser: "The wildest man in London" was dead, as one breathless American account would detail, linking his death to a tragic play Loughie was said to have seen during the days before his death. There were even ghostly tales of apparitions, some inside Rosslyn Chapel and seen by a groundsman at the same time as Loughie lay dying in the garden back in London.

The social exploits of London's upper class were mostly documented by newspapers in gossip columns which celebrated beauty and style, where the worst that could befall one was to be ignored. But such a dramatic demise proved much more exciting. *The Times, Guardian, Daily Express* and regional papers all gave extensive coverage to news of the tragedy and the inquest, which quickly followed. It was irresistible. It even found its way into Australian papers because his links to Sheila, daughter of the late Harry Chisholm, made such good fodder. He may have been "tall and well built with a winning smile", as one account pandered, but his physical attributes did not protect him from his character flaws.

The inquest took just one day, hurriedly convened two days after his death and one day before his funeral. Dr Lennane was the chief witness, not only because he had been with Loughie all day but because he was also the young man's GP and was aware of his fragile state of mind.

He described the young lord as a hypersensitive man who was keenly aware of his impact on others. He said Loughie had suffered a nervous breakdown three months earlier and had been hospitalised for depression, although there was nothing in his behaviour that day to presage such a dramatic event: "He was perfectly cheerful all day from the time I saw him until I left him," said the doctor. "He was in good spirits."

Neither was there any suggestion of drug or alcohol use, other than the brandy and soda, which, the doctor revealed, was strictly for medicinal purposes. Reports of the pair having been at the notorious 43 Club in Soho appeared inaccurate although it was clearly a haunt, infamous for its gambling and whores, which had contributed to Loughie's demise.

The coroner, a Dr Scott, was puzzled, as is shown by the following reported exchange.

Scott: "I must ask you why you took all the care of him, why you went to his room two or three times?"

Dr Lennane: "I was told he was wandering and wanted to go out. It was a little difficult to understand him sometimes. He had not a very precise way of talking."

Scott: "You cannot throw any light on his nervous condition?"

Lennane: "No."

Scott: "Have you ever known him do anything irregular or unreasonable?"

Lennane: "No. I have never known him to suggest suicide at any time."

Scott: "Have you prescribed sleeping draughts for him?"

Lennane: "Not for some years."

Scott: "Did he complain of being depressed?"

Lennane: "No. There was some slight depression about trivial things but I talked him out of it."

Instead, Lennane offered the suggestion that the death might have been a terrible accident caused by another coughing fit. In trying not to disturb the rest of the house, perhaps Loughie had opened a window, lost his balance while coughing and fallen out. It was a desperate theory, in an attempt to save what was left of his friend's good name.

And what of the mysterious phone call made during the card game? Could it throw any light on the tragedy? The woman

Loughie had telephoned was in court, dressed in black, and gave evidence, but for the moment she remained unnamed. She was the owner of a flat in which he had been staying, but which he was now being forced to vacate. She said the lord's manner had been normal, and he had merely wanted to give her a forwarding address—yet another reminder of his fall from grace for a young man who was facing a series of closing doors.

Was that the answer? Had he finally had enough and had nowhere to go?

But not all doors had closed. In fact, a new one had recently opened: a city publisher had engaged him to write about his exploits in London gambling clubs, firstly as a serial and then to be published in book form, perhaps similar to his father's memoir. Rosslyn's *My Gamble with Life* had been published in New York only the year before, (and had been described by reviewers as self-congratulatory). Its release was much to the horror of his family; the earl's sister, the Dowager Duchess of Sutherland, had travelled to the United States on a quest to block its publication because it "rattles indecently forgotten skeletons of the Rosslyn clan". She had failed.

Loughie's London publishers could clearly see potential in the father–son connection. "He [Lord Loughborough] was always very cheerful and was quite a promising writer," the unnamed publisher commented when told of the death.

But was the possibility of becoming financially self-sufficient enough to give him hope? Perhaps the fact that he had two young children by his marriage to Sheila, and that he had told friends he intended to marry again and was about to propose to an unnamed young woman, might have been reasons to live, and it could be put down to an accident.

The mystery only deepened later in the day, when the identity of the woman in black at the back of the court was finally revealed. Heiress Iris Thornton was not only Loughie's landlady but, so she believed, his wife-to-be. A tearful Miss Thornton had brought one of his last letters for the coroner to read, in the hope it might persuade the court that his death was an accident. He was happy about the future, she insisted, pointing to a sentence which read: "I missed my happiness once, but now everything is alright."

Miss Thornton told the court a convoluted story. She knew her beau was a fragile and damaged man, and perhaps she loved him for it. She wanted to save him. She had accepted Loughie's faults and had kept a careful eye on him in recent months while they planned a life together, with her family's money offering him financial salvation. But she had made a mistake when she asked him to vacate her flat that day. Her hope had been that it would force him to return to the safety of his father's house, away from the temptations of London. Instead, she feared it may have contributed to his mood:

He had telephoned me three times that day and the last words he spoke were "Goodnight, Angel". He only rang up to tell me where he was staying. Oh, how I wish I had not insisted on his leaving the flat that day. I don't think I was quite as nice to him as I might have been but I wanted him to go home and spend a quiet weekend with his father. It would have meant so much to both of us. It was silly of him to go and play cards and I was afraid that, away from me, he might start drinking.

She believed it had been an accident. "I wanted to come here and prove it was an accident. Why, he promised to ring me up at ten o'clock the next morning and, if he was very good, I was going to let him come down for the day."

Miss Thornton attended the coroner's court in the company of Lady Teddington, who also gave evidence but thought differently to her friend: "From the circumstances, as I know them, there can be no doubt that this terrible act was one of sudden despair—despair at another little turn of fortune's wheel which he feared might snatch his happiness from him, and in his nervous and highly strung condition he could not face in the fulfilment of his hopes."

The jury took only a few minutes to weigh up the scenario, siding with Lady Teddington's view. They pronounced that Lord Loughborough had committed suicide, brought on by depression and "a temporary unsound mind".

⚬⚬⚬

The day after the inquest Harry Rosslyn went to Runnymede to see his former daughter-in-law and beg her to go to the funeral and allow the boys to be pallbearers. Sheila was reluctant: "I thought both these ideas unsuitable because I had divorced Loughie and the boys were too young. However, to please Harry and also because I knew that Loughie would have gone to the ends of the earth for my funeral, I agreed to go. We were both extremely sad, and wondered if in any way we could have helped Loughie more. We both decided we had done all we could."

The Guardian newspaper covered his funeral two days later at the family chapel at Rosslyn. About a hundred people attended, including Sheila Milbanke, who sat with her two "golden-haired" sons beside her former father-in-law. The coverage had turned from sensational to atmospheric:

> Candles burned low on either side and beautiful floral crosses lay on top of the coffin, one from Lord Rosslyn and the present Lady Rosslyn, stepmother of Lord Loughborough, and the other bearing the inscription "In loving memory of my darling boy— mother". The chapel was dimly lit by candlelight but the sunshine, streaming in the window, displayed the wonderful beauty of the carved stonework for which Rosslyn is world-famous.

Sheila stood at the graveside with the boys: "I had ordered masses of Lily of the Valley for Loughie. The scent of them made me sick, with memories my eyes were blinded with tears . . . so many memories. I thought: 'Head high, walk very tall' which always comes to my rescue."

On the train back to London, Sheila sat lost in thought: "It was the same train I had taken after my divorce more than three years before, after the imaginary ornaments that I had tried to hang on Loughie, as one hangs ornaments on a Christmas tree, had fallen off one by one. It was not his fault, I mused, that he couldn't live up to my idea of what I wanted him to be. I remembered how, many years before, my mother had warned me against this trait in my character."

Tony and Peter were in a carriage next door: "I thought I would peep at them and see how upset they were after such a bad experience. They were playing a game called Peggity and screaming with laughter. Oh, glorious youth."

Sheila was still absorbing the tragedy a few weeks later, when the *Daily Express* columnist Tom Driberg, aka "The Dragoman", spotted her one evening in a restaurant. In a piece written about whether the waltz was back in favour (Driberg thought not) the columnist described the scene: Sheila, "tanned by the Antibes sun", was wearing black in stark contrast to others in bright colours. He also noted her demeanour: "Lady Milbanke did not dance, but sat quietly at the table with her husband." Driberg would have been keenly aware of the Loughborough tragedy and that others would be reading his column. Sheila wanted it known that, in spite of her social commitments, she was in mourning.

18

THE "IT" GIRL

General Sir Bryan Mahon and Sir John Peniston Milbanke, Buffles' father, shared much in common, although the two men probably never met. Both had distinguished military careers and were feted for their bravery in combat, particularly in the Boer War where Sir Bryan was awarded a Distinguished Service Order and Sir John a Victoria Cross.

And both served in the Dardanelles, although this was where their stories went separate ways. Milbanke was killed in action and Mahon, who didn't agree with the tactics of his superiors, was transferred to run the Irish command and survived. He then married Sir John Milbanke's widow.

Dame Amelia Crichton had married Baronet Milbanke at the end of 1900 and, in a happy but all-too-brief marriage, bore two children—John Jr and Ralph—before her husband was killed in action in 1915 during the pointless skirmishes of

Gallipoli in the Great War.

Five years later she married 58-year-old Sir Bryan and moved to Ireland where he was a member of the Privy Council. They lived in a rambling house named Mullaboden in County Kildare, south-west of Dublin, which she had inherited from her father and where they occasionally hosted John and Ralph, or "Buffles" and "Toby" as they were known, now young men who found London more to their taste. The Dowager Lady Milbanke, as she preferred to be called, died in late 1927 and Sir Bryan followed three years later, his two stepsons by his bedside when he finally succumbed to a long illness on September 29, 1930.

Sir Bryan's death marked something of a fillip for Sheila and Sir John. The shock and sadness of Loughie's death the year before was now fading and the passing of Buffles' parents proved a fortuitous windfall at a time when the Great Depression was beginning to bite. But instead of selling Mullaboden, the couple decided to add a country manor to their social life, as a place where they could host friends from London. It also offered a respite from the increasingly harried capital. Sheila entertained in the autumn, as the London Season was drawing to a close, and then later in winter. Cecil Beaton quipped in a piece he wrote for Vogue: "Sheila Milbanke has become a champion knitter and, with the help of pattern books, makes socks, sweaters and caps. She has developed a complete fireside manner."

She also quickly became a local celebrity and was photographed with her two sons, now aged fourteen and thirteen, when in 1931 she decided to invest in the Irish racing industry, which was struggling in the gloom of the Depression. It was perhaps inevitable—given her family background in horses, and the lure and prestige of Ascot and Epsom in the English summer—that Sheila would eventually dabble in thorough-bred racehorses.

Annoyed that Buffles and Toby had secretly bought some racehorses, she went to the Dublin Horse Show and bought a yearling, chosen "chiefly because he nibbled the carnation in my buttonhole", and placed it with the flamboyant Irish trainer Roderic More O'Ferrall, who had his stables next door to Mullaboden.

The modest 55-guinea investment was social more than serious, announced to the local media as a signal that she and her husband intended to spend much more time in Ireland now that Sir John had inherited Mullaboden. And she proved to have a keen eye for horse flesh when in the following year the gelding, now a strapping two year old named Dr Strabismus, won his first race at the odds of 50 to 1. He would go on to win three in a row, the prize money repaying tenfold his purchase price and the horse being declared the best two year old of the Irish racing year, with a promising career ahead.

The media coverage was enthusiastic and always seemed to describe the animal as "Lady Milbanke's horse", as if the owner-ship was an important aspect of his race form. The English racecourses beckoned and he was now entered into a lead-up event to the famous Grand National steeplechase. Dr Stra-bismus began as one of the favourites in the West Derby Stakes, immediately before the big race, and finished a creditable second. He then finished midfield in the Irish 2000 Guineas, which was enough to show he had promise, although it might take time for him to fulfil it.

But her dalliance with racing would be short-lived. After the gelding easily won a stakes event back in Ireland, Sheila chose to sell him on a winning note to an excited Indian businessman keen on taking him back to Bombay. The price of £1100 was the highest sum paid that season: "I invented my own racing colours and made quite a lot of money. I sold 'The Doctor' eventually and retired from the turf gracefully, I hope."

Sir John Milbanke's boxing career had all but ended in 1930, when he had stepped into the ring with a London professional named Ernie Jarvis, the nation's second-ranked flyweight. The Boxing Baronet had his hand broken, or "knocked up". Henceforth, he would concentrate on his growing financial career outside the ring and he began dabbling in the world of gambling.

In October 1932 he and three partners announced their involvement in a Monte Carlo-based sweepstakes project, which promised 25 per cent of the take to British hospitals in the hope of winning government and public support. It was front-page news in the *Daily Mirror* on October 11, 1932, which trumpeted: "At long last a sweepstake is going to be run on the Continent from which British hospitals and charities will benefit." The article included pictures of the esteemed businessmen who would front the scheme—Sir Charles Higham, Colonel Wilfred Egerton and Sir Walter Peacock with the much younger Sir John Milbanke as an inset.

The first £2 million sweep would be on the Grand National steeplechase and would raise £500,000 for hospitals. It was a grand plan, supported immediately by a combined hospitals board, but it would splutter and die when its Monte Carlo backers objected to English hospitals benefitting, instead of French facilities. Buffles backed off quickly, although he would always be known as the man who attempted to bring national sweepstakes to England.

In June 1933 the Milbankes caved in to the reality of the continuing economic malaise and reluctantly sold Mullaboden, its grounds and much of its stash of antiques, which had been built up over several generations. But with this sale came an opportunity: they poured the proceeds into a new project, a family home in St John's Wood, a suburb in north London that had been among the first to abandon the traditional London terrace in favour of larger, semi-detached villas with large gardens.

For Sheila it was an attempt to marry the convenience of city living with space, inside and out, for children and dogs and, as usual, she set a trend. Their move from Belgravia was soon followed by others such as Lady Ravensdale, the novelist Dennis Wheatley and later by Freda Dudley Ward.

———

If Sheila Chisholm's wartime entry into London society had been originally fuelled by the novelty of her being a young Australian, and her Roaring Twenties stardom had been nurtured by prominent family and friends, then the profile of

Lady Sheila Milbanke in the 1930s was of her own making. As the musical taste turned from jazz to swing and fashion from elegance to glamour, it seemed there was little she could do or wear that didn't make an impact.

From being tanned: "The bronzed complexions that are to be fashionable this summer have already appeared on some women. Lady Plunket is one of them. She is combining a brown skin with a rather high colour. Lady Milbanke is another who has adopted this fashion"; to having bare legs in public: "One of the smartest women at Cowes this year is the Australian beauty, Lady Sheila Milbanke. She goes about stockingless most of the day, and, like most of the smart younger set, sports a jaunty white beret in preference to other hats". Even wearing a wig caused a stir:

> Society is not likely to take up the silken wig as a new fashion, despite its alluring colour scheme possibilities. This at least appears to be the majority verdict upon the chance of Lady Milbanke who created a mild sensation by appearing at a West End dance club in a wig of golden coloured silk. Miss Tallulah Bankhead: "Women with naturally nice hair would not, I think, want to hide it, apart from fancy dress balls and the like. I should imagine that Lady Milbanke was indulging in a lark."

(Sheila also recalled the incident: She had won the golden wig at a fancy dress and accepted a bet to wear it in public at the Embassy Club: "I couldn't resist doing so. News must have been scarce at the time because the *Evening Standard* came out with the front-page headline 'Lady Milbanke goes blonde!'")

The columnists were not just reporting her attendance at a restaurant or a dance but what she was wearing and how it fitted with trends—"long-drop earrings, which are so fashionable at the moment", an all-green dining room in her home, and her hair in curls, "more fashionable now that an uncompromising shingle".

Clothing houses began using her to show off their new fashions in newspaper photographs:

> Lady Milbanke, who was formerly well known in Australian social circles as Sheila Chisholm, is wearing one of Jean Patou's newest sports suits of brown wool, with a blouse of green, beige, and brown plaid tweed, matching scarf and brown felt beret . . . Lady Milbanke is wearing one of the newest Mary Stuart hats. She is just as lovely as ever. She once said that one of her beauty secrets was her capacity to sleep anywhere and at any time . . . Lady Milbanke's becoming beige costume came from Paris Trades in London. She was among the popular young London hostesses at Le Touquet.

She had become one of the first so-called "It Girls", the term coined initially by Rudyard Kipling in his 1904 short story, *Mrs Bathurst,* when he wrote: "It isn't beauty, so to speak, nor good talk necessarily. It's just 'It'", and later by another English novelist and script writer Elinor Glyn in her 1927 novel, *It.* Lady Glyn, who happened to be an acquaintance of Sheila's, wrote as an introduction to the subsequent Hollywood movie of the same name: "With 'It' you win all men if you are a woman and all women if you are a man. 'It' can be a quality of the mind as well as a physical attraction."

The term also echoed Cecil Beaton's view on the changing nature of beauty, in that women required a personality, and not just genes, to be beautiful. Sheila Milbanke had it all—she was an increasingly significant woman in the world's most important city. She was not just "Lady Milbanke, wife of . . .", as many women were often described, being mere adjuncts to their husbands. She was Lady Milbanke the tireless charity queen or the stylish hostess or, quite often, the Australian—as if these were integral aspects of her character, and her beauty.

London society had been hit by a wave of American "dollar princesses" in the latter years of the 19th century, when dozens of young women made their way across the Atlantic in search of a husband and the heady social power of a title. European aristocracy, and particularly a British title, had become a "must have" that could not simply be bought; however, the cynical claimed that this was exactly what happened as an estimated 200 young women, mostly from self-made, moneyed families, found love. By 1899, prompted by the future King Edward VII's frank admiration for their uninhibited vitality and self-confidence, society magazines had begun covering "Anglo-American beauties". There was even a club called the Society of American Women.

There would be many who would leave their mark, like Jennie Jerome—the mother of Winston Churchill, who became one of the first "princesses" when she married the Duke of Marlborough in 1874—or Nancy Langhorne, who became Lady Astor in 1906 and in 1918 was the first woman to be elected to the British Parliament. But it was an uneasy acceptance, as the Duchess of Marlborough would write in her diaries:

> In England, the American woman was looked upon as a strange and abnormal creature with habits and manner something between a red Indian and a Gaiety Girl.
>
> Anything of an outlandish nature might be expected of her. If she talked, dressed and conducted herself as any well-bred woman would . . . she was usually saluted with the tactful remark; "I should never have thought you were an American"—which was intended as a compliment . . . Her dollars were her only recommendation.

Even though most American princesses were eventually accepted in society, they would continue to create ill-ease and to be dismissed by some as mere social climbers, particularly when Wallis Simpson appeared in 1934 and inveigled her way into the bed of the Prince of Wales, thus threatening the monarchy.

But Sheila was different. From the moment the newlywed Lady Loughborough arrived in London in early 1916 she wore her birthplace as a badge, often mentioned alongside the description of her latest frock, or her hat or fur coat. At the time, there were only a handful of Australian women who had married into high society; these included Lady Huntingdon, who was formerly Margaret Wilson, daughter of a Victorian MP; the Countess of Portarlington, born in Adelaide as Winnafreda Yuill; and Lady Lindsey, formerly Millicent Cox, daughter of a Sydney dentist.

Perhaps best known was the Countess of Darnley, who was formerly Florence Rose Morphy, a Melbourne nanny and music teacher who had tended the injured finger of the English cricket captain Ivo Bligh during the 1882 tour of Australia and won his heart. Bligh had been presented with a small terracotta urn by a group of Melbourne women after England's victory in that Test series and the Countess of Darnley kept the urn on her mantelpiece until the death of her husband in 1927 when it was donated to the Marylebone Cricket Club, where it became cricket's most famous symbol.

The Australian ranks had hardly swelled by the 1930s, although debutantes and their mothers continued to make their way to London for the Season each year, often making a beeline for Sheila who might offer an entrée. For example, in 1931 a group of young Australian women accompanied her to the Dublin Horse Show. For most it would be an introduction to society and no more, after which they would head back home in August, when the social rounds came to an end. But some would remain.

In 1938 *The Australian Women's Weekly* would commission a feature on "Australians who shine in London" but the magazine could barely name more than half a dozen. "The amazingly youthful and beautiful" Sheila Milbanke was photographed at the Ritz; the gushing article lavished praise on the women who "have won a reputation as brilliant hostesses. There is a quality about their dinner parties, house parties and entertainments which sends fashionable London flocking to their doors."

Sheila Chisholm's powerful persona was best illustrated by a peerage survey, published in 1939, which attempted to rank the importance of titles. As the wife of the Earl of Rosslyn she would have been among the more senior women in London society, but as Lady Milbanke, wife of a baronet, her ranking was a lowly 27,130.

The seniority of her title didn't seem to matter as she sat among the guests in Westminster Abbey to attend the wedding of the Duke and Duchess of Kent, nor when she was nicknamed "Mascot" by the Earl of Derby because she was sitting next to him when his horse Hyperion won his own race, the Derby. Sheila was again in the royal box at the Theatre Royal in Drury Lane to watch close friend Nöel Coward's play *Cavalcade*—"I had known him in his infamous days. He is completely unspoiled, kind and generous," she would later recall. She watched the love affair of Aly Khan, son of the Aga Khan, with Joan Guinness and became "Aunt Sheila" to their son, the current Aga Khan. She holidayed with Prince Paul of Yugoslavia and his wife Princess Olga of Greece and Denmark and stayed at Blenheim Palace "with the Marlboroughs", as well as Leeds Castle, the former home of King Edward I, with Lord and Lady Braille. Christmas was usually spent at Himley Hall with Lord Dudley.

Her home in Talbot Square became a frequent venue for parties, usually featuring a performance by the latest West End star, and she often stayed at a house in Sunningdale, just outside London, where she sat with American songwriter Cole Porter while he composed some of his best-known songs: "It fascinated me to sit in the room while he played and sang as the words and music came into his head."

The Derby Ball, created initially as a one-off event, had become not only an annual fixture on the social calendar but the city's most significant charity event of the year. Lady Milbanke was its permanent chairwoman, enjoying the ear of Edward, the future King of England, and his brother George the Duke of Kent, whose wedding invitation at Westminster Abbey in 1934 she would keep as one of her prized possessions. She supported the events of other charity queens and in return they flocked to hers, whether it was at Grosvenor House or the May Fair Hotel.

The high-profile guest appearances and one-off events at the ball continued to spur its ticket sales. In 1932, on the same page as *The Irish Times* congratulated Lady Milbanke for her foresight in buying Dr Strabismus and published a photograph of her horse being patted by jockey Tommy Burns after a convincing six-length victory, the newspaper welcomed to the UK the famed American pilot Amelia Earhart as the first woman to cross the Atlantic.

Just as had happened to Charles Lindbergh five years before, Ms Earhart was quickly drawn into the Milbanke circle and drafted to appear at the Derby Ball, due a few days before Dr Strabismus made his debut at Epsom. The ball that year was an enormous success, attended not only by the Prince of Wales but by a slew of entertainment celebrities, including Fred Astaire, who had recently returned to London. But Ms Earhart, "whose

boyish curls and charming smile attracted a good deal of attention", as the *Daily Express* described her, was the focus of the
now traditional gushing media coverage.

The ball's theme turned to cricket in 1933, when Sheila staged
a "Grand Googly Competition" hosted by English great "Patsy"
Hendren, who was about to face the Australians in a home
Ashes series after missing out on the infamous Bodyline Tests
of 1932–33. And so it continued for the rest of the decade—the
ball always supported by royalty and a clutch of show business
celebrities, often from Hollywood like Gary Cooper in 1932, or
Broadway and West End stars of the day.

It also had its controversial moments, which only added to the
lustre of the occasion as the paying public were able to witness
the rare sight of the wealthy and powerful behaving badly. In
1935 the guest of honour, the famous American Woolworth's
heiress Barbara Hutton, became upset when no one would
outbid her offer of 300 guineas for a blank canvas to be painted
by the famous equestrian artist Lynwood Palmer. Ms Hutton's
disgust that "a better effort was not made for charity" was
front-page news in the *Daily Mirror*—Hutton photographed
alongside London's queen of charities, Lady Milbanke.

19

VIVID, GAY, UTTERLY CHARMING

When domestic sales of its face creams and other beauty prod-ucts slumped in the mid-1920s, the American company Pond's commissioned market research to stem the tide. The agency found that middle-class women were ignoring the locally made beauty products in favour of European brands such as Chanel and Helena Rubenstein, which they thought were better simply because they were imported and more expensive.

The research company also interviewed prominent and wealthy society women, whose buying habits were, surprisingly, the opposite. Although they could afford the imported brands, most preferred to pay less for the locally made product. The company realised that, if it could win the endorsement of those women who appeared in the newspaper and magazine society pages, and who thus wielded enormous influence in fashion, then it might strike advertising gold.

Pond's began using women prominent in US society to build their campaign; however, there was more to such women than just their wealth. For example, Alva Vanderbilt, wife of the industrialist William Vanderbilt, was a fabulously wealthy New York socialite who was known as much for her support of women's rights and child labour reforms as her money. Likewise, another woman they chose was Cordelia Biddle Robertson, who was a Philadelphia socialite, author and philanthropist who had established charities for artists and disadvantaged youth. They were women of substance as much as style.

Their campaign was a success. Pond's recovery in fact coincided with a sales boom across the business generally, with other firms, such as Max Factor and Elizabeth Arden, also prospering. Cosmetics were becoming more socially acceptable as the allure of Hollywood began to take hold, but the celluloid stars did not have a mortgage on glamour.

When Pond's expanded into Europe and opened a factory in London, it brought with it the same advertising strategy, choosing a mixture of royalty and socialites to endorse its products. Sheila Milbanke and Diana Cooper were among the first socialites chosen; their images were shot by the most distinguished fashion photographers of the day, including English Cecil Beaton, Madame Yevonde and Dorothy Wilding, in a style that mimicked the lighting, poses and clothing of the movie stars.

Sheila would make no mention of the campaign in her memoir, perhaps embarrassed because it was money that was her motivating force. Money was never spoken of in polite circles but the truth was that as Lady Milbanke, even with her own family endowments, she did not have the financial rescue net afforded her when she was married into the Rosslyn family.

It might also have been the public recognition the campaign would have brought her. She had always enjoyed being on the stage and at one point had expressed a desire to become involved in screen acting. And although she declared a modesty about her appearance, it was clear that she was aware of her looks and enjoyed the attention of men and the comparisons with other beauties of her time, such as her friend Diana Cooper, as well as being recognisable to the general public.

Age was no barrier, because the campaign and the products were not focussed on the first blush of youth, but on maintaining eternal beauty. When the first advertisements were published in 1932, Sheila was thirty-seven years old; when she appeared in her last, to coincide with the coronation of King George VI, she was aged forty-two.

The advertisements pictured her in a demure pose, hair carefully shaped into a wave, and dressed simply in a black dress and single string of pearls, so all the attention would be on her face and skin rather than on her jewellery or clothes. Some of the ads were succinct, while others were presented as a conversation with the reader:

VIVID, GAY, UTTERLY CHARMING IS
LOVELY LADY MILBANKE
This is how she cares for her rose-petal skin.

"Yes, I've travelled a great deal," said Lady Milbanke, "and I've learned how simple it is to keep one's skin soft and fresh even in a bad climate."

Lady Milbanke is tall and slim, like a willow, with soft brown eyes and nut-dark hair. Her complexion has vivid carmine tints that some brunettes are blessed with. Her skin is satiny smooth.

Other ads contrasted her brunette hair and darker skin with the complexions of pale blondes, or highlighted how her cosmetics complemented her lifestyle—"engaged in outdoor sport or dancing in London's smart restaurants". One ad even sported her flourishing signature as a personal endorsement.

And it wasn't just face cream she was promoting. A gas cookware company quoted her cook—a Mrs Easton—to endorse a new oven and how it roasted a chicken, in fact a whole roast meal, to perfection.

The post-war social freedom of London produced not only a generation of moneyed aristocrats eager to break the heavy shackles of Victorian and Edwardian society but a surge of creativity across the arts. Modernism was born and its impact was felt from the art galleries of New Bond Street to the dance floors of Soho and the theatres of Covent Garden. Fashion followed the upbeat lead of jazz and the Charleston, and F Scott Fitzgerald told its story through *The Great Gatsby*. The changes were fed further by rapid advances in technology, which, for example, introduced colour to the cinema and to still photography.

Inevitably, it also produced a generation of artists who

revolutionised their craft. Miss Yevonde Cumbers was one such: an enterprising but indulged daughter of a London ink manufacturer, she was profoundly influenced in her teens by the suffragette movement. She stumbled into photography accidentally, apprenticed herself to the leading portrait photographer of the day and in 1914, at the age of twenty-one and having taken just one photograph, opened her own studio under the name Madame Yevonde with a £250 gift from a doting father.

Women's rights had become a powerful force in her work, exploring not only female sexuality but women's role in society. Portraits had evolved from swan-necked beauties in extravagant gowns staring awkwardly, "pouter pigeon" style, at the camera. Now her clients adopted more relaxed poses, often looking away from the camera and using props and lighting to bring out their individual personalities.

Madame Yevonde had quickly gathered together some well-known clients by doing free portraits of them; she had then won acclaim and work from such magazines as *Tatler* and *The Sketch*, followed by *Vogue* and *Harper's Bazaar* in America. Her big breakthrough had come when she was asked to take the official portrait for the engagement of Lord Louis Mountbatten to Edwina Ashley in 1922. Subsequently her clients included Barbara Cartland, AA Milne, Nöel Coward, Vivien Leigh, George Bernard Shaw, Somerset Maugham and a host of society women who flocked to her studio in Victoria Street.

In the early 1930s, Madame Yevonde began experimenting with colour photography using a process called Vivex. Battling initial hostility among both photographers and the public, she began using colour for her portraits; in 1932 she staged the first colour photographic exhibition in Britain. But her most famous project would come three years later and involve Sheila Milbanke.

On March 5, 1935, a great ball was held at Claridge's in Mayfair, with guests dressed as Roman and Greek gods and goddesses. The event, held to raise funds for the Greater London Fund for the Blind, featured Venus arriving in a shell drawn by cupids. Goddesses paraded, attended by nymphs and fauns. Madame Yevonde had not attended the ball, but she carefully chose some society women (whether they had attended the ball or not) who she believed best embodied the attributes of certain goddesses.

She created dramatic studio shots of each of them using colour, costume and props to build a surreal air around her subjects: Lady Warrender, organiser of the Olympian Ball dressed as Ceres, goddess of agriculture; the Duchess of Wellington as Hecate, goddess of crossroads; Lady Diana Mosley as Venus, goddess of love; the Viscountess Ratendone as Euterpe, muse of delight; the actress Gertrude Lawrence as Thalia, the muse of comedy; and Baroness Dacre as Circe, goddess of magic.

Sheila Milbanke was Penthesilea, the Queen of the Amazons. Hers was regarded as the most striking of the twenty-two portraits—dramatic and beautiful, with her eyes closed and her ruby-red lips slightly open. Her head was thrust back in a pose to capture the moment when, according to Greek mythology, Penthesilea had been speared by Achilles at the Battle of Troy. Animal skins barely covered her neck and breasts; her own weapon and the spear that had killed her formed the shape of a cross in the background.

It was a statement about the heroism and strength of women. The exhibition was an instant success, with visitors flocking to the studio to view it. Not only would it be regarded as one of the most powerfully expressive exhibitions of the medium of photography, but it would secure for Madame Yevonde her place as an important figure in the history of photography.

A CURIO SHOP IN TABLEAUX

Lady Crowther's Tableaux will be a feature of Princess Christian's matinee at the Palace Theatre on Friday, December 7. They are described as a series of Objets d'Art Vivants, and well-known people will take part in the unusual representation of a curio dealer's treasures. Lady Cynthia Asquith, Miss Kitty Kinloch and the Hon. John Lytton will represent "A Luca della Robbia"; Miss Jean Kinloch and Miss Barbara Lutyens "an Old French Fan"; Miss Violet Keppel "a Mezzotint"; Mrs Underdown "a Wedgwood Plaque"; Lady Idina Wallace "a Persian Miniature"; Mrs Gerald Leigh "a Missal Page"; Lady Loughborough, the Hon. Mrs Fane and Mrs John Lavery "a Triptych"; Lady Diana Manners "a Cameo"; Mrs Henry Howard "a Green Jade Figure"; the Countess of Drogheda "a War Poster" and Mrs Ralph Peto "the Lady of the Lamp". The entire proceeds of the performance will be handed over to the funds of the Housing Association for Officers' Families and the Florence Nightingale Hospital.

Sheila

It was a small item in the social columns of *The Times* on November 24, 1917, and yet the snippet threw together three names that would begin and end one of the great scandals of English society. Lady Idina Wallace, better known by her maiden name of Sackville and cousin to the writer Vita Sackville-West, was at the centre of the *White Mischief* story that had also featured Alice de Janzé and Raymond de Trafford. Ultimately her exploits would be used as the inspiration for characters in three novels.

Idina was rich and beautiful. In 1917, she was the mother of two young sons and married to an army captain named Euan Wallace, who would become a war hero and recipient of the Military Cross. Yet her world fell apart a little over a year later when her husband began an affair with another of the Tableaux women.

Barbara Lutyens was the eighteen-year-old daughter of a prominent architect and she had come to lunch at the Wallaces' a few months earlier as a friend of Idina's younger sister. Euan Wallace, home on leave from France, was immediately smitten by the leggy brunette with ice-blue eyes; before he returned to the Front a fortnight later, he had begun an affair with this woman seven years his junior.

Idina had at first fought to save her marriage but, by the time of the Tableaux evening, she knew that she had lost her husband to the younger woman, which must have made the event a somewhat tense night. It wasn't that Idina cared about her husband taking a younger lover; after all, discreet affairs were accepted in a society torn by war, and she was no angel herself. Her real fear was that Barbara's aim was to marry her husband and she would be left on her own. Her solution was to end the marriage on her own terms. She began a relationship with a penniless Scotsman named Charles Gordon and granted Euan Wallace a divorce a few days after the end of the war. She then hastily married Gordon and, at the suggestion of her friend and travel writer Rosita Forbes, sailed to Kenya to start a new life.

In doing so, Idina agreed to give up her children—three-year-old David and two-year-old Gerard—a decision she took to ensure they had the emotional and financial stability of a home in London rather than the wilds of Africa, where she would become famous as the high priestess of a hedonistic lifestyle that featured wife swapping and drugs. It would be fifteen years—and thanks to the intervention of Sheila Milbanke—before she saw her children again.

In May 1934, Idina was in London, having left Kenya in an attempt to end her fourth marriage. The relationship with Charles Gordon had fallen apart in 1923, as had another marriage, to Josslyn Hay, the Earl of Erroll, whom she divorced in 1930. Then she wed Donald Haldeman who, unlike her previous two husbands, was not keen on his wife's philandering lifestyle. Now she wanted out.

More than seventy years later, Idina's great-granddaughter, author Frances Osborne, would write in her 2009 book *The Bolter* about Idina's reunion with her elder son, David:

Amid the melee of cocktail and dinner parties that marked the beginning of the London Social Season, Idina received a note from a friend that would turn this new state of affairs on its head. The name of the friend was Sheila Milbanke. Sheila was a glamorous society beauty, generally described as "quite the nicest thing ever to have come out of Australia". Being Australian, she was engagingly unconcerned by some of the rules of British society and approached life and the people around her in a straight-forward, matter-of-fact way.

Sheila was friends with Euan Wallace and Barbara (whom he had married and by whom he had had another three children); she had spent a lot of time with David and Gerard, who were a few years older than her own sons. Barbara had legally become the mother of her two stepsons and called herself their mother; Idina had no visitation rights, but Sheila was convinced that she should be back in their lives.

Gerard, aged eighteen, was a well-adjusted prize-winning student studying to be a pilot at Cranwell, but David was struggling emotionally. He too was an extremely bright young man, now aged nineteen and studying at Balliol College at Oxford, where he was reading the Greats, including Philosophy, Latin and Ancient Greek. But, in Sheila's words, he was "burning with both brilliance and anger", rebelling against the beliefs and lifestyle of his parents; his father was now a high-profile Conservative MP, while Barbara was playing political hostess. David had told Sheila that he could no longer have a rational conversation with them and was considering becoming a celibate "Christian Socialist". Sheila believed that he needed his birth mother—someone who could understand the "fire" burning within him, as he described it in his own diary, and who would listen to him.

David and Idina met at Claridge's—the same venue where, seventeen years before, Idina, Barbara and Sheila had dressed as "curio dealer's treasures" at a charity function. Sheila meantime took Euan and Barbara out to lunch at the Ritz Hotel around the corner so mother and son could be alone. Idina sat smoking a breakfast cigarette and sipping a cocktail nervously until she saw the young man, wearing a red carnation in his button-hole so they could recognise one another. She would not be "Mummy", as she once was, but "Dina". The pair sat talking for several hours while she told him about the collapse of her marriage and her intoxicating new life in Africa, and then listened to his angst about the world and its ills. She wondered how his intellect and passion might allow him to fit into an increasingly complex world.

Sheila Milbanke had been right—Idina Sackville needed to be reunited with her son, for her own sake and his, and it would have a positive impact on both their lives. David would alter his views over the next few years and decide he wanted a political career to help change the society he railed against.

But he would not live to see them through. War would take him and his younger brother, Gerard, with whom Idina would also be reunited. Gerard, a pilot, was shot down in 1943 and David was killed by machine-gun fire in August 1944 while an army major serving as a diplomat in Greece.

It would not be Sheila's last personal intervention to aid a flawed and fractured friend. It was also typical of her apparent ability to make and maintain meaningful connections and friendships across the various "sets" and generations of London society—from the brash and youthful Bright Young Things to the art and literature world of Beaton, Evelyn Waugh and Nöel Coward, from the entertainment sphere of Charlie Chaplin, Fred Astaire and Sophie Tucker to the politics of Duff Cooper, Philip Sassoon and Winston Churchill and, ultimately, the power of "Buck House".

20

WHEN THE CAT'S AWAY

Darling Mr Coo,
What am I to do?
You go to Bognor every Sunday
And send me orchids every Monday
I never see you so to speak
Although you bunch me once a week.
My husband's a boxer
Your wife is a beauty
So what can we do
But attend to our duty?

In late 1934 Sheila Milbanke penned a verse on a square sheet of paper torn from a notebook and sent it secretly to the husband of one of her best friends, Lady Diana Cooper. "How would the late Lord Tennyson like this metre?" she asked on the back of the paper, clearly referring to its doggerel nature rather than the sly but obvious message of mutual attraction.

Sir Alfred Duff Cooper, Viscount of Norwich, Ambassador to France and member of parliament, was well known for his philandering ways. This was not unusual—in fact, it was far too much the norm for anyone to freely admit it. Adultery was rampant in high society and yet "Duff", as he was known to friends, had less reason than most to have a roving eye and hands. He had married Lady Diana Manners, regarded as the great beauty of her generation—a flamboyant society hostess with wealth and charisma in equal portion.

It had been a marriage born of sadness in many ways. They had both been members of a pre-war fashionable set of English aristocrats and intellectuals who called themselves the Coterie. Its members included Raymond Asquith, son of the prime minister and a famed barrister; the dramatist, poet and novelist Maurice Baring; the war poet Patrick Shaw-Stewart; lawyer Edward Horner; socialite Nancy Cunard and her friend Iris Tree. War destroyed the group and took the lives of Horner, Shaw-Stewart and Asquith. Duff Cooper had been one of the few surviving men of the group.

Duff, son of a GP, and Diana, daughter of the Duke of Rutland, were married in 1919 in a ceremony (which Sheila attended) which stopped the city and they had a son, John Julius, ten years later. But Duff would have at least five known affairs, including with the writer and American diplomat's wife Susan Mary Alsop, by whom he had an illegitimate son.

It is clear that he would gladly have added Sheila Milbanke

to his list of conquests, although their friendship had got off to a rocky start in 1916 when she had first arrived in London. As she recounted in her memoir, at a dinner at the home of the Duke and Duchess of Sutherland, given in her honour as an introduction to London society: "I sat between Geordie [the duke] and Duff Cooper. I had never met Duff before and he made me feel shy. I could not think of anything to say so I racked my brains and finally, for no reason, stupidly remarked: 'I hate people with big heads, don't you?'

"He stared at me and said: 'Mine is the largest in England.'

"His head was big, which I had not noticed. He never spoke to me again that evening. He went back to France and Carroll Carstairs told me that one evening in a dugout Duff saw a full-page photograph of me in the *Tatler*. He looked at it, tore it out, tore it into small pieces and ate it, muttering as he munched: 'I am eating one of the silliest girls I have ever met.'"

Two decades later all was forgiven, and Duff Cooper felt the opposite about Sheila, and the once-silly girl was now a target of his illicit affections. Duff had begun the game a few months earlier, when he wrote to tell of his devotion and reveal that he had eaten a photograph of her years before. She wrote back:

Darling Duff,
Your "devotion" could never be a bore or an embarrassment. I am so fond of you. If you think it nonsense and midsummer madness perhaps you'd better laugh yourself out of it a tiny bit, but not enough to have quite "calm dull feelings of friendship as in the past". I can't

bear to remember that when you ate my photograph years ago, it never even gave you indigestion!
Sheila

But her poem clearly suggested an interest on her part, or at least a delight in the attention, and during the next month there was a series of letters and notes back and forth as Duff Cooper attempted to woo her and she kept the hook baited. Ultimately she resisted the temptation. Even so, this literary dalliance was important enough for him to keep her notes and poems among his possessions. She would not return the compliment.

In mid-December he offered to buy her a Christmas present and she replied:

Darling Duff—thanks for your very sweet letter. I am very touched that you want to give me a Christmas present. I should love one (I'm funny that way!) but absolutely wouldn't go and buy one myself. What I should like better than anything is any sort of little animal made of that pale pink stone (I think it's quartz).
Love and best wishes for everything beautiful in 1935.
Sheila

A few days later the gift arrived and she wrote again:

Thank you darling Duff for my pink lady. I am crazy about her. She is too beautiful. I didn't mean anything half so grand when I said a little pink animal! But I love her. I am in London for one day and then go to Apsley for 2 weeks. Violet has asked me to stay for the

Belvoir Ball but I doubt that I shall be able to fix it. But may see you there.
Love and best wishes for 1935.
Sheila

Later, another note from her, this time with a little more candour:

Darling Duff,
Dear froggie could only have come from you. Thank you so much but you mustn't send me any more presents till next Xmas. I have been in bed with a vile cold. Don't forget lunch here next Thursday, 21st.
Love Sheila

Her fifth note in this series was simply dated "Sunday":

Darling Duff,
Thank you ever so much for the orchids. I can't make up my mind if I would rather you loved me more and saw me less or loved me less and saw me more.
Sheila

On the second page there was another ditty, this time with a warning from the past:

My darling Duff it's very plain to see
In every way you quite agree with me

I'm all for pure love without even kisses
For what one's never had one never misses!
Let's take a warning from our old friend Serge
And "beware of sex appeal and body urge".

Serge, of course, was Prince Obolensky, who had followed Sheila to Australia in 1920 and on the Port Said docks had declared his love. Even though she ultimately rejected Duff's advances, she was playing a dangerous game, just six years after marrying Sir John Milbanke. Was she unhappy, realising that it was a mistake to marry a younger man? Or was she just titillated by the attentions of an older man? There was no indication of the former, even though her husband was abroad for weeks at a time, travelling as an investment banker with a company called the British Foreign and Colonial Corporation.

Of all Sheila's close friends and even her English relatives, Diana Cooper would be one of the few who remained faithfully married to her first and only husband. She accepted Duff's philandering ways, explaining his many lovers to her son in this way: "They were the flowers, but I was the tree." Sheila had already been unfaithful during her turbulent marriage with Loughborough; Freda Dudley Ward would marry twice and have a fifteen-year affair with the Prince of Wales; Poppy Thursby (formerly Poppy Baring) and Edwina Mountbatten both remained married, but were promiscuous, as were the Dukes of Sutherland and Westminster; Millicent, Duchess of Sutherland, married three times and the Countess of Warwick (the wife of Lord Brooke) was known as the "Babbling Brooke" because she couldn't keep quiet about her liaisons. And so the list went on.

———•••———

Her exchange with Duff Cooper would not be the only time that Sheila would resort to verse to explain a subtle sexual quandary. One Easter in the 1940s, alone at the Milbanke property Brook House in Berkshire, she wrote to a friend, Georgia Sitwell. At the end of the letter she added a ditty she had written about being the wife of a club member at London's most famous gentleman's club, White's. It was entitled "To all 'White's Club Wives' from and by one of them!"

I'm just a little White's Club Wife,
my husband's very kind
I wait outside "the club" for hours
I really don't MUCH mind

I watch the big St James's clock
to pass the time away
but I know he's talking business,
and it isn't every day!

The policemen often grumble
and say the cars "must scram"
but when I tell my husband that
he doesn't give a damn.

Sheila

We seldom go to nightclubs
he doesn't like it much
he still prefers his billiards
with "old Baghdad" and such.

He is often late for dinner
and he says he's met a bloke
and he simply had to listen
to a very funny joke.

But we really mustn't grumble
for when the cat's away
it gives the "Little White's Club Wives"
a lot of time to play.

White's was among the most exclusive clubs in London, opened in 1693 by an Italian immigrant, Franco Bianco, to sell one of the rarest pleasures of the time—hot chocolate—and originally known as Mrs White's Chocolate House. By the early 18th century it had been turned into a gentleman's club and had become notorious for its gambling, criticised by the author Jonathon Swift as "the bane of half the English nobility".

It would continue to be both a pleasure and a problem for the idle rich as well as a place of legend, with members such as the dandy Beau Brummell, and exotic betting including the outcome of battles during the French Revolution and the Napoleonic Wars. Perhaps the most famous was when Lord Alvanley bet £3000 with a friend named Pierrepoint as to which raindrop would first reach the bottom of a window pane.

Loughie had been a member, courtesy of his father, as was Buffles, who had begun to tire of the endless round of balls and dinners, instead preferring the club and his male friends. It came to a head one night when they had dined in a private house along the prestigious Carlton House terrace before making their way to Buckingham Palace for a royal function: "All the men were in court dress or in uniform and the ladies wore tiaras and much finery. We arrived at the ball and as we were walking up the staircase Buffles turned to me and said: 'The whole place stinks of mothballs. I am going to play billiards at White's.' And he did!"

There were dents and scuff marks appearing on Buffles' shining armour as the binding ingredient of their relationship—physical attraction—began to wear thin, although Sheila seemed willing to look past them, perhaps mindful of her continuing regret about the demise of Loughie.

Buffles had lost a court dispute over payment of fees for stabling and managing his polo ponies and was also involved in an early morning scuffle outside a central London nightclub. Buffles and two others were arrested and charged with "making use of insulting words and behaviour". They appeared at the Marlborough Police Court a few days later, where the arresting officer gave evidence that he'd noticed them outside the Cabaret Club in Noel Street just before 1 a.m.: "The men on the door refused them admission. They became abusive and refused to go away and I was obliged to take them into custody. They had been drinking." The magistrate placed them on a six-month good behaviour bond.

Then there was his gambling, although a moderate version of the tragic Loughie's, observed at a new beachfront casino in Cannes, and which then appeared in the social pages of the *Express*:

Everyone, it seems, was there. This implies, I need scarcely say, the presence of Sir John Milbanke who sat at the principal baccarat table, partly hidden by a wall of ten thousand franc plaques. Nor, in spite of all the trumpets blown by the syndicate holding the bank, did the wall crumble away. The alternative reputation of "Buffles", the boxing baronet, is thus enhanced by his prowess as a baccarat bank-buster.

But there were also times that Sheila was proud of her husband, recalling the night that forty couples stayed with the Duke and Duchess of Westminster during the running of the Grand National: "Winston Churchill was among them, as was his son Randolph who was about 18 and very beautiful. He was, however, also tiresome and argued with everyone. One evening he became so obnoxious that several of the elder men decided to de-bag him [pull down his trousers in public] and fling him in the lake to teach him a lesson and improve his character."

Then Buffles intervened, insisting that because his father had been a protector of Winston Churchill at high school he would do the same for his son. Sir Claude de Crespigny took up the challenge: "They chose my huge bedroom for the event. I had gone to bed and was half asleep when Buffles told me what was about to happen. They fought for some time, stripped to the waist with no boxing gloves. I can't remember who the referee was. Anyhow, Buffles won, on points, so no one could touch Randolph."

Even so, Sheila could not resist the attention of other men who continued to crowd around a woman nearing her fortieth birthday, such as the night in 1935 that a young aristocrat named Seymour Berry asked her to dance at the nightclub Ciro's. He was "dark and attractive" and at twenty-six years old was almost fourteen years her junior: "I told him I had been trying unsuccessfully to force Buffles onto the dance floor all evening. 'They must be mad,' he replied. We danced for a long time."

Seymour would appear frequently over the next few years at functions and weekends, showering Sheila with gifts including a treasured Yorkshire terrier nicknamed the Vocal Muff and the Barking Chrysanthemum because of her high-pitched bark: "She was photographed several times for *Vogue*."

He was not alone. Sheila would be surrounded by would-be suitors on visits abroad with friends like Jeanie Norton: "There were trips to Paris—crazy evenings when Jeanie and I would get back to the Ritz about 5 a.m. and be seen to the lift by . . . various young men. They would buy dozens of red roses as we left Montmartre and scatter the petals on the floor to make a path for us to walk on. The night porter always enjoyed this—so did we."

Sheila

The friendships were always coy or merely flirtatious and, insisted Sheila, not a threat to her marriage despite the shadow of doubt that had begun to encroach into a relationship dulled by the routine of marriage: "Buffles had a good job as a financial adviser. He was sweet and kind to me and a wonderful stepfather to Tony and Peter, who were now both at Eton, and adored him. Our lives were full but we hardly seemed to be alone together anymore."

21

YOU'D BETTER ASK MRS SIMPSON

The first week of April 1934 was promising for the bloodstock agency H. Chisholm and Co. The Saturday opening of Sydney's autumn racing season had been a great success; the hopeful early signs of economic recovery from the Great Depression were reflected in the numbers through the Randwick turnstiles and the fashions were flaunted.

Men wrapped up against the misty rain in camel hair coats and Donegal and Harris tweeds while the women ignored the weather conditions to show off their millinery, from velvet, wide-brimmed Mae West hats and tiny skull caps to creations inspired by the Dutch bonnet and Tudor cap, the curate's hat, the pillbox and halo, the fez, Tyrolese, the mortarboard and even the military forage cap.

Over the next six days, crowds flocked to the company's yards, built conveniently next door to the racecourse, for three sales.

In the first sale, hundreds of spectators and prospective buyers spilled out into nearby passageways as they eagerly snapped up the 104 promising young horses paraded.

Then, three days later, the crowds returned when the Chisholm family's partners, William Inglis & Son, with whom the family company had merged a few months earlier, were forced to seat buyers on the grass alongside the 138 horses up for sale. The final sale of the week—another 140 lots—started slowly as the rain came down but brightened with the weather in the afternoon, and by the evening all but a handful had been bought at the best prices in years.

When Harry Chisholm died in 1927 neither of his two sons wanted to leave their own rural properties to run the operation—Jack was up north in Queensland running cattle, while Roy ran brood mares down south at Braidwood, near Goulburn, where he was a successful amateur rider and polo player. Instead, both brothers were content to have the family business managed by the managers who had been put in place by their father. But that had changed as times got tough in the Depression years and Roy had reluctantly agreed to move to the city permanently, selling the Braidwood property and buying a house in Macleay Street, Potts Point, just up the road from his mother, Margaret.

But this settled family situation was about to change. On the evening of Friday April 6, Roy Chisholm was feeling tired but satisfied as the yards were being cleaned; the animals, penned for the night, would be picked up by their new owners the following day. But before he could go home, Roy had a meeting with his insurance agent to complete documentation for the policy, which had fallen due. His sons, Bruce and Tony, then aged seven and ten respectively, were at home with their mother and thus not privy to the conversation that followed, but it would become part of the sad family folklore in years to come. Bruce still remembered the night seven decades later: "I know that Dad had an argument with the insurance agent and sent him off, saying he would think about it over the weekend and re-insure on the Monday. But the whole place burned to the ground on the Saturday and everyone lost their money."

Bruce Chisholm knew the Randwick yards well. The brothers had often spent time there helping out and watching the horses, some of whom were among the nation's finest racehorses. One event that would always shine in his memory was the morning Roy Chisholm hoisted his then three-year-old son onto the back of the red wonder horse, Phar Lap, and led him slowly around the exercise ring. The champion had just finished eighth in the 1931 Melbourne Cup (after winning the 1930 race) and was being stabled ahead of a journey to the United States where he would win the world's richest race before dying suddenly, creating a sporting legend.

The champion thoroughbred Chatham, winner of eighteen major races, was one of 200 horses housed inside the yards and at the nearby stables opposite Centennial Park. When Roy Chisholm went home that night, he was unaware that he'd walked past a smouldering cigar butt, which lay hidden in the coir matting he'd installed in the ring to make it easier on the hooves of the horses. Investigators would blame one of the buyers as the likely culprit for flicking or dropping the cigar, which smouldered for hours before its heat took hold and created a small flame. Then, fanned by a rising breeze through the building, the fire had grown and swept toward the stables, where the horses, sensing the danger, began to rear and shriek.

In the early hours of the morning Mrs Sweeney, wife of the stable foreman, who was sleeping, with her two-year-old son, in a bungalow next door to the stables, was woken by the noise and the glare. As she recounted a few days later to a reporter from *The Sydney Morning Herald*:

> I saw flames leap through my bedroom window and the curtains catch alight. I screamed "Fire!" to my husband, who was sleeping in another room, and took my son out to the back yard. The fire had got a hold on the side of the house. The window panes cracked with the heat, and some of the furniture in my bedroom and the living room was charred. My husband dashed buckets of water onto the flames, and threw burning cushions and other articles out of the windows. The wind was blowing the fire from the stables straight on to our house at first, but afterwards, fortunately for us, its direction changed. The heat in the house was terrible.

The timber sale ring, plus the adjoining offices and dining room, were a sheet of flames when the first fire truck pulled up thirty minutes later; the night sky was lit up for miles around. A group of apprentice jockeys and stable hands in another part of the complex were woken by the desperate whinnying of the fear-maddened horses in the stables alongside them.

Fifteen-year-old Cyril Heath roused his colleagues and the staff, and then watched as stable manager Bob May and two firemen dashed along the narrow passage between the yearling stables and the sale ring. Half choked by smoke and scorched by the intense heat from the flames alongside and above them, they wrenched open the stable doors and began dragging the young horses out into the open.

One horse was dragged out of its burning stall into the passageway, only to break away and run madly back into the burning sale ring. Its body was found the next day. Two other yearlings were roasted to death in their stalls, the men unable to reach them as they and a growing band of staff and volunteers pulled the other horses to safety. Among them was Chatham, who would go on to win the Doncaster Handicap a week later.

Two city fire brigades joined their colleagues from Randwick. A change in the wind's direction saved other businesses and horses that flanked the Chisholm yards, but even so it took more than three hours for the three brigades to bring the blaze under control. By then it was too late to save Roy's establishment: dawn revealed the blackened, charred remains of the sale ring and stables. The remains of his dead horses were a horrific sight. Six months later the land and its still-blackened buildings were sold at auction, raising barely £2500. A family dynasty lay in ruins.

Life had changed suddenly and irrevocably for the Chisholms, and Roy's young family in particular. They were far from destitute but Roy had to find work, a psychological struggle for a man now aged in his mid-forties. Or perhaps it provided an excuse to get back to the land, which he now must have wished he'd never left. It came as no surprise when he went bush "looking for country" with a cousin as the Randwick land was being sold.

At first Roy looked for pastoral land in central Queensland, near where Jack had settled after the war, before travelling across to the Northern Territory where he found a promising station at Roper River, 450 kilometres south of Darwin.

Roy returned to Sydney and approached another pastoralist, named Tom Holt, who had several properties on the Liverpool Plains, to see if he was interested in buying the Roper River lease in a 50/50 partnership. Roy would run the place as part of the bargain, and so Holt agreed. Roy wanted Mollee and the boys to go with him but she was concerned about schooling in the remote central desert and decided to remain in Sydney until Tony and Bruce had finished their education. They would go to a preparatory school in Edgecliff and then enrol at Scots College in Bellevue Hill.

For Roy, outback station life could not have been more different from his previous existence in Sydney—it was located in harsh and isolated terrain, the nearest humanity being a tiny settlement called Mataranka. But Roy's entrepreneurial spirit had not dulled despite his misfortune and within a year, having travelled to Singapore to establish contacts, he was negotiating live cattle shipments through the port of Darwin to Asia. He later tried to create an abattoir industry.

The Chisholm Arms, as the Roper River station was dubbed by a Royal Flying Doctor pilot, quickly became a haven of domesticity in the wilderness, with flower-laden gardens, kerosene refrigerators and two wireless telephones. For Roy, it had everything but his wife.

It had been a tumultuous time for Mollee, losing not only the business but her parents, who had died within two months of one another later in 1934. She moved into a big apartment in Elizabeth Bay and took a job at the David Jones department store in the city, where she found a niche as floor manager of the dress department, a position that made the best use of her society contacts. She was later poached by businessman Sam McMahon (whose brother William would become Australian Prime Minister) to run his society dress shop.

While Mollee's husband made headlines in the north of Australia as a man attempting single-handedly to rejuvenate the cattle industry, she was back in the social pages as a fashion leader. The story of her friendship with the Prince of Wales got a re-run later that year when Edward's younger brother Prince George, the Duke of Kent, toured Australia. It happened again in 1936, when "David" became King Edward VIII and *The Australian Women's Weekly* ran a feature on the only child in Australia with a royal godparent. Tony Chisholm was almost thirteen years old when the story appeared, photographed sitting in the backyard of their home, his arm protectively around nine-year-old Bruce.

The accompanying story repeated the details of the prince's visit: his meeting Mollee at the suggestion of Sheila, and their subsequent informal and private meetings at Brooksby. The most compelling detail, however, was not in the words but in the accompanying pictures: Tony Chisholm was the spitting image of his royal godfather. He had blond hair, whereas his mother, father and brother were dark, and his head had a gentle tilt with a lop-sided, self-effacing smile. Could he actually be the bastard child of the new King of England? The question was not so much stated as implied. It was clearly not the case, given that Tony Chisholm had been born three years after the prince had left Sydney, but the story would fester for years.

———

Wallis Simpson was a divisive presence in London society from the moment in 1934 when she won the undivided attention of the Prince of Wales. Until then, Edward had maintained a detached relationship with Freda Dudley Ward which had also allowed a string of other brief affairs. His private secretary Alan Lascelles would later describe the prince as being "continuously in the throes of one shattering and absorbing love affair after another (not to mention a number of street-corner affairs)".

In 1930 Edward accepted Sheila's invitation to the Derby Ball but only if Freda also attended—"that's a condition", he wrote—and as late as 1931 he was declaring his love for Freda in letters. But it overlapped an affair with Lady Thelma Furness, an American-born actress and young, bored wife of shipping magnate Viscount Marmaduke Furness, whom he had met in 1929 while handing out ribbons at an agricultural show in Leicester. A few weeks later she attended an ice carnival and dance with the prince and Sheila Milbanke. The affair would last until 1934 when, in January, Lady Furness had to travel to New York to visit her sick sister, Gloria Vanderbilt.

In her memoir, Lady Furness described how she asked her close friend, another American, Wallis Simpson, to "look after him while I'm away. See that he doesn't get into any mischief." Lady Furness had already introduced Edward to Wallis (and her husband Ernest) several years before and had been unaware that her friend had already been flirting with the prince. Thelma's trust was misplaced and by the time she returned a few weeks later, her disloyal friend and secret rival had swooped.

On reflection, the basis of Edward's attraction to the spare American divorcee was obvious. Wallis was not unlike Freda Dudley Ward in appearance—slim and severe—and, more importantly, was almost maternal in her command over him. He had set down his emotional needs quite plainly in an early letter he wrote to Freda in 1918, in which he said in part: "I think I'm the kind of man who needs a certain amount of cruelty without which he gets abominably spoiled and soft!! I feel that is what the matter is with me."

Wallis Simpson took the same, scolding approach with Edward as Freda had done on occasion. This was something many saw as domineering, but it had been a frequent ingredient in the prince's earlier attraction to older women, unlike the much younger and demure Lady Furness.

It was Wallis's overt influence over Edward that polarised those in society who knew of the affair in the three years before it became public and ended in his abdication and exile. And yet most of those in the know were politic enough to keep their feelings hidden from Edward. Chips Channon was one who played both sides, commenting in his diaries after hosting a 1935 luncheon "to do a politesse" to Mrs Simpson: "She is a jolly, plain, intelligent, quiet, unpretentious and unprepossessing little woman, but as I wrote to Paul of Yugoslavia today, she has already the air of a personage who walks into a room as though she almost expected to be curtsied to . . . She has complete power over the Prince of Wales."

Lady Nancy Astor, a fellow American socialite, was less charitable. In a series of entries in her diary, Britain's first woman MP, who was famed for her verbal clashes with Winston Churchill, wrote:

June 5, 1934

Dining at Chips & Honor's was fun—everyone in tiaras and on to the Derby Ball charity—It is Sheila Milbanke's last "go" as chairwoman—she had been at it for seven years—The Prince of Wales let her down by not attending . . . Guess he was busy with his new "bit" Mrs Simpson—it's all so funny as she was Thelma's best girl friend, and now she steals the Prince away from Thelma—Mrs S is a very déclassé American married to a 4th rate Englishman—the Prince is sinking lower and lower in his taste in women.

June 8

At Portia's for weekend at Holwood—Prince George, Marina, Sheila Milbanke and Seymour Berry make up our party. Prince George seems very restless—she is most attractive and sweet (with child). They simply loathe the Prince of Wales' attitude, the world in general and his "pushing" of Mrs. Simpson about. It was a pleasant weekend and I enjoyed the arguments. Wales refused point blank to go to the Court Balls unless Mrs. Simpson was given an invitation. That did make London's older crowd indignant. Wales made a statement several years ago that he hated and was bored by the English nobility—& he certainly shows it—by cutting most of his old friends and "hanging out" with whatever friends happen to be his mistress's at the time.

Lady Astor also predicted that Mrs Simpson would not last long as Edward's mistress and lamented the attitudes of her social contemporaries: "Everyone seems to have a new disease 'Simpsonitis' & 'sucking up' to dear Wally is the thing to do. Emerald Cunard heads the list as the biggest horse's ass, then Duff Cooper—it really strikes me as being ludicrous, all this toadying it is all so temporary."

But by mid-1936, with Edward settling into Buckingham Palace as the new king, she realised that "temporary" had been the wrong word. Although still a secret publicly, there was a growing sense among the royal court that Edward might try to marry the American divorcee, as Lady Astor conceded:

If I ever made a mistake in my life, I did when I said that "Queenie" Simpson would be "out" & a new one in—I'm afraid when a man reaches 42 (as our monarch is) & if he loves a plain woman his own age—it is a thing that will last—(also for the country). Mrs Simpson is lucky & benefits where all the others have lost—She has over 100,000 pounds worth of jewels from him! To say nothing of clothes & furs & things she never had before.

Sheila Milbanke had been ambivalent about Wallis until the eve of the 1934 Derby Ball, an event which she regarded as a personal achievement and which had raised tens of thousands of pounds for the hospital over the years, the equivalent of several million dollars in modern terms. She would joke about it being like delivering a baby because it took nine months to arrange from planning and sending out requests, to organising the ticketing, guests and entertainment.

The appearance of the Prince of Wales was a critical element of its success each year, and he had again promised to attend so his presence was advertised as sales boomed. A few days before the event a friend issued Sheila a warning: "If you want the prince this year then you'd better write and ask Mrs Simpson."

"I was surprised because he had never failed me yet, and come to the ball every year since the Lindbergh occasion," she recalled thinking before replying, testily:

"Why should I write to Mrs Simpson whom I have never met?"

Her friend sighed: "Well, I have warned you."

The morning before the event she rang the prince and asked him about rumours that he would not be attending: "He assured me the rumour was unfounded." But at a pre-ball dinner that night she sat next to Prince George, who passed her a note under the table. She read, discreetly. "It was from the Prince of Wales and was to this effect: *Cannot be at the ball tonight as I am going to the country. Enclose cheque for £100, which I am sure will be more useful to the hospital than my company.*

"I was disappointed to say the least of it. Hundreds of tickets had been sold, mostly because people adored the Prince of Wales and knew he would be there. It was fooling the public. I was not very happy. What should I do?

"It was too late to ask anyone's advice so I decided to make an announcement on arrival. I explained that the Prince of Wales had been unavoidably detained, which was a great disappointment to us all, but that I had a pleasant surprise—his cheque for £100, which I waved in the air. Would anyone care to follow suit? Who else would give the hospital £100? I soon had many cheques."

Although she had rescued the situation from an embarrassing snub, the incident highlighted the change in the relationship between Edward and Sheila, the prince so smitten by Wallis Simpson that he was prepared to end, or at least distance himself from friendships that had once been the centre of his world. It was little wonder that Mrs Simpson was despised by much of London society, and Sheila would be one of the few who, in later years, would forgive.

22

POOR LITTLE RICH GIRL

Sheila Milbanke and Barbara Hutton holidayed together on the French Riviera in August of 1935, as persistent rain further north threatened to ruin the European summer and forced a larger-than-usual flock of holidaymakers south, filling hotels and casinos and crowding beaches from Cannes to Monte Carlo. They met again a month later, this time in Versailles, where they both attended a lavish dinner of oysters and lemon sole at the fabulous Villa Trianon where the hostess Lady Elsie Mendl, better known as the American actress and heiress Elsie de Wolfe, often played gin rummy and drank cocktails in a lake-size bath surrounded by leopard-skin-upholstered banquettes.

Sheila and Barbara had been introduced in June, when the young American attended the Derby Ball and promptly made a scene by accusing others of being stingy during the charity auction. Sheila quickly forgave her this faux pas and perhaps even enjoyed her audacious behaviour. After all, both women were colonial interlopers and uninhibited by an establishment European society that accepted few from outside their comfort zone.

Barbara Hutton, or rather Countess Haugwitz-Reventlow as she had become earlier in the year by marrying a Danish aristocrat, was one of the world's wealthiest women, having inherited the US$42 million supermarket five-and-ten-cent Woolworth fortune on her twenty-first birthday in 1933. This wealth had so far not brought happiness to a life already marred by the suicide of her mother when she was aged just five. She'd been dubbed the "Poor Little Rich Girl" by the US media; they were disdainful of the way in which her wealth was being flaunted at the height of the Depression, including her $60,000 twenty-first birthday party when the average worker earned $1500 a year, a car cost $600 and a house little more than $3000.

Barbara was now twenty-three years old and pregnant to her second husband, the controlling and ultimately abusive Count Court von Haugwitz-Reventlow. The morning after the Mendl dinner party, she visited the fashion queen Coco Chanel, whose salon at 31 Rue Cambon was across the road from the Ritz Hotel in the heart of Paris, where she was fitted for maternity wear.

By contrast, Sheila was about to turn forty, with two teenage sons and an established second marriage. Both women were beautiful, vivacious and opinionated, but it was Barbara's vulnerability that helped them click. Sheila recognised the psychological frailty of the young heiress and the countess sensed the strength and independence of a woman who had emerged successfully from an abusive relationship. A friendship was cemented and it would prove to be among the strangest in Sheila's life.

The media was infatuated by the countess's life. She had been forced to flee her native country the year before, because of the almost daily running commentary on the cost of her lifestyle amid the continuing economic hardship there, but there would be no respite for her in Europe, where journalists leaned over fences to photograph her playing tennis and followed her to daytime hairdressing appointments or shopping sprees on the Rue du Faubourg Saint-Honoré before she went off to lunch at Maxim's. Likewise at night, she would be snapped as she arrived at the opera or the ballet, before dining and dancing at Le Pré Catelan.

By September, Barbara's physicians had become concerned about her health, which suffered from the combination of her hectic social calendar and the stress of all the media attention; they suggested she seek sanctuary elsewhere. She then turned to her new friend, who suggested London as a place where she could feel safe and secluded; Sheila arranged for the count and countess to move into a house in Hyde Park Gardens owned by a friend of hers, Mrs Wakefield-Saunders, until the baby was born..

The move seemed to work and the countess's health gradually improved under the care of Dr Cedric Sydney Lane-Roberts, the chief of obstetrics at the Royal Northern Hospital, where Sheila was still chair of the ladies committee and its principal fundraiser. As a precaution, a home birth was advised; an upstairs bedroom was stripped and turned into a delivery room using equipment borrowed from the hospital, including operating lights hooked up to a portable generator. Sheila oversaw the transformation. Another bedroom on the fourth floor of the Regency mansion became the nursery, and two more would provide accommodation for a nurse maid and baby nurse.

At the last minute the countess demanded to have the baby delivered by caesarean section, a procedure that was becoming more common among the upper class. Her son was seemingly born without incident the next day, but soon afterwards Barbara fell into a coma and began haemorrhaging from a ruptured blood vessel in her abdomen. Her life was in danger and she required an emergency operation; for the second time, the bedroom operating room was needed, this time to save a life rather than to begin one.

The Prince of Wales' personal physician, Lord Horder, was called in and a priest hovered as Sheila arranged for society friends to give blood, in case Barbara needed a transfusion. The media, now aware of the emergency, reported her life-and-death progress daily and prepared obituaries in case she did not wake from her coma. It took four days before she was out of danger.

But the drama was only just beginning. While Barbara was still recuperating, an anonymous hand-written note was delivered to the house, containing a threat to kidnap the child she had named Lance (after the knight, Sir Lancelot). Police foiled what turned out to be a timid extortion attempt from a bungling textile fitter who was after some quick cash, but the countess was very mindful of the infamous kidnapping of Charles Lindbergh's son four years earlier and that was enough for her to begin a hunt for a more secure house.

After searching outside London as far as Cornwall and Northumberland, the Haugwitz-Reventlows found an estate in the heart of the city. St Dunstan's Lodge stood on the outer circle of Regent's Park, a few kilometres north of the city centre, on what had once formed part of the royal hunting grounds. It had since been used by a succession of aristocrats and for the rehabilitation of British servicemen during the Great War, but the main building had been badly damaged by fire and it was about to be auctioned.

They bought the property but, rather than repair the Regency house, they chose to demolish and rebuild. Their red-brick, Georgian-style three-storey mansion boasted thirty-five rooms, including ten bathrooms, indoor and outdoor swimming pools, a ten-car garage, a library, music room, billiards parlour, gymnasium and a cold storage unit for the countess's fur coats. It sat on more than 12 acres, giving it the largest private garden in London after Buckingham Palace. Security provisions were equally excessive—a series of underground tunnels and a strong room, bullet-proof windows, remote control cameras, fences and a kidnap alarm.

Construction took a year, after which Barbara again called on Sheila Milbanke's advice, this time to help design and furnish the vast interiors. More than US$2 million would be spent on items such as the gold room's 24-carat ornaments, the hand-painted 18th-century wallpaper in the garden room, the wall-mounted cases full of rare Chinese porcelain and jade, the green-and-ivory marbled bathrooms and the calfskin-lined nursery for Lance. The hallways were draped with oriental embroideries while several paintings by the Venetian landscape painter Canaletto hung in a downstairs lounge room. Persian carpets covered the oak floors in rooms filled with Louis XIV and XV furniture.

When the small family moved into the oversized house, which Barbara had renamed Winfield House after her grandfather, Frank, who'd founded the Woolworth company, they had to hire a staff of thirty.

But the opulence would not buy them the protection or happiness the heiress desired. Within weeks, newspaper photographers would be perched on platforms built outside the mansion gates, using massive camera lenses known as Long Toms, which had been used by German Zeppelins during the Great War. With these they snapped photos of the family inside their sanctuary, particularly the toddler Lance as he wandered the vast grounds, an only child surrounded by paid carers and warring parents. History appeared to be repeating itself for Barbara Hutton.

Sheila made no mention of Barbara Hutton in her memoir, despite their close relationship and the publicity it received at the time. It was the same attitude she took to numerous friendships with important or controversial figures. She either regarded them as private affairs, and off-limits even for a document to be read by others after her own death, or she simply didn't see the significance amid the wash of famous names.

Around the time she was working on the interiors of Winfield House there were several significant events which she also glossed over, in particular the death of King George V and the ascension to the throne of Edward: "King George V died," she would write. "The Prince of Wales became King Edward VIII. The King is dead, long live the King."

She watched the old king's funeral procession from a window at St James's Palace, although clearly upset that she had not been invited to Buckingham Palace because Edward, the new king, had bowed to his mistress's demand that "all the best rooms in the palace are for Mrs Simpson and her party. We were not invited as she was not a friend of ours."

June 11, 1936
"When royalty comes in, friendship flies out of the window," Sheila Milbanke said on the telephone and how right she is: tonight's dinner has cost me Laura's friendship, at least for the moment. She is still in a rage. I rang her up, repeated my invitation for her to come in after dinner and she rudely refused . . .

As Henry "Chips" Channon noted in his diary, he had been in a panic. Edward VIII, King of England, was arriving for dinner that evening and instead of attending to details of the most important party he'd ever hosted, he was trying to explain to an irate society hostess, Laura Corrigan, why she hadn't been invited but could arrive after the meal.

Dubbed "America's Salon Queen", Mrs Corrigan was a

former waitress who had clambered up the social ladder, firstly as a society reporter and then by marrying a gullible doctor, whom she'd subsequently traded in for the wealthy son of a steel magnate, before moving to London, where she became known as the "Social General". Sheila Milbanke—"calm, lovely, gentle, restful and perfect . . . with a classic, oval face, dark brown eyes and auburn hair, she had a 'smile like a Lely court beauty'", as Channon described her—had intervened on his behalf, but she had not placated Mrs Corrigan. Still, the dinner went off splendidly.

June 12

I woke feeling terribly ill and old and world weary, the result of too much champagne. Everyone rang up to say how successful our party had been. "A wow", as Diana [Cooper] put it. Philip Sassoon, Barbie Wallace and others wrote. Wallis Simpson said the King had much enjoyed his dinner with us. Laura Corrigan was freezingly polite and is still deeply hurt over last night's party but one really invites the King's friends to meet him, not one's own. Oh social rows! There is nothing so trivial and yet nothing so wounding and discouraging.

The son of a Chicago businessman, Channon had arrived in London in 1920 and stayed, becoming a loud critic of the culture of his birthplace as a threat to European and British civilisation. He took citizenship and in 1933 completed the transition by marrying brewing heiress Lady Honor Guinness. Two years later he entered parliament, starting a long but unspectacular political career as a Conservative MP. His nickname, it was said, came from his introduction of the potato chip to London society cocktail parties.

He would become best known as one of the most influential political and social diarists of the 20th century, and an unapologetic social climber—a male version of Laura Corrigan, the woman he did not invite to dinner to meet the new king. "I am riveted by lust, furniture, glamour, society and jewels. I am an excellent organiser and have a will of iron; I can only be appealed to through my vanity," he once confessed.

Perhaps this was best illustrated by the occasion in 1932 when, while still a bachelor, he hired Winston Churchill's nephew John to paint onto the walls of his dining room a fresco depicting eighty of his closest friends as a "Florentine garden party of the Renaissance period". The figures, all in medieval dress, included the Prince and Princess of Yugoslavia, Sheila Milbanke, Poppy Thursby, Prince and Princess Obolensky, Lady Diana Cooper and her husband, Lady Emerald Cunard, Lady Cavendish and Randolph Churchill, who henceforth could gaze up at themselves there as they sat around his table for dinner.

His extravagance would continue three years later, when he and his new wife bought a home at No. 5 Belgrave Square, next door to the Duke of Kent: "It's not too grand and is dirt cheap compared with all the other houses we have seen. It has a distinguished air and we will make it gay and comfortable." He was true to his word, creating a rococo extravaganza, which featured a dining room he described as "a symphony in blue and silver, cascades of aquamarine, approached from an ochre and silver gallery". And he was keen to show it off.

And if his over-indulgence in luxury was not enough to impress, Channon further embedded himself into high society when his only child was born in 1935; he named him Paul, after his friend the prince, and invited the influential to be his son's godparents, among them Sheila Milbanke.

His June 1936 dinner was not the last time King Edward came to dinner, nor the last time that Sheila Milbanke was a conduit. On November 19 he famously hosted another dinner for the King and Mrs Simpson, attended by Prince Paul and Princess Olga of Yugoslavia, and the Duke of Kent and his wife Princess Marina of Greece and Denmark. Just three weeks later Edward abdicated.

England had spent the year under the reign of a rebel king, who had turned royalty on its head from the moment he'd reluctantly accepted the crown and watched the public proc-lamation of his accession from a window of St James's Palace, side by side with his married girlfriend.

King Edward VIII didn't fit the mould of an aloof and imperious monarch, declaring in his later memoir "a modest ambition to broaden the base of the monarchy: to make it a little more responsive to the changed circumstances of my times".

He'd rather dine with a small number of friends in private houses than host a dinner for hundreds at Buckingham Palace; he preferred to sit in a box at an evening performance of musical theatre in Covent Garden than to parade in the enclosure at Ascot on Cup Day. He had relinquished the crown after less than eleven months on the throne, choosing to spend the rest of his life with a woman favoured by few others; he had then driven to Portsmouth in a blue limousine, sitting side by side with his chauffeur, before sailing under the cover of darkness bound for Vienna.

It was a lonely exit, and one that Sheila followed closely, and with mixed feelings. She had watched "with amusement" those in society who had gone out of their way to curry favour with Wallis Simpson and, therefore, the new king: "When the abdication came naturally the sinking ship was deserted and, to my amazement, the rats loudly proclaimed they had hardly known her. It was a disgusting performance."

She and Buffles drove around the empty streets of London after Edward's radio announcement. She wrote: "I could not even dream of trying to describe one's feelings over the Abdication. We all felt it deeply and the Empire was really rocked. Surely, we thought, there must be some demonstration, some excitement somewhere. Nothing. All quiet outside the Duke and Duchess of York's house in Piccadilly, all quiet outside Buckingham Palace. We went home, disappointed.

"Really, the British are extraordinary and unpredictable. This event could not have happened so quietly, so calmly anywhere else in the world."

23

TIME CHANGES MANY THINGS

It was one of the strangest and yet most compelling parties anyone in American high society could recall. On January 16, 1937, gossip columnist and famed New York hostess Elsa Maxwell filled the glamorous Starlight Room on the nineteenth floor of the Waldorf Astoria Hotel in Park Avenue with animals and haystacks for her "Barnyard Frolic". Cattle were hoisted into the room inside a freight elevator, to graze in pens alongside a sty of well-fed pigs, a flock of sheep, some chickens, goats and wandering donkeys.

A robotic cow had been created, with udders that squirted champagne instead of milk, and a moss-covered well that winched up beer and cocktails. Human scarecrows delivered food to the guests; there was milking and square dancing, and even a champion hog caller, who could summon the pigs with his swinish imitations and had been hired as a competition judge. But, after a night of merriment, the hog caller took such offence at "these sassiety ladies smokin' and drinkin' on Sunday mornin'" that he sent his herd charging through the gilded room, scattering the guests. The front-page headline in the London *Daily Mirror* the next day read: "SCREAMING WOMEN CHASED BY PIGS AT FREAK BALL".

The 400 guests, described by the *Chicago Tribune* as "a nice balance between international society, Broadway, Hollywood and the seven lively arts", included not only the glitterati of New York, Las Vegas and Hollywood but selected members of London society, who had made the journey by ship just for the event. Among them were Cecil Beaton, the playwright Nöel Coward, the actor John Gielgud, Douglas Fairbanks' new wife Sylvia Ashley, and aristocrats Lady Colefax, Viscount and Viscountess Adare and Viscount Wimborne. Then there was Sheila Milbanke, whose attendance was trumpeted by the media on both sides of the Atlantic—by the English as a social triumph and by the Americans as if her RSVP was a national honour.

The party was seen as a great success by the press, almost as a sign of a hopeful re-emergence from hard economic times. After all, argued the *Oakland Tribune*, if the social elite were spending money again, even if it was with a sense of abandon, then perhaps the rest of society could look forward with some confidence to better times:

Noses that were so close to the grindstone for years are now lifted higher, and maids and beaux who almost heard the wolf yipping

Pilot Peter Loughborough was killed in a training accident on September 8, 1939, during the first few days of World War II. His mother struggled for years to come to terms with her youngest son's death.

Lady Sheila Milbanke as painted by Cecil Beaton in 1930, at the time he was compiling his ode to London's most beautiful women, *The Book of Beauty*.

A portrait of Lady Sheila Milbanke painted in the late 1930s by the celebrated British society painter and war artist Simon Elwes, RA (1902–1975). © Peter Elwes

Sheila could look as glamorous as the movie star she once wanted to be, as can be seen from this 1935 photograph by Madam Yevonde, which depicts Sheila as Penthesilea, the Queen of the Amazons. © Madame Yevonde Archive

Wartime Sheila, sans makeup and ballgowns, instead wearing the uniform of a volunteer. The six-year conflict had an enduring impact on her physically and psychologically.

Tony Loughborough, by now the Earl of Rosslyn, with his stepfather Sir John "Buffles" Milbanke in 1945, after they had returned home from World War II. Although both were safe, the marriage of Sheila and Buffles was a casualty of the conflict.

Sheila decided in 1948 to become a businesswoman and started a travel agency. She talked her way into opening a desk with two staff at the Fortnum & Mason department store in Piccadilly.

Sheila and her third husband, Prince Dimitri Romanoff, on their wedding day in 1954. The ceremony at a registry office was a far cry from her wedding to Buffles.

To Aunt Sheila,
with much love,
Karim.

Sheila counted royal families from across Europe in her social circles, including Aly Khan, son of the Aga Khan spiritual leader of Shia Imami Ismaili Muslims. Aly's son, Karim, became the Aga Khan in 1957 at the age of twenty. He gave her this photograph two years later, signed to "Aunt Sheila".

Sheila, the grandmother, reads to young children in 1960.

Sheila (second from right) was a frequent guest of the Duke and Duchess of Windsor at their homes in France, including this visit in the 1960s. Edward and Sheila were close friends for half a century.

Even aged in her late sixties Sheila, now Princess Dimitri, knew how to engage with a camera.

at the butler's heels are centering their interests upon celebrating a return of the "Age of Unreason". Like children suddenly released from school, the leaders have responded to their escape from the realities of life by a hysteria of fantastic entertainments.

But others were more cynical. *Fortune,* created at the beginning of the Great Depression and seen as a financial magazine with a social conscience, delivered a scathing critique of American social climbers in general and in particular Laura Corrigan, one of the guests of honour at the Maxwell event. The English aristocracy, opined *Fortune,* was being exploited:

The transatlantic method of climbing has recently been perfected by the discovery that British Society is much more quickly and directly purchasable by Americans (not by their own kind) than is New York. The reason is that the British cannot take seriously the fantastic idea that an American (or any other colonial, including the Australian bushman) could have a social position. They regard Americans as simple hearted savages with a penchant for providing free lunch for their betters. So our transatlantic climber opens a London house, begins giving big dinners for the proper people, and within a year is established as a London hostess. She can then invite her new friends to an American tour at her expense, loading them onto the *Queen Mary*, the first class bulging with barons, earls protruding from the portholes, dukes squatting hopefully on the lifeboats, and the scuppers awash with mere knights, all of them warmly anticipatory of several months' free board, room and laundry.

Among the newspaper tear-outs glued into Sheila's albums of memories is a photograph of her dressed in what appears to be a milkmaid outfit, alongside a darkly, handsome man wearing braces to fit in to the farmer theme who is chatting to her as she fixes her make-up. It was taken at the Barnyard Frolic party and published in an unidentified New York newspaper. At the bottom of the picture, Sheila had scrawled: "1937. Time changes many things!"

Her admirer's name was Stuart Symington, a businessman from Missouri who would rise to prominence as a politician who would serve as the United States' first Secretary of the Air Force under Harry Truman before becoming a US senator; Truman later backed him to be the Democrats' presidential candidate in 1960, but he lost the nomination to John F Kennedy.

Sheila had met him a week before the party, at a dinner organised in honour of her first visit to the US in eleven years. She had arrived to a huge placard on the dock with the message "WELCOME SHEILA" and a band playing "Rule Britannia", arranged by Serge Obolensky and Vincent Astor, two former love interests who would set the tone for the rest of a visit that would last three months.

At first she wasn't sure what to make of Symington. They argued over the abdication of King Edward and Wallis Simpson, whom he had known as Wallis Warfield when they were younger: "I didn't like him at first and felt he didn't like me," she reflected, although there was clearly a mutual attraction.

Sheila was in a vulnerable frame of mind, the marriage with Buffles clearly strained if their individual travel diaries through the second half of the 1930s were any indication. *The Times*, in particular, frequently published passing references to the travels of aristocrats in its "Court Circular" column and immigration authorities kept reasonably accurate records of their comings and goings. Not only was Sheila travelling internationally regularly by herself, or with Poppy Thursby, but Buffles was also travelling increasingly by himself, sometimes for business but equally for pleasure.

She made little mention of it in her memoir but it was clear that they were drifting apart: "Tony and Peter were more or less grown up—Tony at Oxford and Peter at the RAF College, Cranwell. Buffles was busy and often seemed preoccupied. Our lives were in rather a muddle."

The signs had been there some time. The previous year he had travelled, alone, to India and Iceland, attracting some publicity back in London by bringing back a salmon he'd caught and smoked before having it cooked in a West End restaurant. Sheila went to Cannes to spend time with Laura Corrigan, after which she partied at the Cowes Regatta with Poppy Thursby and then took the train to Scotland in September to spend time with her sons at the Rosslyn estate.

She had agreed to the New York trip with some reluctance, "although it seemed an opportunity to get away for a complete change"—a clear reference to the tension between her and Buffles. And now there was another handsome American giving her the rush.

Symington persisted, even when she went on a cruise through the West Indies aboard the Astor yacht *Nourmahal*, sending radiograms each day and turning up at Palm Beach when they landed a few weeks later: "We all went back to New York and he saw me off when I sailed for England a few weeks later. He gave me his book of [Robert] Browning's poems, which he'd had at school. Marked in red ink was:

"Love among the Ruins"
With their triumphs and their glories and the rest!
Love is best.

Sheila travelled back to England confused and hoping to forget about Stuart Symington but the reunion with Buffles back in London didn't help matters. During her absence Tony had almost bled to death from an accident at Oxford, Peter had been in hospital for a week after being knocked out in the boxing ring and the house had been damaged in a storm: "I decided I could never go away and leave them again," she wrote, a vow she did not keep.

Despite her misgivings about their marriage they had a happy summer, frequently travelling to the country to stay with friends including the Duke of Rutland at Belvoir Castle where Sheila delighted in watching Buffles and the duke fishing one evening after dinner still in tail-coats and white ties, and ignored what she would describe as "the ever-increasing rhythm of marching feet and the menace of war machines".

At a time when US society was exuberantly exploring the possibility of new social mountains to climb, London was moving in the opposite direction. The coronation in May 1937 of a second monarch in as many years would spark an array of old-fashioned grand social events on a scale unseen since the beginning of the century, and unlikely to be witnessed again. The Kings and Queens of the Commonwealth and Europe flocked to London for the celebration, and the finery of royalty—originally made obsolete by war, and then by the social freedom of the twenties and the frugality of the Depression—had once again returned to fashion.

Vogue magazine reported breathlessly on the seeming revival of a long-gone age:

No-one dreams of going to less than three places a night. We entertain and are entertained royally, officially and privately. The parties in private houses during this Coronation season are unique in our time, gay and romantic, with the fine old plate, the family livery and the supper cooked in the house. We watched the duchesses moving with their tiaras and trains up the green onyx staircase to dance again the old Strauss waltzes, under floodlit ceilings and a Congress-of-Vienna gaiety.

The French are giving the most overpowering parties with powdered footmen dressed as in Thackeray's time ... the Poles are concentrating on smaller, more numerous and choice dinner parties ... the Spaniards are keeping the flag flying at Belgrave Square and giving large luncheons ... the Japanese, the Scandinavians, the Brazilians, the Argentinians and the Greeks and countless others are all three-party deep. At least two charity balls are scheduled for each night until late July. There are hardy annuals like Lady Milbanke's very smart Derby Ball where there is always a strong contingent of well-known Americans . . .

In Edward's place came a younger king, who accepted not only his brother's crown but his coronation ceremony that had been delayed for a year—a day neither really wanted. But reluctance was all that they had in common. Where Edward was single and gregarious, Albert was a husband and father of two young daughters; a hesitant and shy man, he signalled his more conservative approach by adopting his father's royal name—George—rather than his own. He then judged his brother to have relinquished all rights to a royal title and refused to acknowledge his future wife, Wallis Simpson.

This new turn of events put Sheila Milbanke, daughter of a New South Wales grazier, in a unique position with two Kings of England. She knew both brothers intimately, having had an affair with one of them and having forged an enduring friendship with the other. She would remain a fierce supporter of Edward's rights once he became the Duke of Windsor, and this would later affect her relationship with the new king.

But all that was yet to come. After staying on in the United States in the wake of Elsa Maxwell's party, she renewed old acquaintances and then spent a month cruising the Caribbean aboard Vincent Astor's luxury yacht with a select group from the party, including Laura Corrigan. She finally arrived back in London in March, just as the social events began to swirl in the lead-up to the May 12 coronation.

In 1923 she'd missed Bertie's wedding, arriving a week too late from her failed attempt to save her first marriage in Australia; but now she was on the official coronation guest list, as another new round of Pond's advertisements proudly declared. She also had to finish arrangements for the Derby Ball, which would be held just a fortnight after the coronation.

But there would be more disappointment as Sheila was once again squeezed out of a front-row seat for a royal event. She did not get inside Westminster Abbey, blaming the omission on her husband's middle–ranking title although probably feeling it was due more to the new queen's understandable misgivings about inviting the king's former mistress.

Instead, she and Poppy sat outside Buckingham Palace waiting for the procession. "There was a long wait between processions so we decided to go and have a drink at the Ritz bar," she wrote. "We were still sitting there at the exact moment the new King and Queen were crowned."

London's "magic carpet ride" continued after the coronation, with Loughie's aunt Millicent hosting the main reception for the newly crowned King and Queen, as *Vogue* reported:

One of the great balls was the Duchess of Sutherland's at Hampden House for the new King and Queen, preceded by a dinner at Londonderry House where the great crowd gathered in Green Street, held back by bobbies. Entertaining monarchs at a private house introduces certain challenges, as the King and Queen were conducted by their hosts to special seats in the ballroom, all the women encountered on their way curtseying. A very pretty scene like a wheat-field in a wind as down they bend. With 40 tables of 12 in two dining rooms—the King sat in one and the Queen in another—each table had its own complete set of gold plate and red roses, the royal servants in blue livery and the enormous chandeliers completed the fairytale scene. The colourful scene looked exactly like a Sert fresco: orientally-jewelled Indian princes, Sultanas in saris and sables, foreign rulers and royalties, the black Prince of Ashanti, visitors in native dress or uniforms . . .

In spite of her reservations about Wallis Simpson, Sheila would almost certainly have been invited to the controversial wedding in France between Edward and Wallis on June 3, just three weeks after George VI's coronation, although, like all but a handful of the proposed guest list, she did not attend. After all, it clashed with her Derby Ball, this year held at Grosvenor House, at which Prince Henry (the Duke of Gloucester and later Governor-General of Australia) deputised for his older brother Edward and so maintained the event's royal patronage.

There were other social expectations in the days that followed the ball. She returned to Grosvenor House to attend a reception for the Maharaja of Kashmir and was then noticed at Ascot for the Derby on the same day as the Windsor wedding: "Lady Milbanke's navy blue dress and coat were worn with a black straw hat in a coolie style tied under the chin with a narrow ribbon," *The Times* reported.

But the snub—if that's what it was—was overlooked by the Duke and Duchess of Windsor who invited Sheila and Buffles to stay as guests during their two-month honeymoon, mostly spent at Wasserleonburg, a 14th-century castle in southern

Austria, owned by a cousin of Lord Dudley's—"a pleasant and peaceful summer . . . of mountain-climbing, fishing, golf, tennis, and sun-bathing by the swimming pool," as the duke later reported to a friend.

By mid-September Sheila had returned to London, unaware that Edward had controversially accepted an invitation to go to Germany and meet with Adolf Hitler, in an attempt to negotiate an appeasement deal that would avoid the coming war.

Sheila would recall her apprehension: "We were most of us so interested in the events at home that we didn't hear, or perhaps didn't want to hear, the ever-increasing menace of the war machines that were being built up so blatantly abroad."

But her thoughts soon turned to a threat of a different kind. Ag was ill and had been taken to a private Sydney hospital. She was not in immediate danger and had been unwell for some time; the previous year she'd cancelled "indefinitely" what had become a semi-regular trip to London to spend time with her daughter and grandsons.

The message to Sheila was clear. Memories of Harry Chisholm's death a decade before, when his wife and daughter were on the other side of the world, came flooding back. Her mother was now seventy-two years old, widowed and alone, with her two sons on remote cattle stations in the far-flung north of the continent and her daughter on the other side of the world. Sheila's life was now in London, but it was time to make a trip home.

24

A JOURNEY HOME

The journalist waited patiently for her subject, Lady Sheila Milbanke, who was quietening her Yorkshire terrier Sara Wara, the "morsel of silvery grey hair" who often became over-excited by visitors and guarded her mistress jealously. Like all good journalists, she used the extra time to take in her surroundings: the carefully constructed decor and style of its creator. It was October 1937 and the street trees outside were shedding in layers of yellow, orange and red. The effect was as beautiful in its own way as the spring blaze or the summer greens. Changing, always changing:

The mercurial temperament of this outstanding Australian is best mirrored in the atmosphere of her home. The Milbankes formerly had a country home in Ireland, but have now given it up. No. 82 Hamilton Terrace [St Johns Wood] is a solid mansion standing back from the road, unlike so many London houses. Through a little green door you walk to the front door, through a narrow glassed-in tunnel, roofed picturesquely with the spreading branches of a huge, spreading vine laden with fruit and green leaves. As you enter, the subtle scent of potpourri drifts out from the sitting-room with its family portraits on the walls, for bowls of it are placed at intervals to give off sweet perfume, constantly renewed. There is a collection of rose quartz, lovely things from China collected piece by piece. The dining room, looking out over serene green lawns and trees shedding autumn leaves, is remarkable for its huge, plate-glass window, occupying almost an entire wall, which gives an almost theatrical effect to the room. Lady Milbanke is evidently fond of mirror glass, for I noted several small articles of furniture constructed in this material. Flexible, joined mats of mirror glass for the dining table were also both practical and novel.

Nell Murray had been a keen observer of London society as a journalist for almost a decade, reporting for Australian newspapers from the late 1920s. Most of her chat-style columns focussed on fashion and the arts, but she occasionally strayed into social observations and commentary, particularly when her hackles were raised by what she regarded as "vulgar attacks" on Australians from a steadfastly pretentious and superior English view of the world. She frequently wrote about the changing way in which women were perceived and in a recent article she had marvelled at the "power of fascination" held by women over the age of forty in London society: "The famous beauty, Lady Diana Cooper, still ethereally lovely at the age of 45 or so, is another member of this exclusive coterie which also includes Lady Cunard, Mrs Evelyn Fitzgerald, Lady Adrian Baillie, Lady Louis Mountbatten and Lady Milbanke (formerly Lady Loughborough, an Australian.)"

And now she was interviewing the said Lady Milbanke, this time for a group of papers including *The Mercury* which reckoned its readers would lap up the inside detail of a lady's home. The occasion was the socialite's imminent return to Australia—her first trip home in fourteen years—but it was also a rare chance to peek inside the world of one of the most prominent members of the Mayfair smart set, an Australian who had somehow bypassed the prejudice and slipped almost seamlessly into society. Her origins were well known and at times she was celebrated for her individuality.

The journalist informed her readers that Lady Milbanke was a close friend of the royal family—the Duke and Duchess of Windsor and Duke and Duchess of Kent in particular. She was a woman with perfect manners and impeccable taste but also someone who often dared to challenge society's norms—she was among the first to go hatless or to change into a bathing costume to go swimming during a dinner party.

The previous year—"just for a bet"—Lady Milbanke and her friend, Mrs Peter Thursby (the former Poppy Baring) had taken over the management of the Soho nightclub Ciro's, where the White Lady cocktail had been famously created, by mixing gin, Cointreau and lemon juice. They had wanted to prove they could turn a struggling venue into a thriving business. Just as with Chez Victor the decade before, Sheila had called in her society friends and made a few improvements to the club. "Someone bet us we couldn't make a success of it. We took on the bet—I think it was £100. We engaged the cabarets, bullied the waiters and the band and changed the decorations. It was enjoyable and we quickly spent the money we made in entertaining there." A few months later, having won their bet, Sheila and Poppy withdrew and looked for another challenge.

The two of them were among a group of women who instigated "pay parties", charity fundraisers in private homes, without the costs of the grander balls that had become a permanent fixture on the social calendar. The idea had caught on and was now sweeping the city.

Poppy was accompanying Lady Milbanke on the trip to Australia. The pair looked and acted like sisters, "both petite and dark and vivacious, pioneers of many a fashion that has eventually encircled the world", but there was also a quiet, domestic side to Lady Milbanke's character. She was flying home to see her ill mother but she wanted to be back for Christmas to be with her husband and "two tall sons"—Tony, the elder, was studying at Oxford University and Peter, the younger, was at Cranwell College training to be a Royal Air Force pilot.

"Had it not been for the air service I could not possibly have spared the time to make it," Lady Milbanke said, adding that she was travelling light with "only one tailored suit, two day dresses, two evening dresses and a fur coat" alongside her knitting and a roll of tapestry for her embroidery.

But there was one last social event for Sheila to attend before she left for Australia. Freda Dudley Ward, who had finally divorced her husband in 1931, was about to wed a former Cuban-Castilian racing car driver named Pedro Jose Isidro Manuel Ricardo Mones, who carried the title Marques de Casa Maury. Peter de Casa Maury, as he would become known, had previously been married to socialite Paula Gellibrand, one of Cecil Beaton's favourite photographic models who had given Sheila early advice about her dress sense. The marques's financial affairs were rather up and down: a Bugatti-driving Grand Prix ace, he had owned the first Bermuda-rigged schooner in Europe before losing his fortune in the Wall Street Crash and then remaking it by opening the Curzon cinema chain, London's first art-house theatres, during the 1930s.

Like Sheila's marriage to John Milbanke, the ceremony on October 25 caused traffic chaos in Central London as people stopped and even climbed on parked cars to get a glimpse of a society wedding. Sir John himself gave the bride away and the newlyweds would later move into a house a few doors down from the Milbankes' in Hamilton Terrace.

It had been a hectic time. The day before the wedding, the Earl of Dudley had hosted a send-off party at the Savoy for Sheila and Poppy, as well as for the Duchess of Westminster, who was leaving for the United States. Freda was among the guests, as were the Duke and Duchess of Kent, the Mountbattens and the Duchess of Marlborough.

They spent the night at Southampton and boarded a seaplane for the first leg of their marathon journey. It must have been a hair-raising experience for Sheila, now aged 42, who was used to the slow comforts of first-class sea travel and naturally nervous of the new and seemingly daring mode of transport. Her fears were exacerbated when they were delayed by weather and then forced to take off in thick fog: "It was agony," she wrote later of the experience.

They changed flights in Alexandria, into a four-engine biplane called a Hannibal: "It looked as if it were tied up with string," she recalled with horror. "It only did 40 mile per hour and the cars on the road beneath looked as if they went much faster. All along the route were strewn wrecks of crashed planes, which wasn't encouraging although the sunsets and sunrises were magnificent."

At Karachi, they changed planes again. After a detour over the Taj Mahal—"which looked like a pepper pot"—they headed for Singapore "over bright green jungles where the thick trees looked like pin cushions. One didn't like to think what one's fate would be if the plane came down there."

At Singapore they boarded a de Havilland "Diana" and flew across the Timor Sea at just 120 metres above the water: "I was too bored to be frightened anymore. We looked down into the blue water and saw a school of enormous sharks swimming in formation."

On November 2, after six separate legs over thirteen days, Sheila and Poppy finally stepped off the plane in Sydney, to be greeted by another phalanx of media, eager to hear about the experiences and plans of a woman they regarded as Australian royalty. Despite the disjointed journey it had been an uneventful "boring" trip, she said, hankering for the old days when a six-week ship trip was an adventure in itself.

Still, there had already been two important reunions. The plane had first touched down on Australian soil in the tropical heat of Darwin where her brother Roy had ventured out from the isolation of Roper River Station to greet her, and then again at Longreach in the central west of Queensland, where Jack Chisholm had been waiting to see his sister for the first time since 1923.

Her travelling suit of "tailored linen slacks of coolie blue, hair bound in a neat linen filet and stocking-less feet thrust into open canvas sandals", as reported by *The Sydney Morning Herald*, was perfect until she reached Sydney. Here the driving rain and the puddled airport asphalt ruined her outfit and threatened to dissolve her papier-mâché travel cases (emblazoned with yellow letters spelling out Lady Milbanke's name) and reduce her satchels and hat boxes to mush. Mollee Little, now her sister-in-law, was there as they made their way to the Australia Hotel, where her great adventure had begun one March afternoon twenty-three years before.

But she was here to see her mother and rushed to the hospital only to find that she had been discharged and was now home recovering. The crisis, the details of which she never revealed, was over and she could spend time with Ag planning for the future rather than fearing the worst.

Sydney had changed significantly since Sheila was last "home". The Depression had struck hard, as it had in Europe and the United States, but the city was still growing and evolving at a rapid rate. The population had jumped by almost 40 per cent to more than 1.3 million; the Harbour Bridge, the first sod of which had been turned as she sailed back to London in 1923, was now connecting the city's north and south; and the CBD had grown sufficiently to require its first set of traffic lights, located not far from where her great-great-grandfather, James Chisholm, had built his property empire. Forever handicapped by its forbidding size and isolation, the country was being drawn together by new technology: the Australian Broadcasting Commission had been created to build a national radio network and Qantas Empire Airways, which had brought Sheila and Poppy on the leg from Singapore to Darwin, was beginning to expand its international commercial flights.

Lady Milbanke's reputation had preceded her. Within a day of her arrival *The Sydney Morning Herald* had created a headline out of the frock she wore as she lunched with Poppy and a male friend in the Wintergarden restaurant: "LADY MILBANKE WEARS INDIGO", it screamed.

The same paper then published a feature written by Norman Hartnell, the favourite designer of the new king's wife, Queen Elizabeth; he wrote about his fondness for social formality: "To me dinner is a formal affair, and I designed frocks that I believe were poetic. And they sold and after a while they began being identified with me. I made dresses for Lady Louis Mountbatten, Lady Weymouth, Lady Brougham, Lady Dufferin, Lady Plunket, Lady Melchett and Lady Milbanke. I dressed great beauties. It was glorious to create, to accomplish."

Sheila got caught up in a debate about alcohol and nicotine, when the Victorian Health Minister John Harris suggested that young women were smoking and drinking to excess, and without displaying good manners. Lady Milbanke was among those asked for their opinion. She replied:

> Australian women smoke less than Continental women. Most of the women one meets drink a little, but rarely to excess. I see no reason why they should not drink and smoke. Smoking in restaurants is so universal both here and abroad and is so harmless, really, that I think the protests of non-smokers will meet with little response. Some women smoke in public in an objectionable manner, but in that case the smoker rather than the habit is to be condemned.

The media was fascinated, not just by the clothes Sheila wore and the company she kept, but even the home where she had spent her childhood. When she announced her intention to go back to see the old homestead, a magazine wrote a feature about her birthplace, which had been turned into a bird sanctuary.

Sheila was torn, longing to see Wollogorang and yet dreading what she might find and the memories it might hold for her. Eventually, she borrowed a car and drove out with Poppy: "To my delight, the animal burial ground was intact but everything seemed much smaller than I had remembered. There were no black swans on the lagoon, but it wasn't sunset. I couldn't express my emotions at that moment, even to Poppy, but although she had never known Lionel . . . I believe she understood."

On December 7 there was a dinner party in her honour on the HMAS *Canberra* and two nights later, on the eve of her departure, she was entertained at Romano's nightclub in Kings Cross by Theo Marks, a prominent architect and former colleague of her father's from their time together on the board of the Australian Jockey Club.

Sheila was leaving Sydney with some misgivings, although not enough for her to stay for Christmas. Instead, she promised to return with her husband and children, and cried when Ag gave her a silver boomerang as a parting gift. It was inscribed: "I go out to return".

She was also concerned about her brother and Mollee: "I did not feel happy about Mollee and Roy," she would write. "I wondered if their romantic marriage was really going so well. I felt apprehensive. I loved Roy and Mollee deeply."

Sheila wasn't going back to London, at least not straight away. Her plans had changed because she'd had enough of air travel and could not face another disjointed trip home. There was no hope of returning by Christmas so she and Poppy decided to revert to sea travel and head back to Europe via the United States. They boarded the liner *Montrey* on December 10, bound for Honolulu.

It was a fortuitous decision because the plane on which they had booked to fly one of the legs across Europe crashed and killed all on board: "Better late than never," she wrote to Buffles to explain the delay.

They spent Christmas in Honolulu as guests of the American heiress and philanthropist Doris Duke before sailing for San Francisco on New Year's Eve and finally back to New York, where friends like Laura Corrigan and Serge Obolensky were waiting.

Stuart Symington was also there—"he happened to be in California on business"—accompanying her to Salt Lake City and back to New York, all the while talking about marriage.

Sheila resisted the talk: "We were both already married and both had sons almost grown up. We had not the courage to break our lives and I am not sure that either of us really wanted to do so. I remember telling him that I could never leave Buffles. I said if I did it would kill him. Laughingly, he asked: 'Are you slightly conceited or do I imagine it?'"

25

THE SHADOW OF WAR

Perhaps the most curious document in Sheila Chisholm's personal papers, preserved among thousands held by the Scottish Archives on behalf of the Rosslyn estate, is an invitation to attend an event at the German embassy at 9 Carlton House Terrace on March 10, 1938, a few weeks after she finally returned from her Australian/US trip. The large white card, embossed with the Nazi swastika, said the event would be held between 5 and 8 p.m., hosted by the German ambassador Joachim von Ribbentrop and his wife, Anna.

Sheila joined a crush of politicians and dignitaries, including the new US ambassador Joseph Kennedy, to farewell the arrogant and tactless diplomat who had been recalled to Berlin by Adolf Hitler to be his new foreign minister. He would subsequently be convicted of war crimes at the post-war Nuremberg Trials and be the first of the Nazi hierarchy to be hanged.

Von Ribbentrop had arrived in London 18 months before, just as the English monarchy was about to face the crisis of Edward VIII's abdication. Hitler had given him the task of bolstering Anglo-German relations, by reminding the British of their shared mistrust of communism, and he sought to do this by targeting a select group of aristocrats, dubbed "The Two Hundred Families", whom he naively believed were the "secret" powerbrokers of government behind the royal throne.

He eventually managed to convince a number of prominent people to visit Hitler, but most of English society turned its back on the notion of appeasement with the German Chancellor, even though it was becoming more obvious that war was inevitable. Lady Milbanke's invitation indicated that she was considered a society leader of some importance, probably because of her friendship with the royals and in particular Edward, now the Duke of Windsor, and George, the Duke of Kent.

Sheila had also met the Ribbentrops on a number of occasions, including a shooting weekend on the country estate of newspaper proprietor Baron Kemsley: "I didn't like him but thought, at first, his wife was rather nice and, in a way, pathetic. We talked vaguely of war. I said I dreaded it because we had two sons growing up. She replied: 'What more could a woman want than to have several sons and have them die for their country?' I didn't like her at all after that."

The involvement of Sheila and Buffles in the Barbara Hutton saga had not ended. In March 1938 Barbara had again called on the Milbankes for help; this time, however, it was about money and not interior decorating. The skills of Sir John as an investment banker and financial adviser would become critical as her marriage to Court Haugwitz-Reventlow collapsed.

In the intervening year since moving into the vast yet cold Winfield House, the controlling Court had managed to convince his wife to renounce her US citizenship, in order to avoid tax bills and future inheritance tax obligations that would suck most of the money into the government's coffers.

Although reluctant, Barbara had agreed and travelled to the United States alone in December 1937. During a lunchtime lull at the federal courthouse in New York, she nervously read the short Oath of Renunciation before fleeing back to the ship, aptly named the *Europa*, which left port a few hours later and before the press caught wind of what would be seen as a scandal.

Barbara now regretted her actions and was already making inquiries about reversing the decision, which only fuelled Court's anger. He exploded in fury at Buffles' presence, accusing the banker of taking advantage of his wife.

The influence of the Milbankes on the heiress's financial matters was also commented upon across the Atlantic where Barbara's exploits and excesses continued to make front-page news in papers across the country, many of which shared the same wire copy. For example, *The San Antonio Light* reported: "Today, the Milbankes are reported to have more influence than anyone with the Woolworth's heiress, which has brought about a difference of opinion. For there are those who feel Barbara is being well advised and those who think the 'poor little rich girl' is listening to the wrong people."

The confrontation lit the fuse of a split that came to a head a few months later when Court, who had gone to Paris, was accused of threatening his wife. An arrest warrant was issued and the press reported the spectacular row of wealth and privilege gone wrong as an international stand-off developed. The count broke the deadlock when he returned to London and was arrested and charged with threatening his now-estranged wife. A photograph of Barbara leaving Winfield House, accompanied by a protective and grim-faced Sheila Milbanke, flashed around the world.

The count was bailed and a few days later more than 200 reporters crammed into the grimy Bow Street court—a place normally reserved for violent street crime committed by the dregs of society—to watch the high society theatre.

Barbara claimed, through her lawyer, William Mitchell, that her life was under threat from a pistol-carrying madman and the count's lawyer, Norman Birkett, countered with allegations that Barbara was cheating and sleeping around with Prince Friedrich of Prussia, a student living in London and grandson of the former German Kaiser Wilhelm II.

"Sleeping around, Mr Birkett, is not an appropriate term in this instance," Mitchell replied. "According to the Countess, her husband is a wife-beater, a sexual deviate and a sadomaso-chist. Under such conditions adultery is hardly a luxury; it is a necessity."

Fearing she would have to take the stand and give evidence about her private life, Barbara withdrew her claim and the case was dropped. The marriage was over and so was the heiress's flirtation with European society. Within a year, and as war approached, Barbara packed up and moved back to the United States as she found a pathway to patriotic redemption by making donations to the war effort.

It would be seven years before Barbara returned to London. In the meantime Winfield House was used by the Royal Air Force during the war for its balloon squad and later as a convalescent home for wounded Canadian soldiers. When she visited it on her return, she was shocked the find the house in disarray, with buckled floorboards and broken windows, the wallpaper peeled off in reams and chunks of plaster rubble covering the floor in Lance's old nursery. The next day she offered the house to the US Government for US$1—an act which prompted a letter from Harry S Truman describing it as "a most generous and patriotic offer" and finally mended the rift that had been caused by her 1937 renunciation.

The mansion would eventually be renovated and turned into the home of the US ambassador. But Barbara declined to attend its opening in 1955, remarking to the media: "Winfield House represents a closed chapter in my life, and while I am grateful that the residence now has a new existence, there are too many memories in its walls—both good and bad—that I don't wish to rekindle."

Like most who had lived through the Great War, Sheila feared that the "war to end all wars" would, instead, be the precursor to something far worse. As 1938 dragged on her fears grew: "Hitler never stopped making speeches. Everyone was talking about war again. I couldn't let myself think about it, with Tony and Peter and Buffie and all the people one loved. Luckily, I had the gift of dismissing any unpleasant thoughts that came into my head. I did so now. I had a special imaginary 'thought-whisk' which removed unpleasant thoughts."

Despite the increasing talk of war, or more likely because of it, Sheila continued to be prominent in society circles. The Derby Ball was its usual success, this year with Prince Henry, the Duke of Gloucester, representing the royal family. She attended the celebrations at the Café de Paris when it was announced that Henry's brother George, the Duke of Kent, would become the next Australian Governor-General, photographed dancing with the prince and quoted in the accompanying, gushing article published back in Australia by the *Women's Weekly*: "Lady Milbanke has been a great favourite of the Duke of Kent for many years and doubtless there is very little she hasn't told him about the country to which he is going as representative of his brother, the King."

She and Buffles had parlayed their experiences with Barbara Hutton into an interior design business based in Mayfair. It was an immediate success, winning a contract for the city home of the Earl of Ranfurly and, more spectacularly, designing and building one of the largest dining tables made in Britain. At 20 metres long, the table, inlaid with silver, would seat 74 people on chairs upholstered in silk and velvet. It had been made for an Indian Maharaja and would be the centrepiece for his banquet hall. Despite their early success, the war would lay waste to the venture.

And she continued to travel, much to the concern of Buffles in September when she and a friend went to Vichy, in France, to bathe in the famous healing spas: "In the midst of the cure, our husbands telephoned, saying we must return to England immediately as they thought war was about to be declared. We were annoyed because we wanted to finish the cure. Couldn't we stay a few more days? They were adamant, and home we came."

America beckoned once more in January 1939. The cold winter seemed to have dulled war fears, at least until spring, so she decided to take Tony to New York. It would be her third trip in as many years: "I adored New York, with its air like champagne" and Palm Beach "where the sunshine seemed like a miracle if one has lived long in England".

Stuart Symington tried once more to woo her away from Buffles. She listened: "We had many long talks and we both decided there was nothing we could do about the future. I repeated that Buffles could not live without me! He again teased me and told me I was conceited."

After three months in the US, Sheila left Tony, who had taken a summer job as a runner at a Wall Street brokerage firm and, reluctantly, headed back to London: "I always disliked leaving New York but also enjoyed the thought of getting home. I seemed to be torn continually between two worlds, the old and the new."

Sheila landed at Southampton on Good Friday, April 7, to

be greeted by a white-faced Buffles. He looked ill as they drove to a friend's house to spend Easter and she finally asked if there was anything wrong: "He told me he was involved with another woman," she would reflect. "I offered Buffie a divorce but he said he didn't want one. He also said 'I won't see her again if that makes you unhappy.' This did make me unhappy but, of course, I never admitted it."

It seemed astonishing that Buffles did not want a divorce but was, in effect, asking his wife to sanction a continuing affair with another woman. Then again, she had been contemplating an affair of her own with Stuart Symington. Sheila was tempted to cable Stuart and tell him that the situation had changed, but she didn't: "I'm glad I resisted the temptation," she would write.

Instead, she settled into the summer season, enjoying the seemingly endless round of events—the "eve of Waterloo" summer as it was dubbed, as the inevitable war against Hitler got closer and closer.

Buffles was "on the Continent" in mid-August 1939 when Sheila flew to Italy to join Barbara Hutton on the island of Capri where she had rented a villa with a group of friends. A week earlier Sheila had attended the funeral of her former father-in-law, the 5th Earl of Rosslyn, who had died suddenly after returning from a holiday exploring the Amazon River at the age of seventy. The death meant that her elder son, Tony, who was now back from New York and studying at the British Army officers' school, the Royal Military College at Camberley, automatically assumed the hereditary title.

Among the knot of mainly women at the villa, perched in the

hills above Piccola Marina, was Elsie Mendl, who had just staged another of her wonderfully eccentric balls. The Circus Ball, as it became known, was complete with clowns, jugglers and sword swallowers. As *Vogue* magazine reported: *At midnight, Elsie had appeared along a torch-lit pathway, dressed in pink tights and a spangled tutu, her hair dyed a brilliant electric blue, on the back of a white elephant.* It would become known as the last great ball of the pre-war era, something the women on Capri had suspected. Europe had feared war for the last five years and now it was clear that Hitler would not be appeased and Britain would not capitulate to his demands. Life was about to change.

26

"I'M NOT CRYING; THERE'S RAIN IN MY EYES"

Sheila would always have vivid and haunting memories of the day that her younger son, Peter, graduated from RAF Cranwell as a pilot. She was proud of his "wings" but worried, as any mother would, that if war happened she might never see him again: "We lunched at a hotel in Nottingham, both feeling deeply, trying to be brave and make jokes, not quite knowing what to say to each other. I looked at him carefully, trying to memorise every detail of his dear face. One never knew. After lunch we went to the cinema. The film was Walt Disney's *Snow White* . . . As we came out the newsboys were calling 'Chamberlain back from Munich. Peace in our time'. I burst into tears. The next morning I went to church and thanked God."

It would be another nine months before war finally came to Europe and this time there were no cheering crowds in

Trafalgar Square, just air-raid sirens and a call for Sheila and her neighbours to report to Marylebone Town Hall to be fitted for a gas mask, as she later reminisced: "I have never been able to make anyone understand how air raids made me feel. To me, it is almost like being in love; as one's heart beats fast and one's pulse races—not altogether unpleasant. Perhaps love and fear are stimulated from the same gland!"

A month before the declaration of war, when Sheila had been on the island of Capri, she and the other society women had discussed not whether war was inevitable but when it would begin and where they might go to be safe. Many of the others had chosen the safety of the United States but Sheila, who might have opted for the isolated security of her homeland Australia, had decided to return to London, and to take up a role in the civilian response to the conflict they all expected.

With two sons and a husband going to war it was not a difficult decision for Sheila to return to volunteer nursing, the same role she had taken in Egypt with her mother during the Great War. The maternity wing of the Great Royal Northern Hospital, for which she had raised so much money through the Derby Ball over the years, had been relocated from Central London; there was a need not only to keep pregnant women as safe as possible from the expected bombing raids, but also to rationalise civilian medical services and free up beds for convalescing soldiers. Euan and Barbara Wallace had agreed to convert their grand Sussex manor house, Lavington Park, into a temporary maternity facility, and it was here that Sheila would initially volunteer. The comforts of life in a London mansion would not be difficult to put aside, even if it meant living in a dormitory with six other women and working eleven-hour days assisting medical staff.

She was already there on September 8, just five days after Britain's entry into the war, working the 8 a.m.–9 p.m. shift during which she had helped to deliver a baby girl, which the mother promptly named Sheila. The next morning—her forty-fourth birthday—Sheila was bathing her infant namesake when there was a telephone call from Buffles. After fobbing him off while she finished drying the child, Sheila took the phone:

"Good morning, thank you for remembering my birthday," she said.

There was a silence at the other end, then Buffles said quietly: "I have some bad news for you."

Her heart seemed to stop in that moment: "It's Peter isn't it?"

Buffles sighed: "Yes."

"He's dead." She didn't ask; she didn't have to.

"Yes." It was all Buffles could muster.

The details of his death would remain sketchy, even more than seventy years later. Officially, he was deemed to have died on active service, not in combat but flying a Hurricane L1631 in a night-time accident in the skies above the green fields of rural England.

The official telegram followed the next day, words pasted in strips which ended: "The Air Council express their profound sympathy in your bereavement. Signed Under Secretary of State Air Ministry". It would be one of the first of thousands of telegrams that would have to be sent to distraught parents over the next six years.

Sheila would keep copies of the newspaper tributes that followed what was one of the first deaths of the war: "Erskine was one of the best pilots we had," one unnamed senior officer was quoted as saying. "His zeal and courage were quite amazing. He died young but got more out of life than men many times his age."

Peter St Clair-Erskine, just short of his twenty-first birthday, was a rarity among his generation—a child of the early 20th century who knew only peace in his lifetime. But this statistic did not tell the real story of a young man born on October 30, 1918, amid the euphoria of an end to the horrors of the 1914–18 war.

The guns had been silenced, replaced by bells of rejoicing, but that did not prevent Sheila's younger son from growing up in a period of constant turmoil. His first years were spent in a society struggling to rise from the ashes of conflict and his teen years were economically ravaged by the consequences of the subsequent era of excess.

His private world may have been one of privilege, but that was largely an adult concept in a culture which barely acknowledged children, who were nursed and cared for by paid nannies and maids until the age of seven or eight, when they were sent away to boarding school. The more privileged the family, it seemed, the less children saw of their parents. The notion had always bothered Sheila who lamented that she preferred the American system which kept children in the bosom of the family for longer.

Neither was there enough wealth to hide the difficulties of

his parents' marriage. His mother had always been worried about the family finances, complaining to her errant husband about not having enough money to buy gloves and coats for him and his brother in winter, at a time when his father was continuing to gamble his way into bankruptcy.

Peter and Tony had done what was expected of them. They had attended the right schools and, as the seeds of political discontent began to spread through Europe once more, they had chosen careers that would allow them to play their parts in the anticipated conflict. Peter had gone into the RAF after leaving Eton while Tony had studied at Oxford and later joined the King's Royal Rifle Corps, where his father and grandfather had served.

Sheila was determined to see Peter's body and, against advice, went to Northolt Air Base where the accident had occurred, where she was shown into a tiny whitewashed room: "He was lying there covered with the Union Jack. They told me not to lift the flag—I obeyed this order. I ran my hands up and down his body. It was explained to me later that he was broken into small pieces and put together for my benefit (which was a nuisance for them!)"

Sheila struggled to hold herself together: "Buffles said I must be a brave Australian; a Waltzing Matilda. I tried to live up to this idea of me. We buried Peter with full military honours and with a squadron of RAF [officers] firing salutes into the air. Then the 'Last Post' and pipers. The wailing of the pipes seemed to tear one's heart to pieces."

After the funeral she returned to Lavington, determined to

keep working, despite being "dazed and exhausted with sorrow". She would recall: "One had to pull oneself together and appear to be normal because we had our work to do." If anyone caught her crying she would explain: "I'm not crying; there's rain in my eyes."

Her stoicism could clearly be seen in a letter she wrote a few weeks later to her close friends Georgia and Sachie Sitwell. She was grateful for their best wishes but adamant that life had to move on: "Thank you both so much for your sweet and sympathetic letters about my little Petsie. One's friends' thoughts and love help so much—I am here for a few days (Cram Hill Hotel, Bath) and then return to work at Lavington. Very much love to you both."

Duff Cooper was one of the hundreds who offered their condolences over the next few weeks. Unlike his attempts of five years earlier to kindle an illicit romance, this note was retained by Sheila: "Darling, All my deep sympathy and love are with you. Thank heaven for your high, gay courage that will help you to bear this and to face everything. Duff"

News spread quickly back to Australia, where Peter Loughborough's death was reported widely. In a comment to *The Australian Women's Weekly*, Sheila said: "We've all got to do everything possible to end the struggle as soon as possible. All my family are working, but it was most difficult for me to say goodbye to my eldest son, Anthony, when he went off . . . in the British Expeditionary Force."

Sheila's almost sanguine acceptance of her son's death reflected the attitude of a community faced with the stark truth that war would produce many tragedies and they would almost certainly strike most families, privileged and poor.

The Wallace family, as wealthy as it was, would be among the worst affected. Gerard, the younger son of Idina Sackville, was killed in action in August 1943 and David, whom Sheila had reunited with Idina, was killed in August the following year. Then two of the sons of Euan and Barbara—Edward and John—died in 1944 and 1946 respectively.

Day-to-day life had obviously changed dramatically. This time there had been anticipation of war long before it arrived and the city had not only prepared physically for conflict but also psychologically.

In mid-October 1939, around the time Peter St Clair-Erskine should have been celebrating his twenty-first birthday, *Vogue* published an article—"London under Arms"—which was intended to capture the spirit of the sand-bagged city facing its second "war to end all wars" in a generation:

> This is no kiss-the-boys-good-bye affair. There is no flag-wagging; no champagne hysteria; no jingo braggadocio; no God-speeding the brave boys in Khaki on their way to the front—and glory. We go into it cold sober . . . Too many of us remember the last war, or grew up in its shadow, to have any illusions left on that score. It is an unlovely, bloody business that we must face again so best get on with it and least be said.

To begin with, all theatres, cinemas, nightclubs and dance halls were shut down. But after a while some theatres began opening again, at odd times and in odd places. Audiences trooped out to the fringes of London, to suburban theatres such as Golders Green, where John Gielgud's exquisite production of *The Importance of Being Earnest* was now being housed. Brighton theatres were considered accessible and safe. Cinemas were playing to capacity at 2.30 in the afternoon, and opening their doors at 10 a.m. As *Vogue* observed: "The Café de Paris and Quaglino's are full again—with every other man in khaki and some women in uniform."

Despite her outward resilience, Sheila struggled privately with Peter's death. She had seen death close at hand while nursing in Egypt but this was different. She shifted out of the hospital and into a small hotel outside Bath to be alone with her grief. Hundreds of letters from well-wishers arrived but she could not bear to read them. It was Poppy who eventually, gently forced her to face the reality, reading letters out aloud. They both cried but it was a healing of sorts.

Sheila went back to London, to Hamilton Terrace, and began to see a few friends and return to volunteer work and the war effort. She was even summoned to Buckingham Palace where the King and Queen spent an afternoon with her in private, talking about the past and their children. It touched Sheila deeply: "The Queen has infinite charm," she would write of the day. "It seemed strange to realise that 'Prince Bertie' was now 'The King.'"

In March 1940, six months after Peter's death, she got a cable from her brother Roy. Their mother had died suddenly. The world turned again but her response was typical: "I was beginning to feel slightly recovered and now another blow. I felt I couldn't bear it but, of course, one can."

———

In the European summer of 1939, against a backdrop of a city preparing for war, Tony Loughborough had teamed up with a young American to do the rounds of the parties and hunt for girls. They called themselves "Ross Kennedy" and preferred chasing blondes and women slightly older than their twenty-two years. Tony was eleven days older than Jack, the son of the US Ambassador to the United Kingdom, Joe Kennedy, who had made his entrance into London society at the send-off for Joachim von Ribbentrop back in March 1938.

Tony was keen on Jack Kennedy's younger sister, Kathleen, better known as "Kick", although he had competition among the legion of young aristocrats who flocked to London for the Season. He became close to the family, often joining golf rounds with Joe Senior and his two sons, Jack and young Joe, and listening to the ambassador's views on how to strike a peace deal with Hitler, which had made him unpopular with the British Government and were not unlike the views of Edward VIII. Kennedy Sr found a supporter in the young peer, more because of his belief in free speech than because of any shared idea that Britain should concede to Hitler's demands. It would be an enduring friendship between the two families, both of which were to face tragedies over the next decade.

Tony was staying with the Kennedys the night his brother Peter died. In the space of four weeks between August and September 1939, he had lost his grandfather and his younger brother, followed six months later by his Australian grandmother. He had also assumed a heady title, as the 6th Earl of Rosslyn, but this had meant little to him, given his sense of loss and that, at the time he got the news, he was sitting at the Staff College at Camberley, awaiting the inevitable call to war and possible death.

He was commissioned into the King's Royal Rifle Corps in June 1940, and given the rank of captain, but he was still at the college early in December 1940 when he wrote to Jack Kennedy, who had returned to the United States to study at Harvard University, where he produced a thesis examining the British Government's failure to avoid the current war with Germany. Kennedy's paper had just been published in book form, under the title *Why England Slept*, which provided Tony Rosslyn with his reason for writing:

"My dear Jack," he began and proceeded to congratulate his friend on the thesis which he said was beautifully written:

Most American writers do write beautifully, a fact which has never ceased to amaze me when one takes into consideration the pernicious phrases that they use in conversation. But its chief plus, I thought, was the completely fair attitude which you adopted toward every variety of individual or institution mentioned in the book. There was no prejudice, sarcasm or egotism to be found anywhere, which is most unusual in any author under 70. The result was a helpful, friendly, impersonal commentary on past events which comes as an oasis in the desert to one who has been reading the free press in England, where "freedom" is presumably another word for "licence".

Sheila

The young man then targeted unseen military censors, revealing his keen intellect and desire to express himself freely:

I suppose it would be possible to write you a fairly interesting letter were it not for the fact that the censor's pencil covers over everything one says. I see that your father has been getting into hot water with the press. I don't suppose that that deters him much. As you know, I spend my life looking around for someone who says something different to the next man and, even if he didn't say it, it's something to be known as capable of doing so. I therefore number myself among the large but inarticulate body of people in this country who are sorry that he's given up his post in London. And that is not only because his resignation robs me of the pleasure of seeing his family again.

The letter also revealed his fondness for Kick who, in the sad Kennedy tradition, would die in an aircraft accident in 1948:

You might tell Kick that while passing through Grosvenor Square the other day, I observed that the corner of the balcony where I sat and delivered a lecture on the approaching fate of Europe to her at a dance, has been totally demolished by a bomb. The rest of the balcony is intact so the next time I have occasion to deliver a lecture to her, we'll have to sit at the other end.

Tony would write again in July 1941, asking for a copy of a speech that Jack had given and referring again to *Why England Slept*:

I read your book yesterday again. The moral, if anything written by a Kennedy can be said to have a moral, would seem to be "speak the truth". Am I right? If [British Prime Minister Stanley] Baldwin had spoken the truth before the election, he would have been thrown out. Labour would have gone in. Either their peace policy would have succeeded (result, no war) or failed (result Tories back with mandate to rearm). In other words Churchill was right but too keen. Englishmen don't mind killing people, but they don't like eating them.

Sheila would recall her own friendship with Joe Kennedy before he resigned suddenly as the Battle of Britain raged. "I stayed several times with Ambassador Joe. His wife Rose and the 'Kennedy kids' had all gone to America. Joe was lonely and depressed; he saw too much of Mr Chamberlain! He told me England was finished, and that he could arrange for us all to get out. I replied 'Nonsense!' (or words to that effect!!)"

27

SO COMPLETELY IN
THE HANDS OF FATE

Sheila had known Georgia Sitwell since the mid-1920s, as an acquaintance rather than a central figure in her broad social life. Georgia was the Canadian wife of Sacheverell Sitwell, the youngest of the famous literary Sitwell siblings (he and his sister Edith and his brother Osbert had set London alight in the twenties with their avant-garde poetry). Although Georgia was nine years younger than Sheila, they were kindred spirits in many ways.

The Sitwells were among a set in which Cecil Beaton and Evelyn Waugh were prominent; they and their close friends explored life and art, forever recorded by Beaton's photographs, which were published in magazines like *Vogue*, as if he were mapping a social phenomenon. In their sexual activities they ignored the conventional bounds of marriage and gender. Georgia married "Sachie" in 1925 and, despite their numerous affairs, they remained married and she had two sons by him.

Georgia was not unlike Sheila in many ways—an exotic foreigner who had married into the imposing rigours of London society, and yet someone who was able to retain her individuality. In the 1996 book *The Sitwells*, she was described as "tall, slim and dark-haired with slightly olive skin and wide spaced hazel-green eyes. She had beautiful legs, fine ankles and an attractively husky voice. She was down to earth, highly sexed . . . warm-hearted, loyal, vital and amusing." They may as well have been describing Sheila.

The short letter of condolence she had sent to Sheila after Peter's death seems to have drawn their friendship closer, at least on Georgia's part: she kept among her personal effects a series of letters written by Sheila through the early war years as Sheila struggled with being alone while her surviving son, Tony, fought in Europe and Buffles, an RAF Wing Commander, was moved around the country, from the balloon squadron in Surrey to an anti-gas school in Wiltshire, an island base off Sussex and even an RAF facility at Filey in Yorkshire which had been commandeered from the partly completed Butlin's Holiday Camp.

She also had to cope with the death of her mother, Margaret, who had finally passed away in March 1940, which only heightened her sense of isolation. To compound matters, her brother Roy would die in 1944.

By 1940 Sheila had largely abandoned the home in Hamilton Terrace, St John's Wood, with its four live-in staff, and moved through a series of homes and country hotels, from the rugged and beautiful southern coast of Cornwall to the rolling hills of the Peak District in the north. This was as far from city life as she could get, trading the glitz and glamour of the restaurants and ballrooms for the boring safety of home-cooked meals and small dinner parties, interspersed with volunteer work.

In mid-1941 she made the move permanent by selling the St John's Wood house, which had become uninhabitable after being "peppered" by a German air strike. Instead, she bought the stables and hayloft at the back of a large country property on the fringes of the village of Bracknell about an hour's drive west of London.

She bought the structure initially as a place to store their spare furniture from the Hamilton Terrace house as it was emptied but Sheila fell in love with the area and commissioned an architect to turn it into a large country home. Brook House, as she would name the property, was set back from the main road among sprawling lawns and gardens that would provide her with a sanctuary when the city became too dangerous, so she would not have to keep moving from hotel to hotel and friend to friend.

She also began working as a nurse for the local Women's Voluntary Service—"a small fish in a large pond"—and, later, running a "Welcome Club" for incoming American soldiers who began arriving in their thousands in the latter years of the war: "I shall always remember them with affection—their gaiety, generosity, courage and helpfulness and the fun they made out of nothing. I can hear the village children asking: 'Any gum, chum?' They always got some."

As she buried herself in volunteer war work, Sheila

disappeared from the pages of newspapers like the *Daily Mirror* and the *Daily Express*, which had once published her social deeds several times a week. Very occasionally there would be a mention of her "being seen" strolling in Hyde Park on the arm of her husband, home on leave, but there were no reports of dances and restaurant appearances. As one would expect, wartime austerity had taken its toll on the social whirl of London and restaurants, which once hummed with high-profile customers, were reduced to marketing their past appearances.

The Normandie Grill in Knightsbridge, whose wartime offerings highlighted "wafer-thin minute steak", boiled broccoli and new potatoes, was so desperate to promote its new general manager, who went by the name Sofrani, that it mentioned he used to run the Blue Train Nightclub in Mayfair before adding: "Lady Milbanke was one of the hostesses associated with this club".

A few of her friends, like Lady Diana Cooper, opted to stay in London, moving out of their homes and into hotels like the Dorchester overlooking Hyde Park, which had been opened in 1931 and was advertised as one of the safest buildings in London, with reinforced concrete walls and "gas-proof shelter". But most found sanctuary in the country, like Freda, now the Marquesa de Casa Maury, who moved to Plymouth.

This exodus had long been predicted by politicians like Winston Churchill who, as early as 1934, had reckoned that German bombing raids would kill half a million Londoners and send another 4 million scurrying into the country, where they would need shelter, food and clothes. Sheila, who counted

Churchill among her acquaintances, took heed and left London before the bombs began to fall.

The relative closeness of her relationship with the prime minister is clear from a letter she wrote to him in July 1945, after he lost the post-war election. Churchill, who had gone to school with Sir John's father, kept her missive and it would remain among his personal papers:

Dear Winston,

I feel I had to write to you because I am completely astounded and shattered by the result of the election. The only bright spot is how enjoyable they are going to be as opposition!! I hope you got the card I sent you from Buffles. I have just heard he will be out on 9th August. Perhaps we could all meet sometime soon because you are his Godfather also! I wish I could express what I feel about the whole beastly business but unfortunately I can't.

Yours,

Sheila Milbanke

Her wartime life, particularly during the first few years before Brook House was built, was transient. Summer holidays were no longer trips to wealthy resorts across Europe or the United States but a series of carefully planned movements from friend to friend and village to village, tolerating the inevitable delays of a transport system hampered by makeshift staffing and targeted bombing raids. She ventured to the city only occasionally, to meet her husband or son when they had leave, as can be seen from a series of letters she wrote to

Georgia Sitwell, who was living in the city, through 1940 and 1941:

North Cornwall
December 18, 1940
Darling Georgia,
Thank you so much for your very sweet letters. If it would not be too inconvenient for you, could I possibly come to you on December 28 for a few days?

I long to be near Tony for the New Year and I have the chance of a lift all the way from here by car. I don't mind at all where I sleep—and would be ever so grateful if you would have me then—I have no clothes—and will probably arrive in an old pair of trousers.

Cheshire
January 9, 1941
Darling Georgia—just a line to let you know that I don't think I should get to Northampton before you go on 20th. Elizabeth can't have me till after the 16th—as she has Johnnie and Peter Wallace with her—so as travelling is so awful by train I shall stay in those parts and go to Northampton on my way south. I am very comfortable and happy here—and there are lots of people all round. Poppy lunched here yesterday and am going into Chester tomorrow . . . the days fly—so much love to you.

March 22, 1941
Darling Georgia—thank you so much for your letters and wire. I'm so looking forward to seeing you next Wednesday. I shall go by train

from Crewe to Rugby—arrive Rugby at 5.20 so order a taxi to meet me there. Am going to Portia on Monday for one night—coming back here Tuesday—and then on to you Wednesday—I hope you can get out of your meetings at Oxford—but if you can't I shall be quite okay.

I saw Peter yesterday—Poppy is making whoopie in the south again. Much love darling.
Sheila

Jollywinds
May 2
Darling Georgia—I hope you are not in a rage with me and I have not just put out all your plans by not being here next week. I have several reasons which I shall proceed to tell you. Tony probably told you we were thinking of getting a small home near Ascot and moving the furniture from Hamilton Terrace as I feel it is madness to leave it there and it costs me £600 per annum not living there and I can't afford this house after September—as Buffie has had to cut down my marriage settlement owing to property being bombed in the city. So I must go at once and try and find a suitable house—as you know no one else can ever do those things for one.

Travelling from here at the moment is awful owing to the lines having been blown up so often outside Plymouth—the trains are anything up to 6 hours late—and sometimes they don't go at all. It is not advisable to travel by night at the moment and I am dreading the long day journey up next week (above nine or 10 hours under present conditions). Please come back with me if you can—and stay at least 10 days—it is cold here at the moment—but the weather *should be lovely at the end of May—and the wildflowers are then beautiful beyond description.*

Will write you where I am staying in London—Much love darling—what a boring letter but I want you to understand all my difficulties.
Sheila

But there were also new friendships and, as usual, Sheila had an impact on the men she met. One was an Irishman she would refer to as "Buck" in a letter to Georgia and would refer to in her memoir. He was a friend of the Duke of Sutherland and met Sheila in Cornwall. Although she and Buffles, or Buffie as she referred to him, remained married and saw each other from time to time, they had gone their separate ways in many respects—a marriage in name only—hence the comment about her marriage settlement.

Sheila was clearly attracted to Buck as she was to Stuart Symington, and felt free to act because of Buffles' decision to continue seeing other women. She was lonely and the attentions of the handsome Irishman were hard to resist: "Buck's hair was blue-black, he had the longest black eyelashes I have ever seen and he was tall and very thin." They sat on a Cornwall beach and watched the sunset, "a fat red ball sinking into the sea", and watched to see if they could spy a green flash at the last moment, which was deemed to be good luck: "They called it the 'Green Man' and I saw it twice."

"Buck and I often talked of my Peter. I found that one couldn't talk easily to many people about him . . . I grew to love the planes and the RAF uniforms—they all became muddled up with Peter."

Her grief over Peter's death naturally stirred fears about her elder son, Tony, and in her desperation, she tried to secure his safety by arranging a staff position—from the King. On December 19, 1940, a few weeks after Buckingham Palace was badly damaged in a German air raid, she penned a letter to her former flame which remains in the Royal Archives at Windsor:

Sir,

I have been wanting to write to you ever since Buckingham Palace was bombed because I thought of you all so much & to tell you how wonderful everybody thinks you & the Queen have been and are being.

I have had many letters from America, saying that when you both appear on the screen at a cinema the people go crazy and cheer and scream.

I thought of writing for your birthday and have at last decided to write & wish you all a very happy Christmas & much happiness for 1941.

It seems incredible that a year has passed since you and the Queen were so sweet and sympathetic to me about Peter.

You said then that someday perhaps you could help me about Tony. He got his commission to the 60th Rifles last June & has since been transferred to the 1st Battalion Queen Victoria Rifles. I dread the thought that he may go abroad next year when they are fully trained.

I know it is awful of me when everybody else has suffered such fearful loss too, but he is really the only thing I have got in the world. I suppose he is too young (23) to be attached to you in any way? Or failing that get a job as ADC to some general in England. Please forgive me for writing to you like this and never tell anyone (except the Queen) because Tony would never speak to me again if he knew.

I have taken this house for the moment as I have not been at all well but hope to go north after Christmas and spend the year with Tony.

Please be very kind and think this over if you have a moment— which you probably haven't!

Again, so many fond wishes for 1941. I have the honour to be Your Majesty's most obedient servant.

Sheila Milbanke

There is no record of the King's answer but at any rate, Tony would not spend the war in an office job; rather he would rise to the rank of captain with the King's Royal Rifle Corps and then join the GHQ Liaison Regiment, better known as Phantom, whose role it was to gather battlefield information during military operations to provide "real-time" assessments from the front line. He was later attached to the 3rd Canadian Infantry Division and was mentioned in despatches in 1944 for meritorious action.

As well as Buck, there were many other new friendships which emerged for Sheila during the war years; among them was Daphne Vivian, the Marchioness of Bath, who had run wildly with the Bright Young Things—something she played down in her later memoir, which would be described by Evelyn Waugh in his memoir as "marred by discretion and good taste . . . as though Lord Montgomery were to write his life and omit to mention that he ever served in the army".

Daphne and Sheila holidayed together at Treyarnon Bay in Cornwall in the early 1940s where Daphne's ten-year-old son, Alexander, experienced what he subsequently described in his memoir as "my first self-consciously romantic relationship" with his mother's 47-year-old friend. He continued:

Sheila was similar to Daphne in many ways: a coyly flirtatious brunette with straight shoulder length hair, and a warmly personal way of chatting and confiding, even with children, so that her subject was made to feel special and uniquely rewarded by her attention. The two of them would play a comic act with me. When I composed a short lyric, in grudging acceptance of the newly imposed war-time diet, (of animals trapped by our own gamekeepers) they would perform a little dance around me, singing out the words to me in silly girlish tones.

"Rabbits for lunch, rabbits for tea,

rabbits are good for you and me!"

I decided that I was in love with Sheila and, just before returning home, I found a stone which happened to be in the shape of a heart. Daphne was encouraging the liaison, so was happy to buy for me a small tin of glossy red paint, in which colour I immersed my "heart". Then I wrapped it in brown paper, and left it on her doorstep as a valentine. On re-meeting Sheila some years later, she was to surprise me greatly by taking me upstairs to her bedroom and revealing how she still treasured this heart in a little casket, especially dedicated to its preservation.

The war years were a haze of fear and boredom for Sheila. She watched Plymouth being bombed in 1941 from the roof of a rented house called Jollywinds, cried with friends whose children and husbands were killed and practised shooting her revolver after listening to Churchill speeches—"I felt a strange stirring of pioneer blood bubble in my veins."

There were near misses, once when she decided against going to the cinema in Plymouth only for the building to be bombed. She just missed being hit one evening while dining in the officers' mess at an aerodrome, and on another occasion an incendiary bomb missed her car by a few feet. Her old home in Talbot Square was flattened during an air raid, killing all those inside.

There were also moments of determined resistance, Sheila often visiting Emerald Cunard who was living on the seventh floor of the Dorchester where she continued to give luncheon and dinner parties during the air raids: "Sometimes one could hardly hear oneself speaking for the barking of the [anti-aircraft] guns in Hyde Park," Sheila remembered, adding: "Emerald remained unmoved."

On another occasion, she agreed to go to London and attend a party at Ciro's, the club she and Poppy Thursby once managed for a bet: "About 9 p.m. the bombs began to drop and the band disappeared," she would write. "The noise was terrible and the room gloomy. I left the table, found the band sitting in the basement and asked them to come back and play, quite forgetting I was not still running the place. They returned and played loudly, slightly camouflaging the noise of the bombs and guns. We danced and felt quite gay. A bomb dropped near but Ciro's escaped. One seemed so completely in the hands of fate."

Fate played its hand in her favour on the night of March 8, 1941. She had been staying in London and was considering travelling to the home of a friend named Elizabeth outside the city, but was torn by an invitation to go to one of her favourite haunts, the Café de Paris, advertised as "the safest and gayest restaurant in town", 20ft below ground, and where the singer and band leader Ken "Snakehips" Johnson was the main act: "I tossed a coin, heads Elizabeth and tails Café de Paris. It was heads," she would recall.

Time magazine reported what happened that night as a German air raid enveloped the city:

The orchestra at London's Café de Paris gaily played [The Andrews Sisters' hit] "Oh, Johnny, Oh, Johnny, How You Can Love!" At the tables handsome flying Johnnies, naval Jacks in full dress, guardsmen, territorials, and just plain civics sat making conversational love. The service men were making the most of leave; the civilians were making the most of the lull in bombings of London.

Sirens had sounded. Most of London had descended into shelters, but to those in the cabaret, time seemed too dear to squander underground. Bombs began to fall nearby: it was London's worst night raid in weeks. The orchestra played "Oh, Johnny" a little louder.

Then the hit came. What had been a nightclub became a nightmare: heaps of wreckage crushing the heaps of dead and maimed, a shambles of silver slippers, broken magnums, torn sheet music, dented saxophones, smashed discs. A special constable with the rather splendid name Ballard Berkeley was one of the first on the scene. He saw "Snakehips" Johnson decapitated and elegantly dressed people still sitting at tables seemingly almost in conversation, but stone dead.

———

Buffles, now a squadron leader in the RAF, and Tony, a captain in the King's Royal Rifle Corps Phantoms, were called away suddenly on D-Day, June 6, 1944. There was no explanation for Sheila: "I never expected to see either of them again. I was so proud of them, and so frightened for them."

All she could do was wait and watch the daily armada of planes as they flew over Brook House—"Liberators, Lancasters, Lightnings, Fortresses, planes of every description flying toward the Continent, flying 'over there'. In the evenings they would return, the sunlight gleaming on them and turning their wings to silver and gold. Thousands and thousands of planes; day after day, night after night. It was glorious, it was thrilling, it was terrifying. One didn't let oneself dwell too much on the results of those journeys."

Even as the end of the war approached Sheila found it difficult to celebrate until Buffles and Tony had returned from Europe where they were now stationed as "Liberators", helping to free the survivors from the Nazi concentration camps and rescue the captured Allied soldiers.

By April 1945 her mood lightened as the POWs began returning to London and she agreed one night to attend a party thrown by Sir Michael Duff: "I had a bad cold but was determined to go all the same as there hadn't been a ball for years. Some of the men were in dinner jackets and some in moth-eaten tails, and most of the white ties were yellow, having been put away since before the war."

The Duke and Duchess of Marlborough held a celebration dinner for Winston Churchill late on the evening of May 8, 1945. It was a public holiday, declared Victory in Europe, or VE Day, and the city was alive. The dinner was held at a Mayfair club and Sheila went along, alone. She stood at one end of the room, quiet and reflective about the past six years during which she had lost her younger son and almost certainly her marriage: "I was unhappy and lonely," she would write.

Then she noticed Churchill across the room, surrounded by well-wishers: "I hadn't seen Winston for ages and I don't believe he recognised me at first. Then he came across the room and spoke to me: 'My dear, I had forgotten the calm beauty of your serene brow.' My evening was made!"

28

A FEELING OF UNCERTAINTY

On October 2, 1946, a few weeks after her fifty-first birthday, Sheila Milbanke arrived in New York aboard a Pan Am flight. Her travel documents over the years had been consistent but not entirely accurate; she always described herself as an English housewife with no profession, 5 feet 7 inches tall, fresh complexion and hazel eyes. But she tended to be hazy about her birth year to immigration officials at either end of the journey. "About 1898" was her common entry in the official record of arrival. After all, it seemed entirely reasonable for a lady to fudge her age by three years.

London, a year after the war, was rebuilding—not just physically, but recasting its notion of society and its values. England had been virtually bankrupted for the second time in a generation, but this time repeated bombing raids had smashed its capital city. The pitted landscape there was a constant reminder of the cost of conflict. The wartime coalition government had been disbanded in the spring of 1945 and Clement Attlee had swept Churchill, despite his hero status, from government in the ensuing general elections. The country's widespread desire for social reform resulted in the creation of the National Health Service, which ended the need for events like the Derby Ball, which was never held again.

A year later the Attlee government extended its post-war rationing to include bread for the first time; it began to implement its radical vision of a cradle-to-the-grave welfare state as the country huddled closer together under its coat of austerity. Survival of the Great War had caused a celebration of life and created the Roaring Twenties but this time there seemed to be a collective weariness.

There were rare examples of the old days, such as this report in the *Daily Express*: "The Duchess of Kent is being seen out a good deal in the West End lately. She has been in several of Australian Lady Milbanke's parties at the new and fashionable Orchid in Brook Street, London's gayest and most elegant night club." But, by and large, the upper class kept their diamonds locked away and remained subdued.

In May, a year after the war had ended, Sheila travelled to Paris to visit Diana Cooper and Duff, who was now the British Ambassador to France. The war had changed everything: "Paris made me sad. I tried to recapture the past, which was a mistake—one should never try to recapture the past. I had not been out of England for seven years, and was glad to get home. I felt ill, tired and war weary. World War II was over and Peter had been killed but Tony and Buffles had survived, thank God!

"The doctors said my heart was affected, that I must be quiet, take things easy, never get tired and avoid worry and shock. Rest, complete rest was needed . . . Where can one find all that except in the grave?"

Back in London she and Buffles drove past St James's Palace one night to find it and other grand homes where they had once partied had been badly damaged by incendiary bombs: "They had been tidied up and looked rather like ancient ruins that might have been there for centuries," she would recall soon afterwards when she began her memoir. "As we stood in that haunted, moonlit street I remember so vividly the lights and laughter and the loves of pre-war days—all gone now, cold and dead like this deserted cul-de-sac. As the past came rushing back I felt an icy chill—my eyes were blinded with tears and all the friends and those years gone forever, never to be recaptured."

Sheila health problems were compounded by her troubled marriage. Life with Buffles was becoming unbearable. He had returned from war a changed man and, as many others had done, turned to alcohol to numb the anguish of conflict. For Sheila, it brought back the sad memories of Loughie all those years before: "Buffles and I seemed to have drifted so far apart. I was worried about him constantly. The war had changed him completely. He was drinking which turned him into a complete stranger. We talked things over in his sober moments. He said he couldn't account for his state of mind unless it was the result of the war and the frustrations and endless difficulties which had come with the long-awaited peace."

Tony, now approaching 30 years old, wanted his mother and stepfather to stay together: "He was so wise and helpful," Sheila recounted. "We all decided that I should take a trip to America, get well and on my return Buffles and I would try to readjust our lives. [Buffles] was sure he could give up drinking and end his war romance. In fact, he said he would leave for Belgium after seeing me off to America and fix everything."

But bad weather delayed her departure and a restless Buffles didn't wait to see her off: "I was hurt and unhappy as I left London and stepped into the huge Pan American Constellation alone. Our butler, John, saw me off."

Her mood changed on board when she sat down next to William Averell Harriman, the US businessman and politician whom she had got to know during his time as US Ambassador in London. He was returning to take up a position in the Cabinet of President Harry Truman as Secretary of Commerce. It took just six hours to cross the Atlantic, a "calm lake" below while they watched, transfixed by the colours of the Aurora Borealis above.

Sheila checked into the Plaza Hotel on Fifth Avenue when she arrived in New York, stating on her immigration documents that she was visiting two close friends, Mrs Howard Dietz, wife of the famed songwriter and producer, and Mrs Herbert Agar, wife of the Pulitzer Prize–winning journalist.

But it was Vincent Astor and his wife Minnie who met her, hosting a welcome party that night at the Astor family's

2800-acre estate, Ferncliff, at Rhinebeck on the Hudson: "I was extremely touched. I could never have believed that I had so many friends," she would write.

Over the next week she wandered the streets of New York, eyes goggled at the city with its shop windows laden with food and clothes that hadn't been seen in England since the start of the war, as if America was on another planet: "Actually, all that food made me feel slightly sick. It was almost obscene with the rest of the world starving. I must frankly admit that after a few days I almost began to forget, and to believe I had been living a nightmare for seven long years and that I had woken up at last."

Sheila's arrival was soon noticed by the US media, ever vigilant to spot an English aristocrat, and particularly one who needed no introduction She was simply Lady Milbanke, even in a society that had no real notion of titles or royalty. Sheila was photographed in a Plaza suite decorated by Elsie Mendl for a spread for *Vogue* magazine and spotted lunching at the Ritz with Mrs Dietz: "Both were smart in the uniform black suit that chic women here practically live in from Fall to Spring—the only relief, gay hats spilling flowers or feathers. Mrs Dietz wore a tiny Kelly-green cloche and Lady Milbanke's little black hat had black ostrich plumes."

Stuart Symington came to visit while she was at Ferncliff. He was now Under Secretary for Air and embarking on a spectacular political career. Vincent arranged for them to be alone: "Stuart hadn't changed in appearance but I imagined he had probably changed in character. He had gone a long way in eight years. He had been rather a playboy, and we were both rather socially inclined in the old days. I imagined he had become much more serious. So had I."

It was a time for renewed acquaintances, spending time with Serge Obolensky, who had served in the US Army during the war as a Lieutenant-Colonel in the US Paratroopers, making his first jump at the age of 53 and being credited, with three other soldiers, of capturing Sardinia in 1943. Back in New York after the war he was now vice chairman of the Hilton Hotels Corporation: "He does not change much with the years," Sheila wrote of the man with whom she almost eloped. "I am always happy to see him."

As she was packing to go back to London, Tony rang to advise his mother against going home too soon: "I advise you to stay on until spring," he suggested. "It is going to be cold and dreary here this winter". Sheila took it as a warning that Buffles had not kept his promise: "There was meaning in his voice, it sounded like a warning. It was almost an order."

Instead, she travelled across the country, moving from the earnest creativity of New York via the glitterati of California to the rich idleness of Florida. By January 1947 she was in Los Angeles as a guest of John Cheever Cowdin, the chairman of Universal Pictures in Hollywood, and his wife Andrea. A local paper reported her presence: "When she was here 20 years ago Rudolph Valentino greatly admired her and danced with her many times."

She visited Valentino's grave to lay flowers and stayed a few days with Douglas Fairbanks and his wife Mary Lee at their home in Pacific Palisades. David Niven lived next door, sad and lonely after his wife's death, and she mingled at parties with movie stars like Clark Gable—"I thought him charming!"— and Deborah Kerr. Serge Obolensky came to visit and the Duke and Duchess of Windsor were in town with mutual friends—"I began to like her," she wrote of Wallis.

(The depth of Sheila's eventual friendship with Wallis Simpson was perhaps best reflected in a hand-written will drawn up by the Duchess in the mid-1950s, but never executed. In it Wallis described how she wanted their household effects and personal items to be dispersed, mostly given to museums or sold off. But some "special friends" would be allowed to choose some jewellery. Seven women were named, including some relatives. Sheila Milbanke was the only woman from their pre-war days in London who was on the list.)

One day the scriptwriter Charles Brackett, already an Academy Award winner who would write *Sunset Boulevard*, took her to see a cemetery. As she stood admiring the scenery set against the "purple-blue [San Gabriel] mountains in the distance", the sounds of the Brahms hymn "Cradle Song" filtered out from the chapel—one of Peter's favourites.

She left, moved by what she had seen and heard, and raised it the next day at a lunch attended by several people including the English novelist Evelyn Waugh, who was in Hollywood to negotiate film rights for his 1945 novel *Brideshead Revisited*. The discussions had gone badly and the idea was abandoned, leaving Waugh dispirited, so when Sheila mentioned that she'd been to "an extraordinary cemetery" called Forest Lawn, he became curious.

Waugh's close friend and biographer, the author Christopher Sykes, wrote about the meeting in his 1975 biography of the writer:

> Sheila was one who shone in the fashionable London world of the twenties and thirties, and was among Evelyn's friends. She was a most amusing and amiable woman and held to be one of taste. Sheila told Evelyn that she had been shown a graveyard, just outside Los Angeles, which for sheer exquisite sensitive beauty surpassed anything she had seen of that kind. In its power of faith and consolation it was unique. It was religion and art brought to their highest possible association.

Sheila squired an enchanted Waugh around the facility the next day. After that the author went by himself each day for a week, spending hours at a time while an MGM limousine waited. He would not only wander the grounds that he later, in his memoir, described as "Tivoli Gardens for the dead", but he spoke to the staff—particularly to the chief embalmer about his work, painting loved ones.

It was "a deep mine of literary gold", he told his agent, before heading back to London where he spent the next four months penning his new novel *The Loved One*, a satirical story about the Los Angeles funeral business and Hollywood and British expatriates, in which Forest Lawn became Whispering Glades.

Sheila's year of birth had foreshortened to "about 1900" on May 28, 1947, when she boarded the liner SS *America* for the week-long journey home across the Atlantic, opting once again for sea over air travel. As the boat left the harbour she was handed a cable from Buffles, telling her that he had ended the affair and would be at Southampton to meet her: "I thought everything was going to work out for us. I felt well again and able to cope with our lives. I was excited at the prospect of getting home."

She stood on the back deck watching the New York skyline recede, the sound of Frank Sinatra's voice in her ears singing *September Song,* which he'd just recorded about life and death and wasting time.

Suddenly the joy was gone, replaced by a sense of foreboding. "For the first time in my life I had an apprehension about the future; a fear of loneliness, a strange restlessness and a feeling of uncertainty."

Three days out at sea she was told to go to the radio room. There was an urgent telephone call from her son in London: "I have some terribly sad news for you," Tony began. "You must be brave and strong. Hold onto something. It's about Buffles."

"Is he dead?" It was the only conclusion she could reach.

Tony hesitated: "Yes."

The line crackled, his voice fading away on the waves: "Can you hear me? What arrangements do you want made? Are you all right?"

Sheila felt speechless, numb and unable to think what to say:

"You make the arrangements. Don't worry about me."

The operator cut in, coldly: "Time's up." The line went dead.

The day after she had left port—at about the time she felt the unease—Buffles had been a passenger in a taxi driving through the centre of the Belgian city of Ghent when it collided with a tram. He received severe head injuries and was flown back to London, where he was treated in a Chelsea nursing home, but died a few hours before Tony made the call to his mother. Sir John "Buffles" Milbanke, the handsome Boxing Baronet, financier to the wealthy and Sheila's husband of nineteen years, was aged just forty-five.

He had survived six years of war and was heading home to his wife after ending a long-standing affair to start a new life. The certificate of death would state that the head injuries sustained in the accident had been compounded by hypostatic pneumonia and that he had died without regaining consciousness.

Sheila Milbanke had lost a son in the first days of the war and now a husband soon after the conflict had come to an end. The grief was overwhelming as she was swamped by memories which smothered any regret about the slow disintegration of their marriage: "Blank days, sleepless nights flooded with memories. The years seemed to slip away and we were young again, and so much in love, galloping our horses into the sunset, racing each other; always competition and that strange sex antagonism.

"I couldn't believe Buffles was dead; that fate had stepped in and changed my life. He had been so vital, it seemed as if he were still away at the war. He had such charm, such arrogance mixed with tremendous sweetness. I felt bewildered and lost without him. I was stunned and utterly miserable. I thought to myself: 'Head high, walk very tall.'"

For once, there were no friends aboard and Sheila was alone with her thoughts for three days until the ship reached Southampton. Tony was there to meet her. She had decided that although Buffles was not a member of the Rosslyn family, he should be cremated and his remains kept at the Rosslyn chapel: "I felt Buffie would be less lonely than his own burial ground at Mullaboden."

Tony commissioned a single stained-glass window to be installed in the chapel. It depicted an airman standing on the White Cliffs of Dover and bore both the St Clair and Milbanke family mottos—"Fight" and "Resolute and Firm" respectively. It was dedicated to "Pilot Officer Peter St Clair-Erskine, who died on active service 1939, and to his stepfather, Wing Commander Sir John Milbanke, who died in 1947 from injuries also received during World War II"—a mistruth clearly designed to carefully cover his infidelity and the manner of his death.

Duff Cooper was among those who offered condolences, as he had been with Peter's death eight years before. She replied to him on July 23, a short note that seemed to echo her sadness about their marriage: "Dearest Duff, Thank you for your wonderful letter. I am very sad and bewildered by the whole affair—I mean Life! and Death. Love Sheila".

She stayed at Brook House, comforted by dozens of condolence letters. She finally ventured out when another face from the past beckoned. Edward, the Duke of Windsor and his stern Duchess insisted that she stay with them at their villa in the south of France: "They had a charming villa called La Croe at Cap d'Antibes. It had large grounds and a swimming pool set near the sea. One could also bathe off the rocks. The view was beautiful.

"I will never forget how charming they were to me. They seemed to be deeply in love with each other after 10 years. Their lives were made up of love and laughter, fun and sense, and they helped me a great deal. She is a perfectionist and a great character. She has lovely, strange eyes. I am devoted to them both."

Among the guests in nearby villas that summer was a Russian man she had known, on and off, since the early 1920s when she went to parties at Prince Felix Youssoupoff's flat in Kensington. She'd only had eyes for Serge Obolensky at the time, but Dimitri Romanoff, another of the exiled princes, had become a friend whom she'd seen occasionally over the intervening years. He was a kindred soul.

Reality returned when she got back to London after the summer. Buffles, who had taken a senior management position with the famous engineering firm Vickers after the war, had written his will barely six months before the accident. The document, witnessed by his housekeeper Mrs Streeter and maid Miss Thorn, generated a degree of mystery. For a man who had a reputation for financial competence and had once entertained the dream of creating a national lottery, his estate was relatively modest—£9600, most of which he left to his stepson, the Earl of Rosslyn, and to his wife Sheila, with a token £100 for his butler.

But there were also two payments to female friends, which would reveal the identity of the women he had been seeing. He bequeathed £500 to the Countess Marie Goethals, wife of the Belgian nobleman Rene Goethals, who lived with her husband in a castle outside Ghent where he was killed.

More intriguingly, the sum of £100 was left to Princess Weikersheim who had fled Austria with her husband at the beginning of World War II and settled on a property in Surrey. The Milbankes and the Weikersheims most probably met when both couples attended two society functions in July 1939, but Sheila seems not to have remembered that occasion, if one of her later letters is any indication. Writing to Georgia Sitwell in 1941, she confided: "Was glad to get a glimpse of 'the Princess' at last and thought her very fascinating."

The mystery is further deepened by an unconnected document that would surface more than fifty years later, in a book about Soviet espionage. The authors of The Crown Jewels: The British Secrets Exposed by the KGB Archives published a series of raw, and at times unsourced, documents that gave an account of KGB attempts to infiltrate British society. One of these documents referred to the possibility of agents blackmailing high society figures:

Another method is that of blackmailing wives. A Mrs Beaumont Neilson is the lover of a suspect called S De Trey. He encourages her to run heavily into debt. As her husband is vice-chairman of Vickers . . . De Trey blackmails Mrs Beaumont Neilson for information about Vickers and its associated firms. Mrs Beaumont

Neilson is now living in the house of Buffles Milbanke, who was some months ago in charge of the aerial defences of Vickers. His girlfriend is Pupe Weikersheim, daughter of Count Windischgraetz.

Like the princess—who had attended Sir John's memorial service in London—Mrs Beaumont Neilson did exist. It seems that by then she was estranged from her businessman husband John, so her capacity to exert influence over him would have been minimal; she had lived for some years in a flat in Maida Vale, not far from the Milbankes.

The death of Buffles would indirectly trigger another sad series of events over the next two years, culminating in an end to the title Baronet of Milbanke. At his death, the title had automatically passed to his younger brother, Ralph, known as Toby, who was a larger-than-life character in London's social world and often rode his horse "Tiger" across the city to visit friends, leaving the horse tethered outside their houses. In 1939, for a bet, he had hit a golf ball from Tower Bridge to the steps of the famous White's Club, where he was a member.

Toby also held a pilot's licence and became a war hero like his father. In September 1940, while serving as a second lieutenant with the Royal Armoured Corps, he was awarded the Military Cross, "for gallant and distinguished services in action in connection with operations in the field". He was wounded three times during World War II, serving in North Africa, and returned home shattered psychologically. In November 1949, two years after becoming the 12th Baronet of Milbanke, Ralph shot himself in the head, alone in the Mayfair apartment that had been left to him by his mother. He had no wife and no children, so the title died with him and remains unclaimed.

The village of Bracknell lies deep in the forests of Berkshire where one of Henry VIII's hunting lodges once stood and where he banished his first wife, Catherine of Aragon, until he organised an annulment of their marriage.

In the nineteenth century, the playwright Oscar Wilde stayed and worked at a local estate and later named one of his most famous characters, Lady Augusta Bracknell from his play *The Importance of Being Earnest*, after the village. Lady Bracknell represented the hypocrisy of the Victorian age and in particular of those who married into the aristocracy from the lower classes and then adopted a pious position against those who might follow them up the social ladder.

But, unlike Lady Bracknell's attitude toward change, the village of Bracknell would prove a place of renewal. In the early 1950s it was identified as a "new town" by planning authorities, which wanted to relieve the housing crisis caused by the wartime bombings by building a series of satellite towns around London's perimeter. Bracknell, which had a railway station, was among those chosen.

Sheila would live in Brook House until the early 1950s. A guest book among the photo albums kept by the family shows a constant flow of visitors through the years until the house was compulsorily acquired as part of the "new town" vision, and the only modern signs of the property are two streets named

Milbanke. Despite their largely separate lives, Buffles had also come to regard Brook House as his home and had sat in the study overlooking the grounds one day in mid-December 1946, writing his will, struggling to find a way to end his marital affairs and rekindle his marriage.

Sheila was eventually drawn back to London where she bought a large apartment in Mayfair and resumed her pre-war life, if slightly quieter and attracting much less publicity. There would still be moments when she caught the attention of the media, such as the day she organised a brass band to welcome Vincent Astor ashore at Plymouth to the strains of "Rule Britannia", and the occasional snippet noting that she was hosting the Duke and Duchess of Windsor for the summer at Biarritz or simply that she was leaving for a six-week holiday in Florida. But the heady days of public attention were largely over, not that it had ever mattered to a woman whose memoir would barely mention her personal fame. It was as if she was aware of those outside her windows, figuratively speaking, but rarely chose to peek outside.

Despite this, Sheila remained at the head of the high-society social circuit, as Charles Hepburn Johnston's diaries noted: " . . . we found ourselves firmly embedded in the 'Sheila-Wheeler set' so called because it more or less revolved around Sheila Loughborough/Milbanke, London's Australian-born fun-dictator of the twenties and thirties, still going strongly in the fifties."

Sir Charles would also meet Sheila in the United States and he described a dinner party at the home of Winston Guest, an international polo player, businessman and second-cousin to his namesake, Winston Churchill:

Dinner two nights ago at Winston Guest's. Candles, flowers, champagne, frog's legs, duck. I sat next to "Cee Zee" Guest, who is a sort of mixture between Susie Stirling and Pat Wilson. The newspaper millionaire W.R. Hearst junior arrived unexpectedly after dinner—rather awkward because his ex-wife was there, but Sheila made it all right because as soon as she saw him she called out "William Randolph!" and got him in a corner talking travel business.

There would also be losses. Eileen Sutherland and Jeanie Norton had both died during the war and Laura Corrigan had followed in 1948. King George VI—her "Prince Bertie"—died on February 6, 1952 from lung cancer but she wrote only a few words in her memoir: "The premature death of King George VI early in 1952 made everyone very sad."

It seemed strange to have written so little about a man who had meant so much but, given that she would have expected that others might one day read her memoir, it probably said more about her loyalty to his memory.

Instead, Sheila wrote to the new queen, Elizabeth, to express her condolences. The two families had known each other through the 1930s and Tony had established a friendship with the young Princess Elizabeth, which would be retained over the years with polite correspondence and even an exchange of birthday cards through the 1970s.

Sheila

The Queen eventually replied to Sheila in April, in a black-lined envelope closed with the royal seal:

Dear Lady Milbanke,
Please forgive the long delay in answering your kind letter of
sympathy at the death of my father, which touched me deeply. Owing
to the endless number of letters I have received, it has taken me some
time to answer them all. We have been greatly strengthened to know
that the thoughts and prayers of so many people have been with us
and sharing our sorrow. Thank you once again,
Yours sincerely,
Elizabeth R

Four years later there would be further correspondence between them when Sheila decided to pass on some of the letters that had flashed back and forth between her and the princes Edward, Albert and George after the Great War. The Queen's response was succinct: "It was very kind of you to send me those letters of my father's and my uncles. They were most interesting and amusing."

Soon after, driven by the death of Bertie, Sheila gave up smoking, quoting King James I who in 1616 had described tobacco as a "black stinking fume". She also rejoined the Women's Voluntary Service, this time to help the plight of refugees of the 1956 Hungarian Uprising.

———•••———

Women may have won the vote and equal rights to divorce but even in the late 1940s society still regarded the home as the place for married women, particularly in upper-class society. Ever one for pushing boundaries, Lady Sheila Milbanke decided in 1948 to become a businesswoman and opened a travel agency.

The seeds had been sown at the end of a trip to New York that year, during which she had been inspired by the attitudes of her American circle of friends that life had not ended, but was just beginning. She sailed back to London aboard the *Queen Mary*: "I stood alone on the deck and watched the fantastic skyline disappear into the rosy mist of dawn," she wrote. "I wondered 'Does life begin at fifty?' It reminded me of the quote in the book *Point of No Return*, by John P Marquand, which said '50 is a period of life when time begins altering faces in all sorts of disagreeable and incongruous ways'. I whisked away that thought and wondered if dreams were better than facts."

She began the business soon after returning to London, initially buying shares in a small company owned by a friend, and then talking her way into opening a desk with two staff at the Fortnum & Mason department store in Piccadilly. What had begun as a search for a new purpose swiftly became a creative joy. Interviewed in 1951 she reminisced about her success and expansion: "We invented all sorts of enjoyable slogans. We started with a manager and one assistant. Now we have a counter and a window at Fortnum & Mason plus a large office . . . and employ a staff of 18. I am the chairman and the directors include the Duchess of Marlborough, Lord Ashcombe and Sir Anthony Weldon."

The business had given her a new lease on life, she told *The Australian Women's Weekly*: "I have started a business career because I believe life begins at 50 and ends at 91. All the people of my age are happier if they have an interest in life, especially if they are widows; otherwise they become bores."

As she slowly disappeared from the social pages of the newspapers that had once doted on her beauty and fashion sense, Sheila parlayed her contact book—which contained names like Emerald and Nancy Cunard, whose family owned the famous shipping line—into a thriving business, outgrowing the department store and moving into its own offices, Milbanke House, in New Bond Street.

Eventually Milbanke Travel was producing its own holiday magazine, with package tours north to Norway, east to Romania, Bulgaria and Greece, and south to the Costa del Sol, Tunis and Tangiers. The company offered services for everything—flights, cruise ships, hotel rooms, car hire, travellers' cheques and even beach charges.

Sheila had insisted that the Duchess of Marlborough join her on the board of directors "because women need representation nowadays". Ultimately she removed herself from the day-to-day management and concentrated on her client list, where there was room for flair. In late 1952 she launched a project with her friend the Maharaja of Cooch Behar which offered twelve-day tours for paying guests hunting tigers from the backs of elephants.

Such hunts had been traditional for over a century but, when India's aristocrats began to feel the financial pinch, just as their English counterparts had done half a century before, they started to open up their lands to commercial enterprise. The hunting grounds of the maharaja's estate lay in the province of Bengal in the north-east of India. The new project chiefly targeted moneyed Americans and offered five separate hunts in the season, between January and March; the trappings of luxury included a retinue of manservants and cocktails at sunset, surrounded by the sights and sounds of the Indian jungle that Kipling had known and popularised.

Sheila launched the project in New York, during what had now become her annual pilgrimage to the United States. *The New York Times* lapped up the story; under the heading "Lady Milbanke and the Cooch Behar Tigers" it ran a long interview with her, in which she explained: "It all began at a dinner party last summer when the Maharaja mused with faint melancholy 'How am I going to keep my elephants?' You know, one is always anxious to earn some dollars these days. It's a unique opportunity that has never been done before."

She likened these expeditions to the traditional hunts on grand English estates; when asked if she could guarantee a tiger, she replied: "There are an awful lot of leopards and panthers there, and I should say one would be awfully unlucky if he didn't get a tiger." And did she hunt? the reporter inquired: "I couldn't shoot a fly," Sheila winced gently.

Years later, in May 1967, as her health began to wane, Sheila agreed to sell her share of Milbanke Travel to the British hotel and restaurant company Forte. By then it had grown into an operation with several entities, with eight branches across the country and a staff of 200. There were also operations in the United States and Australia, which made it one of the largest independent travel companies; during the previous year it had generated a turnover of £5 million and sold 40,000 holiday packages. Sheila Milbanke had left a unique mark on the business world, just as she had done on so many other worlds into which she had ventured.

29

A PRINCE OF RUSSIA

The lasting memory Prince Dimitri Romanoff would have of landing in England in 1919 was not of his rescue from almost certain death at the hands of Bolshevik revolutionaries but, as he would later write, watching the "flow of tears" as his grandmother Maria, the Dowager Empress of Russia, hugged her sister Alexandra, the Queen Mother of England, on the docks of Portsmouth Harbour.

Dimitri was seventeen years old when he and his family arrived in London aboard the HMS *Nelson*. He had been born in a thousand-room palace with the sound of cannons celebrating his birth; he'd been raised amid the untold wealth and splendour of one of the world's great dynasties. But his family had been displaced by revolution and terror and now they had to start a new life in exile. His surviving family members had lived under house arrest for two years, sleeping in their clothes with few possessions and little food as they waited to be either rescued by the Allies or delivered for slaughter into the hands of the revolutionaries. They were among the thirty-five direct relatives of the royal Romanoff family who would escape.

It was only when German troops—their former and future enemy—freed them that he was told of the murder of his uncle, Tsar Nicholas II, and his family. The same fate would almost certainly have befallen them, given that his mother was the Tsar's sister, Grand Duchess Xenia Alexandrovna, and his father was the Grand Duke Alexander Mikhailovich, head of the air force and navy and close advisor to the Tsar.

After another nine months on the island of Malta, they were brought to London, where King George V and Queen Mary were waiting on the platform at Victoria Station to usher them into the bosom of Buckingham Palace. Such was the familial network of the European dynasties that the King of England was the first cousin of the Tsar of Russia and of the Kaiser of Germany.

"We were driven straight to Buckingham Palace, where we were met on arrival by the Prince of Wales, who was standing at the entrance to the palace. He escorted us to our rooms. That first night in London did not seem so strange. The atmosphere of one palace is much like another and being in one in London with our English relatives helped obscure the reality of the situation," Dimitri would recall many years later.

Dimitri's unpublished memoir, written in 1970, gives an intriguing account of life in Buckingham Palace over the next few months, under the grace and favour of the British royal family: "We dined with King George and Queen Mary nearly every evening. Not having evening dress [we] were obliged to wear dark suits to dinner, which were inappropriate as the King always changed into white tie and tails ... The King had a special way of eating pears: 'What are you doing?' he demanded when I began cutting my pear in the conventional manner. 'I'm trying to eat a pear,' I replied.

"He then proceeded to show me his own special way of tackling a juicy pear. He would cut it in half then scoop out the fruit with his spoon, leaving the skin standing on the plate. As the meal progressed the King's language would grow increasingly colourful and I always marvelled at Queen Mary's patience. King George's physical resemblance to Emperor Nicholas was emphasised by his habit of sucking his moustache whilst eating his soup, which produced a drawing sound. The first time I saw him do this I turned to my mother and whispered 'Just like Uncle Nicky.'"

The death of "Uncle Nicky" and his family was also raised around the dinner table. King George laid the blame squarely at the feet of Prime Minister Lloyd George: "He told my mother that at the beginning of the revolution, during the time of the provisional government, everything had been made ready to take the Emperor and his family into exile. [Revolutionary leader Alexander] Kerensky was willing to allow them to leave and in fact was keen that they should.

"A British cruiser was standing ready at Murmansk but at the last minute Lloyd George decided against the evacuation. Kerensky, with the intention of safeguarding the family by getting them away from the centre of events, had them sent to Siberia. The one opportunity for the family to leave Russia from the north had passed. I twice heard King George refer to Lloyd George as 'that murderer' in the presence of my mother."

During their two-month stay, Dimitri enjoyed a privileged insider's glimpse of the everyday life of the royal family. He was amazed at the King's frequent forays into Hyde Park, galloping through the palace gates alone on horseback, while the princes wandered freely and unnoticed through Green Park. He befriended the two oldest princes and was also witness to the King's abrasive relationship with his children. Edward occupied a suite of three rooms on the top floor at the front of the palace: "He was always getting into trouble with the King and could not seem to do anything which pleased him."

But Edward was not the only child to suffer their father's sharp tongue and inflexible nature. Bertie's desperate efforts to overcome his stammer were hampered by the King's impatience; he laughed openly at Prince George's attempts to grow a moustache and poked fun at the size of Princess Mary's feet, claiming they were bigger than his.

It was inevitable that Dimitri would drift into the tangle of impoverished Russian royalty who either lived or lounged and partied at the Hyde Park apartment of Felix Youssoupoff, who was his brother-in-law and married to his older sister, Irina. Dimitri was among the youngest of the crowd and flirted at its edges; he noticed the beautiful English society women who became entranced by the excitement and colour of the Russian enclave. Among them was Lady Sheila Loughborough, who had captured the attention of another of his relatives, Prince Serge Obolensky.

But life had to move on. A family that had once lacked for nothing now had to forage for everything. Success had to be of Dimitri's own making, and London did not seem big enough for him to achieve that. In December 1923, at the age of twenty-two and after studying at Oxford, he left with friends on what was supposed to be a short holiday to New York. Instead, he stayed there for seven years, thoroughly engrossed by the character of the city and its people. He was intrigued by the tailor who had adopted a Russian surname to sound exotic; he spent evenings watching gangsters like Al Capone and his thugs in a basement speakeasy, drinking illegal grog with police officers; he even dined with the Queen of New York, Grace Vanderbilt, in her Fifth Avenue mansion. His was a world of extremes: a name and heritage worth nothing, and yet a ticket to every society event in the world's most exciting city.

He initially worked in the foreign exchange department of the National American Bank of Manhattan, where he almost immediately attracted publicity as a lost Russian royal—"Mr Dimitri, a dark complexioned, brown-eyed and not unhandsome youth"—who had fallen on hard times. He was "very attentive and faithful to his duties and highly regarded," the bank president told *The Washington Post* when the story broke. Dimitri, embarrassed by the publicity, insisted to the newspaper that he had no intention of seeking American citizenship: "I will always be Russian and one day I will go back, but not while the Bolsheviks rule."

That job didn't last and he began working for a businessman who was manufacturing an early-model household refrigerator; he moved south to Baltimore. By day he worked on the factory floor, where he was known as Mr Alexander, and by night he lived in the cultured environs of the Maryland Club, where he was Prince Dimitri. But, inevitably, a local newspaper eventually exposed his double life.

He moved back to New York and the world of high finance, working for a Wall Street stockbroking firm, FB Keach and Co., as the market first boomed before crashing in 1929. He would recall the heady days when "one was assured of a profit within a couple of days". A businessman walked into his office one day and produced three $10,000 notes with which to open an account, such were the flood of money and the carefree spending habits. In the days before the crash he encouraged a friend—the legendary investment banker, philanthropist and patron of the arts, Otto Kahn—to buy 100,000 shares in a copper company at $1.50 per share and to sell out two days later at $4 per share. Kahn followed his advice and took his $250,000 profit. The market crashed a week later, and Dimitri watched as the stockroom ticker-tape spat out losses for six hours before closing to keep up with the financial carnage.

In 1930 he moved to a rival firm, GMP Murphy, and was offered a job in the company's London offices, which he took. He resettled in Europe, although his working life was anything but settled. He switched between the financial world of London and the more relaxed lifestyle of continental Europe; he even managed the Chanel boutique in the French tourist mecca of

Biarritz in the summer of 1931, during which time he met and later that year married another Russian exile, Countess Marina Sergeievna Golenistcheva-Koutouzova.

Before the revolution their two families had known each other well and Dimitri had first met the woman he called Myra when she was a child of eight. But she was eighteen years old now and modelling for Chanel; Dimitri, now aged thirty, fell instantly in love. They would spend the next eight years between London and Paris, where Dimitri worked again as a broker, and they had a daughter, Princess Nadejda, before World War II exploded.

Dimitri enlisted with the British Royal Navy and served as a lieutenant commander during the evacuation of Dunkirk, during which he made four trips across the channel aboard the paddle steamer *Queen of Thanet* and helped to rescue 4000 men, including 2000 from another rescue ship, the LNRS *Prague*, which had been hit by German bombers. He finished the war as an admiralty liaison officer with the Greek Navy and then turned his management skills to good effect when he was appointed secretary of the elite Travellers' Club in Paris, which stood in the Champs-Élysées below the Arc de Triomphe and in the heart of the Parisian social and political milieu.

But this lifestyle would ultimately mean the end of his marriage. He divorced Myra in 1947 and abandoned Paris, heading for London once more. This time he became a sales representative for the Canadian distillery, Seagram's, a job he still held in 1954 when he rekindled a lifelong friendship with Sheila Milbanke.

Sheila

Dimitri and Sheila would both describe the origins of their union in a very matter-of-fact manner, perhaps because it was a relationship of shared moments and friendship rather than of heart-pounding love. They had known each other for more than thirty years in a world filled with extraordinary people and amazing experiences.

Dimitri's memoir recounts a meeting between him and Sheila orchestrated by the Duchess of Windsor in August 1954, seven years after they had renewed acquaintances in the wake of Buffles' death. Dimitri had just come from an extravagant tour of the Greek islands in the company of a clutch of European royals. The cruise, organised by King Paul and Queen Frederika of Greece, was essentially a tourism promotion. The liner *Agamemnon* had left from Naples in mid-August for a ten-day tour of Greece and its ancient wonders and island magnificence. It was viewed by the media as a love boat for the young royals from Europe's dead or dying dynasties.

There were thirty-seven of them under the age of twenty on board: apart from the Greek monarch's three children, there were the crown princes and princesses of the Netherlands, Italy, Bulgaria, Denmark and Yugoslavia, as well as the children of a dozen counts and countesses of European provinces. There was at least one marriage that would eventuate from the cruise: King Paul's oldest child, Princess Sophia, met Prince Juan Carlos of Spain on board; they were both sixteen years old at that time and they married eight years later.

After they docked back in Naples, Dimitri took the train to Rome, "where I met my old friend Sheila Milbanke," as he would later write. "I had known her since 1919 when we met at Felix's flat in Knightsbridge. I had seen her through the years and we were always good friends. I had to return to Athens on business for Seagram's and we later met in Paris. We were invited to spend the weekend with the Duke and Duchess of Windsor at the Mill, their country house near Gif-sur-Yvette, and soon after Sheila and I became engaged. I proposed to her by saying 'You're going to marry me, aren't you?' and she agreed. Wallis said later 'Think what you like, but I fixed this marriage.'"

Sheila was equally perfunctory. In her memoir, she wrote of Dimitri visiting her at Brook House which was not far from the splendours of Hampton Court Palace where his mother, the Grand Duchess Xenia, now in her late 70s, lived in a "grace and favour" apartment next to the famous maze.

After one visit, Tony stated the obvious: "I think Dimitri is falling in love with you."

"Nonsense," she had replied. "He is my great friend, and friendship is more important as one grows older."

A month later she and Tony flew to Italy to holiday with friends at Praiano on the Amalfi coast in a villa perched halfway down a cliff: "200 steps down from the road and 200 steps to the sea; blue sea and blazing sun, and Capri in the distance. I adored it."

They then headed for Rome where she met Dimitri: "He proposed to me. I said 'Perhaps' and then joined friends at Montecatini near Florence. Dimitri and I met later in Paris. He proposed again."

"You are going to marry me," he told her.

"No," she replied firmly.

"Yes," he countered.

"Yes," she consented.

They were wed, quietly, at the Marylebone registry office on October 29, 1954, on what would have been Peter's 36th birthday. There were just two witnesses—a far cry from her second marriage, which had caused a traffic jam along the Strand—and spent their honeymoon in Spain. The following May they went through a ceremony before Archbishop Nikodim, head of the Russian Orthodox Church outside Russia, in a chapel at Hampton Court Palace.

It was a marriage of companionship and friendship in many ways, their lives having crisscrossed and touched often over the years. Although their backgrounds, triumphs and struggles had been very different, their friends and experiences made them as compatible as any couple who had spent a lifetime together.

They had both been drawn to the energy and opportunity of the United States and had mutual friends in that country, although there was no evidence they had ever crossed paths during their travels. In his memoir Dimitri wrote about Rudolph Valentino's casket being swamped with flowers as the actor lay in state in Campbell's funeral parlour in Columbus Square, but he was probably unaware of Sheila's fleeting romance with the screen star eight months earlier. Like Sheila, he was friends with Vincent Astor and had been invited to spend a few nights aboard his yacht *Nourmahal*, on which Sheila would also cruise some years later.

Both had been invited to dinner parties thrown by Gloria Vanderbilt and Mrs Randolph Hearst, and they had attended fancy dress balls hosted by Elsa Maxwell. But never were they there at the same time. Dimitri had been acquainted with the heiress Barbara Hutton, whom he met on several occasions while holidaying in Cannes, but this had been at least two years and one husband before Sheila became embroiled in her life. Perhaps their former lives had come closest to touching through their separate friendships with Serge Obolensky, who had settled in New York, and with the exotic couple, Alfred Duff Cooper and Lady Diana Cooper, whom both counted as among their dearest friends.

As a couple then, Dimitri and Sheila had many entries in common in the address books they maintained at their home at 20 Wilton Street, within sight of the garden walls of Buckingham Palace. There were two versions—the larger address book sat in the front room downstairs, near the telephone and overlaid with frequent scribbled updates, while a smaller, neater version was in Sheila's bedroom. Their pages are filled with names famous from almost half a century of English society.

There was Viscountess Astor in Sandwich, Lord Beaverbrook in Arlington House and Chips in Belgrave Square; a private number at Kensington Palace for the Duchess of Kent, as well as contacts for the Duchesses of Marlborough and Westminster and the Maharani of Jaipur. Cecil Beaton lived in Pelham Place, Nöel Coward in Belgrave, the Sitwells in Towcester and Douglas Fairbanks Jr in Chelsea.

Of her closest friends, the former Freda Dudley Ward was in Kensington and Poppy Thursby in Grosvenor Place. Sheila's neighbours included Lord and Lady "Dickie and Edwina"

Mountbatten at No. 2, Viscountess Wimborne at No. 5, Lady Metcalfe at No. 16, the Duchess of Rutland at No. 21 and the Duchess of Sutherland at No. 33.

In New York there were numbers for Gilbert and Kitty Miller on Park Avenue and Serge Obolensky at the Ambassador Hotel, while at Palm Beach there were the Vanderbilts and "Mrs Kennedy, Rose, Joe and Jack". Wallis and Edward were in Paris, along with the Countess von Bismarck and Prince Youssoupoff.

And yet there was also a charming homeliness about some of the entries, with the celebrated names appearing in among reminders of their everyday life: the number for "Buck" House (4832) was below Boodle's club in Pall Mall, where Dimitri was a member; Countess Cadogan was next to a number for the local chemist; the various contacts for Lady Diana Cooper were above Cartier and the Earl of Derby was squashed between the dressmaker and the dentist.

There was still a role in society for the pair, who were occasionally noted among the guests at a fashionable ball or a society luncheon; they even organised the performance of a play in aid of one of Queen Elizabeth's charities. But travelling and socialising together would be their delight —a more relaxed version of the habits of a lifetime. Sheila had been back and forth to the United States a dozen times by 1959, when they travelled to New York as a couple. New York was a shock for Dimitri, who had last been there in 1930 as the Depression struck. The Empire State Building and the Waldorf Astoria were now among the structures on the expanding skyline, so foreign to European cities. The traffic and noise had also exploded.

They stayed at the Manhattan Hotel on Seventh Avenue. During a meal at the fashionable restaurant La Côte Basque, which had recently been opened by the haughty French restaurateur and host Henri Soulé, they were introduced to Marilyn Monroe and her then husband, the playwright Arthur Miller. Dimitri would later write of this meeting: "Although she gave the impression of being a dumb blonde she most certainly was not. She wore no makeup and her hair was rather messy, and she did not look particularly beautiful."

They spent weekends with the Windsors in their Paris home near the Bois de Boulogne, where Edward's royal standard hung in the hallway, and at their country residence, the Mill, at Gif-sur-Yvette, where they mingled with other guests. Among them was Richard Nixon who, some years later, would hold a reception for the exiled royals at the White House.

And there were memories, as Sir Charles Johnston would note of a 1958 trip to Winchester for a family christening:

On Wednesday I drove down with Sheila and Dimitri . . . for the christening of Sheila's grandchild, the little Loughborough, in Winchester Cathedral. Afterwards we drove round in search of a house called Lank Hills where Sheila lived as a bride of eighteen during the first war when her husband was adjutant at the Rifle Depot. We found it—a mouldering Gothic revival lodge at the end of an overgrown drive. "We used to have such fun in the garden," said Sheila, "with Prince Bertie, and the Prince of Wales, and Freda (Dudley-Ward) and Jeanie (Norton) . . .

But it was their journey to Australia in 1967 that proved the most memorable for them. It was a homecoming for Sheila, of course, but for Dimitri there was also a sense of return. His father, the Grand Duke Alexander Mikhailovich, had visited Australia twice, including during the country's centenary celebrations in 1888, when he attended the opening of Centennial Park. At that time he had written home to his cousin, Tsar Nicholas: "If it were not for my duties in Russia I should never leave this paradise."

30

SMELL THE WATTLE AND THE GUM

Sheila began compiling her memoir a few months after the death of Buffles Milbanke. It must have seemed the right thing to do as life was passing by and she wondered what was left for her. She was in her early fifties and had now lost two husbands as well as a son.

It begins with a longing for the "strange magic" of Wollogorang: "I have a desire to write all I can remember in a sketchy manner, so I will attempt to skip through the years to amuse myself and you, I hope. Perhaps it will make you laugh a little and maybe even make you sad. I have just read Proust, which starts with a quotation from Shakespeare: 'When to the sessions of sweet silent thought I summon up remembrance of things past.' This seems appropriate." The initial chapters are full of details and whimsy, the memories of a childhood and the dreams of a young, vibrant girl who could see far beyond the boundary fences of her father's farm.

She called it "Waltzing Matilda", subtitled "A Sketch", and clearly wrote large sections and then put it aside—it seemed for several years—before starting again. There are errors, some simple mistakes in time and others recalling events that other records show didn't happen. For example, she wrote about both brothers, Jack and Roy, being in Egypt at the same time during the Great War as well as a childhood friend named Lionel who died at Gallipoli, broken-hearted that she had chosen Loughie rather than him.

Australian war records show that Roy only joined the army in January 1918, long after his sister had settled in London and had a baby boy and would soon be pregnant with another. Lionel, according to official records, never existed—perhaps it was a pseudonym.

There is frankness at times, about some of the men who admired her and her choices and expectations, forever chasing the elusive emotion of love. On the other hand, there is an avoidance of some issues, particularly of her relationship with "Bertie" when it is clear from other sources and events that there was a close relationship which flirted with a love that was never allowed to flourish.

Her marriage to Dimitri not only gave Sheila a husband with whom to see out her days but the daughter she never had—Dimitri's daughter Nadejda, "who might have been my own". She would also have a granddaughter when Tony married Athenais de Mortemart, a descendant of the famed mistress of Louis XIV of France, the Sun King. Tony and Athenais would have two children, Caroline born in 1956 and Peter, the current

Earl of Rosslyn, who was born in 1958.

In an entry written when her granddaughter was seven months old, Sheila pondered: "I wonder what her fate will be? Please God, save Lady Caroline."

Sheila's last entry in her memoir is dated January 14, 1960 and begins: "Now this is the end of my story." It tells of attending the wedding of Lady Pamela Mountbatten, daughter of friend and neighbour the Earl of Mountbatten, and the famous interior designer David Nightingale Hicks. The weather was terrible, with snow and ice which plunged their grand home, Broadlands, in Hampshire, into darkness: "The ceremony at Romsey Abbey was wonderful but the guests froze, except for the royal family who had installed huge electric heaters over their heads (most unfair!!) Luckily I was wearing snow boots. The special train was comfortable and we had an excellent luncheon. We were met by motor coaches and had good seats in the Abbey. The organisation was perfect. We had to keep jumping up as the Royals arrived. Headed by the Queen Mum looking sweet, Princess Margaret looking annoyed, the Duchess of Kent and Princess Alexandria both looking beautiful, footed by the Duke of Edinburgh and the Prince of Wales, both looking older.

"We arrived at Broadlands for the reception and the house was in pitch darkness. Dickie and Edwina were receiving guests in the dark except for a candelabra held in front of them by a butler. Dickie and Edwina were serene and charming, and smiling as if nothing had happened. We then pushed our way through a door into another room where we found a buffet lit by a few candles. We gratefully grabbed a glass of champagne.

"Arrived in London at 8.30 after a nine-hour icy day. Dimitri—who could not or would not go—greeted me by saying 'I told you so'—a typical husband's remark! Now this is really the end of my tale (seem to have heard that before!!!) The End?"

Her Highness Princess Dimitri lived for another nine years after the Mountbatten wedding but made no more entries in her memoir. She died on October 13, 1969, from a combination of heart failure and lung cancer, compounded by pneumonia, but this was barely noticed by media that had once doted on her. In death it seemed she had been forgotten. The *International Herald Tribune* published one of only two brief obituaries:

> She was Margaret Sheila MacKellar, daughter of Harry Chisholm, of Sydney. In 1915 she married Lord Loughborough, heir to the Earldom of Rosslyn, from whom she obtained a divorce in 1926 and who died in 1929. Their son is the sixth Earl of Rosslyn. In 1928 she married Sir John Milbanke, 11th baronet, who died in 1947. He was an amateur boxer. Between 1918 and 1939 she was a noted hostess and a frequent dance partner of the Duke of Windsor when he was the Prince of Wales. She bought a majority of shares in a Piccadilly travel agency. Her marriage to Prince Dimitri, whose maternal grandfather was Czar Alexander III, took place in 1954.

A more appropriate commentary on her life would be published as a passing reference fourteen years later. The obituary of her great friend Freda read in part:

The Marquesa de Casa Maury who died in London yesterday aged 88 will be better known to future generations as Mrs Dudley Ward. She lived into the last quarter of the twentieth century but it was her life between the wars, which will give her a place in history. She was one of a group of exceptionally beautiful young married women—a group that included Mrs Richard Norton, Lady Milbanke and Lady Louis Mountbatten—who played a part in the liberation of the old aristocratic society and were to be seen in the restaurants and night clubs of London. Mrs Dudley Ward belonged to the generation, which bridged the gap between the manner of the old world and the new.

But she did not die alone. A few days before her death, a young relative visited Sheila in her hospital ward. It was just after her seventy-fourth birthday, and the room was filled with people—ageing friends and compatriots from the early days all laughing and making merry: "They were spitting cherry pips in the air like children. It was a party; they were celebrating her life."

And what of Australia?

The last few lines of her memoir discuss how Dimitri's family had escaped from Russia in 1919: "None of them has ever returned to Russia," she wrote, before adding as an afterthought: "Funnily enough, I always thought I would return to Australia—but quite different—although same thoughts of one's country."

Sheila

In 1967, when she arrived in Sydney on her last trip, a *Herald* reporter asked Sheila if she missed her homeland. She replied: "I've missed Australia very much. I dream about it, you know, and I can smell it, quite clearly, with the wattle and the gum trees."

Margaret Sheila MacKellar Chisholm was cremated and her ashes spread across the grounds of Rosslyn Chapel. The following year her son ordered a commemorative stained-glass window, which was placed in the chapel's baptistery and dedicated to his mother. The window depicts the figure of St Francis of Assisi, the patron saint of animals, surrounded by birds, a lamb, squirrel and rabbit. "My mother loved animals all her life," he explained.

In the bottom left-hand corner is a kangaroo.

NOTES ON SOURCES

The journey to uncover the life story of Sheila began thanks to the eagle eye of my commissioning editor, Richard Walsh. Buried in William Shawcross's 2009 official biography of the Queen Mother, Richard spied a few paragraphs describing the relationship between Prince Albert and "an unhappily married, beautiful Australian"—Lady Loughborough, nee Sheila Chisholm.

Richard sent me an email in July 2011 quoting the intriguing snippet and adding that the detail had made him "salivate", adding "I think there is a book somewhere in all this that is crying out to be written." I too was hooked when I read the small entry on Margaret Sheila MacKellar Chisholm in the *Australian Dictionary of Biography*.

From there, however, the task became very difficult and the research path over the next year felt more like a treasure hunt than a biographical project. There was no one left alive who would have known Sheila in her heyday, so her life had to be reconstructed, fragment by fragment, after a meticulous trawl of international newspaper archives and online databases. My search took me to the National Archives, British Library and British Newspaper Archive in London, the Rosslyn Collection at the Scottish National Archives in Edinburgh, the Churchill Library in Cambridge, the New South Wales State Library in Sydney, the National Archives in Canberra and the Georgia Doble Sitwell collection at the Harry Ransom Center at the University of Texas in Austin. Permission was sought—and granted—to search the royal family's archives held at Windsor.

Hugo Vickers, the noted author and royal historian, kindly provided important references to Sheila from the diary of Sir Charles Hepburn Johnston, the former UK High Commissioner to Australia. I would also like to acknowledge the help I received from John Harris at the Royal Australian Historical Society and Roberta Carew, archivist at the Kambala girls' school in Sydney.

I found mentions of Sheila in the biographies and autobiographies of famous contemporaries, including King Edward VIII, Evelyn Waugh, Lord Beaverbrook and Lady Diana Cooper. She featured, again in passing, in books by more recent authors writing about the lives of friends such as Fred Astaire, Rudolph Valentino and Nöel Coward. All these snippets, along with mentions in hundreds of social columns and articles in newspapers and magazines—ranging from the Fleet Street dailies and magazines such as *Vogue* to smaller, regional UK newspapers—became important, if tiny, parts of a jigsaw puzzle that allowed me to get a sense of the human being behind the famous "It" girl—as well as her place in London society.

During the early part of the 20th century, the lives and loves of the British aristocracy proved irresistible the world over. In the United States and India, local newspapers could not get enough of reports from "special correspondents" in London who filed social news via the wire services, while Australia lapped up any mention of the woman reported always as "formerly Sheila Chisholm of Sydney".

Most valuable too were the letters of Prince Edward to his married lover Freda Dudley Ward, not just because they provide a contemporary voice but because they were written without the kind of discretion and self-censorship that would normally dampen such correspondence. It is a great pity that he did not keep any of her replies.

The Scottish archives also maintain an extensive collection of the Rosslyn family's records, among them a small collection of personal files, all folded neatly and probably originally held in the top drawer of Sheila's bedroom bureau. Here, the importance of the letters sent to her by Prince Bertie is very clear, as is the carefully conserved card from Rudolph Valentino. Here too it is sad to note that most of the letters between Bertie and Sheila were long ago destroyed, an act that his brother, Prince Edward, had reminded her to do so very frequently.

Ultimately however, the most important and valuable resource in writing this book was her family's decision to grant me access to her unpublished memoir. The document, poignantly titled 'Waltzing Matilda', was written when she was well into her sixth decade and is chronologically incomplete, missing (or discreetly skimming over) a number of important relationships and significant events in her life.

I was given access to the memoir only after I had finished writing the first draft of this book. I am enormously grateful to the current Earl of Rosslyn and his family because it was so important to give a first-person voice to Sheila's thoughts, joys and fears. I am also indebted to a friend, James La Terriere, who arranged the introduction to the Earl whom, by chance, he knew from their school days at Eton.

I would also like to mention two other family members. I am grateful to Sheila's nephew Bruce Chisholm, Roy Chisholm's son, who is now in his eighties, with whom I chatted on several occasions about memories of his aunt when he visited her in London during the 1950s—a gentle woman, as he recalled— and his memories of the night in 1934 that the family stables burned down at Randwick.

The Australian family of Sheila has been shy of publicity because of the incessant stories of the years of Edward and Mollee, and the paternity of Bruce's late brother, Tony. If it gives them any comfort, it is clear from my search of records, including numerous media stories of the day, that Tony was the son of Mollee and Roy Chisholm.

The other relative I found was Penny Galitzine, granddaughter of Dimitri Romanoff, who kindly gave me access to her grandfather's unpublished memoir. The yellowing document of 280 pages, carefully typed but clearly a first draft, with hand-written corrections and notations, lies at the bottom of a cardboard box stored in the roof of her home in a small town outside Eastbourne in southern England.

The pages haven't curled in the three decades since Dimitri's death because of the weight of the photographs and negatives on top of them—unfiltered, mostly amateur images taken of the last few years of his life with his second wife, Sheila.

Although the wealth and splendour of a European title has long disappeared, the Galitzine family's pride in their aristocratic background remains strong. The house is filled with memories of another age—long-dead Russian relatives in their finery populate haunting black-and-white family portraits of families who fled or died in the revolution of 1917.

Among them, on the lounge room wall, is a very different and striking portrait. It is clearly the face of Sheila, drawn in the 1930s, her hair cut sharply ending with shoulder-length ringlets, as had been vividly described by Cecil Beaton for *Vanity Fair*. There is a faraway look in her eyes—almost a sadness which might, romantically, be read as a wistfulness for her home on the other side of the world.

There are signs in the house of her longing for Australia. Carefully mounted on the staircase wall are a series of sketches of Australian animals that once decorated Sheila's home—a kangaroo, platypus and koala among them. And on a coffee table is the small, hallmarked silver boomerang given to Sheila by her mother in 1937 as a reminder to keep a promise and return to Australia with her grandchildren—a journey never made as war intervened.

The boxes and plastic bags Penny has dragged from her roof space were unsorted, but very much treasured nonetheless. She is resolute that they should be kept, not discarded, but she is unsure as to exactly how they should be displayed. When the contents are tumbled out onto the kitchen table, the task of sorting through them looks enormous and problematic. The photographs, mostly undated and early Polaroid, communicate a sense of contentment—they are of an ageing couple still travelling and exploring old places and new, as the pace and demands of life slow.

The scenery behind them provides clues about where they were taken, mostly in Europe—summers in Italy, spring in the south of France, autumn in Monte Carlo. Almost always there is a lunch or dinner scene, to toast enduring friendships. Several contain familiar faces. There is the jazz singer Sophie Tucker, with whom Sheila socialised during the 1920s, and several taken with the Duke and Duchess of Windsor at their home in southern France, his trademark lopsided smile unchanged despite years of social exile.

There are also images from Sheila's younger days among the pile: one is a mesmerising image of the young married woman soon after arriving in London in 1916; another is of her posing innocently in a tennis outfit, perhaps from as far back as her student days at Kambala. Others reveal the sense of fun of the couple: Sheila's depicted as a white rabbit on a card titled "Time to Travel the Milbanke Way" and on another with her head glued to a kangaroo.

Penny's memories of Sheila are vivid but limited to the year her family spent in London in 1968 (she grew up in Canada) when she was fourteen years old and she and her two sisters,

Marina and Alexandra, would visit on alternate Sunday afternoons. Sheila and Dimitri's house in Wilton Street was a stone's throw from Buckingham Palace and was set up for entertaining, even though they were now both into their seventies. There was a dumb waiter, which brought up from the kitchen in the basement food that was cooked and served by two live-in staff members, and a bar at the top of the first flight of stairs with a machine that frosted drinking glasses.

"I can see why Sheila and Dimitri fell in together," Penny told me. "They were both irreverent and had a sense of humour. They enjoyed each other's company and must have had a gas. Sheila was a great organiser and my grandfather, whom I call Apapa, was a man who needed to be organised. He was probably not the easiest person to live with. He was very set in his ways, a bit stubborn and someone who either had lots of money or no money at all. He had great schemes, most of which came to nothing, and great connections. It was an all-or-nothing existence.

"Sheila was always dressed immaculately, usually in pearls and earrings; quite discreet and nothing flashy. Understated. She was a great socialite and they had a huge number of friends. They both loved going out to dinner or to Apapa's club, usually in their car which had tiny gold crowns above the door handles inscribed with a "D", like a cipher."

When they weren't travelling, they would entertain old friends, many of them ageing society hostesses, including Diana Cooper, widowed after the death of Duff in 1954 and dismissive of the title Viscountess of Norwich, which she announced in *The Times* she wouldn't answer to, because it "sounded like porridge".

"The house always smelled like French cigarettes. They were just over the top—all these glamorous people behaving not like old women but like girls, as if time had stood still and they were still in the 1920s and '30s. Diana was notorious for driving her Mini Cooper and parking it anywhere she damn well pleased. I don't think she ever got a ticket. She would arrive, usually wearing a big hat and long gloves, which would never come off during lunch. Apparently ladies who lunched always kept their gloves on."

By 1968, however, Sheila was in poor health. She would often remain in her room on the third floor and Dimitri would explain this away by saying she was indisposed.

"She was always immaculate, but there was a frailty about her. She loved my sister Marina, who was very pretty. I was more of a tomboy. They would sit at Sheila's dressing table and paint each other's faces, trying nail polish and scents and make-up or trying on her jewellery. Maybe she missed not having a daughter."

But there were also times when Sheila would descend the stairs and delight in taking the sisters to St James's Park to feed the ducks. Sometimes they would visit the Brompton Oratory, a 19th-century Catholic church in Kensington: "I have this strong memory of her lighting candles in the cathedral, and that each one represented a person. She lit a lot of candles."

Sheila Chisholm was an Australian woman who lived through one of the most interesting, if turbulent, periods of the 20th century. The story of her life, and loves, suggests she embraced—and embodied—a particular kind of 'Australian-ness' and a spirit that defied and perhaps helped loosen the strictures and mores of Anglo-English relationships of the time.

SELECTED READING

Amory, M. (ed.), *The Letters of Evelyn Waugh,* London:
Weidenfeld & Nicolson, 1980

Bradford, S., Clerk, H., Fryer, J. and Gibson, R., *The Sitwells and the Arts of the 1920s and 1930s*, Austin. TX: University of Texas Press, 1996

Chisholm, A. and Davie, M., *Beaverbrook: A Life*, London: Hutchinson, 1992

Cooper, A. (ed.), *Mr. Wu and Mrs. Stitch: The letters of Evelyn Waugh and Diana Cooper*, London: Hodder & Stoughton, 1991

—— *A Durable Fire: The letters of Duff and Diana Cooper 1913–1950*, London: Collins, 1983

Cooper, D., *The rainbow comes and goes the lights of common day trumpets from the steep*, London: Hart-Davis, 1959

—— *Old Men Forget: The autobiography of Duff Cooper,*

London: Readers Union Rupert Hart-Davis, 1955

Davy, M. (ed.), *The Diaries of Evelyn Waugh*, London: Little, Brown, 1976

Day, B. (ed.), *The Letters of Nöel Coward*, New York: Alfred A. Knopf, 2007

Driberg, T., *Ruling Passions*, London: Jonathan Cape, 1977

Earl of Rosslyn, *My Gamble With Life*, London: Cassell, 1928

Ellenberger, R., The Valentino Mystique: The death and the afterlife of the silent film idol, Jefferson, NC: Mcfarland & Company, 2005

Giles, S., *Fred Astaire: His friends talk*, New York: Doubleday, 1988

Godfrey, R. (ed.), *Letters from a Prince: Edward, Prince of Wales to Mrs. Freda Dudley Ward*, London: Little, Brown, 1998

Greig, G., *Louis and the Prince: A story of politics, intrigue and royal friendship,* London: Hodder & Stoughton Educational, 1999

Heymann, C.D., *Poor Little Rich Girl: The life and legend of Barbara Hutton*, Fort Lee, NJ: Lyle Stuart Inc, 1984

Jenkins, A., *The Twenties*, London: William Heinemann, 1974

Jennings, D., *Barbara Hutton: A candid biography of the richest woman in the world*, London: WH Allen, 1968

Leider, E., *Dark Lover: The life and death of Rudolph Valentino*, London: Faber & Faber, 2003

Marr, A., *The Making of Modern Britain*, London: Macmillan, 2009

Meyrick, K., *Secrets of the 43: Reminiscences*, London: John Long, 1933

Morgan, J., *Edwina Mountbatten: A life of her own*, London: Harper Collins, 1991

Nobbs, A., *Kambala: The first 100 years 1887–1987*, Sydney: Kambala Centenary History Committee, 1987

Obolensky, S., *One Man in His Time: The memories of Serge Obolensky*, New York: McDowell, 1958

Osborne, F., *The Bolter: The story of Idina Sackville*, New York: Vintage, 2008

Pine, L.G. (ed.), *Burke's Peerage, Baronetage & Knightage*, London: Burke's Peerage Ltd, 1959

Shawcross, W., *Queen Elizabeth: The Queen Mother*, London: Macmillan, 2009

Spicer, P., *The Temptress: The scandalous life of Alice, Countess de Janzé: Passion and Murder in Kenya's Happy Valley*, London: Simon & Schuster, 2010

St. Clair-Erskine, P. (Earl of Rosslyn), *Rosslyn Chapel*, Rosslyn Chapel Trust (Roslin, Scotland), Edinburgh: Lothian and Edinburgh Enterprise Limited, 1997

Sykes, C., *Evelyn Waugh: A biography*, London: Little, Brown, 1975

Taylor, D.J., *Bright Young People: The rise and fall of a generation 1918–1940*, London: Vintage, 2008

Tucker, S., *Some of These Days: An autobiography*, London: Hammond, Hammond & Co, 1948

Vickers, H., *Elizabeth: The Queen Mother*, London: Hutchinson, 2005

Wheeler-Bennett, J.W., *King George VI: His life and reign*, London: Macmillan, 1958

Sheila

Wilson, J.H., *Evelyn Waugh, a Literary Biography*, Madison, NJ: Fairleigh Dickinson University Press, 2001

Ziegler, P., *King Edward VIII: The Official Biography*, London: Collins, 1990

—— *Diana Cooper, the biography of Lady Diana Cooper*, London: Hamish Hamilton, 1981

Ziegler, P. (ed.) *The Diaries of Lord Louis Mountbatten 1920–1922*, London: Collins, 1987

INDEX

INDEX